Praise for *Career Self-Care*

"*Career Self-Care* is a must-have guide for today's new world of work. Minda Zetlin helps you navigate toxic bosses, unreasonable demands, and feeling stuck in a job you hate. If you're ready to take your career to the next level, this book will help you get there."

— **Barbara Corcoran**, Shark and executive producer on ABC's *Shark Tank*, founder of the Corcoran Group, and host of the podcast *Business Unusual*

"A personable, practical guide for improving your work life. Minda Zetlin has spent much of her career helping people pursue success without sacrificing their well-being, and her book highlights how you can take better care of your career and your health."

— **Adam Grant**, #1 *New York Times* bestselling author of *Think Again* and host of the podcast *WorkLife*

"*Career Self-Care* teaches you how to reach your biggest goals. It will help you become your best, most effective self and keep you focused on the things that matter most."

— **Eric Partaker**, CEO coach and 2019 CEO of the Year, Business Excellence Forum UK

"In *Career Self-Care*, Minda Zetlin weaves fascinating stories, including her own life story, with valuable insights for women (and men) to make their own self-care their priority. Doing so enables us to show up as our best self in every aspect of our career and our life outside of our career. This is especially crucial for leaders because when they don't practice self-care, they are in essence signaling to their teams that the same is expected of them."

— **Shelmina Babai Abji**, author of *Show Your Worth: 8 Intentional Strategies for Women to Emerge as Leaders at Work*

"*Career Self-Care* provides unique real-world, actionable solutions for any and every possible situation that readers may experience in their careers. The meticulous exercises that Minda Zetlin presents in this book should serve as a contemporary compass for professionals seeking to improve their self-care."

— **Dr. Eli Joseph**, faculty member,
Columbia University and Queens College, and author of
*The Perfect Rejection Resume: A Reader's Guide to
Building a Career through Failure*

"*Career Self-Care* is not about finding balance between your work and personal lives — it's about learning how the two can integrate and enhance each other to help you reach new heights in both."

— **Robert Glazer**, #1 *Wall Street Journal*
and *USA Today* bestselling author of *Elevate*

CAREER
SELF-CARE

CAREER SELF-CARE

Find Your Happiness, Success, and Fulfillment at Work

MINDA ZETLIN

New World Library
Novato, California

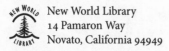

New World Library
14 Pamaron Way
Novato, California 94949

Text design by Tona Pearce Myers

Library of Congress Cataloging-in-Publication Data

Names: Zetlin, Minda, author.
Title: Career self-care : find your happiness, success, and fulfillment at work / Minda Zetlin.
Description: Novato, California : New World Library, [2022] | Includes bibliographical references and index. | Summary: "A collection of pragmatic self-care methods for balancing the competing demands of career, well-being, and personal fulfillment. Includes exercises and questions for reflection"-- Provided by publisher.
Identifiers: LCCN 2022005806 (print) | LCCN 2022005807 (ebook) | ISBN 9781608687329 (paperback) | ISBN 9781608687336 (epub)
Subjects: LCSH: Career development. | Work-life balance. | Success in business. | Success.
Classification: LCC HF5381 .Z37 2022 (print) | LCC HF5381 (ebook) | DDC 650.1--dc23/eng/20220207
LC record available at https://lccn.loc.gov/2022005806
LC ebook record available at https://lccn.loc.gov/2022005807

First printing, June 2022
ISBN 978-1-60868-732-9
Ebook ISBN 978-1-60868-733-6
Printed in Canada on 100% postconsumer-waste recycled paper

New World Library is proud to be a Gold Certified Environmentally Responsible Publisher. Publisher certification awarded by Green Press Initiative.

10   9   8   7   6   5   4   3   2   1

To my mom, Erlinda Cortes Brobston, born Mary Boone (1924–2015), who made all of this look easy, and to my husband, Bill Pfleging, who makes my own career and self-care possible.

Contents

Introduction

How to Use This Book: Any Way You Want

How do you feel about your job, your career, your work life, and your outside-of-work life? Is your job a source of misery and frustration? Is it time to make a change? Are you working as hard as you can at a profession that excites you, doing your absolute best to find the next step up, and then the next after that? Do you have a career that you love and a home life that fulfills you? Is it a constant battle to find time for all the things you really want to do? Even though all of it is wonderful, do you still feel overwhelmed?

I've felt all those things at different times in my life and career, and I've struggled with them all. But for more than a decade, I've had an incredibly fun job writing for the website of *Inc.* magazine, exploring all the different ways successful people, and those who aspire to be successful, can better manage their jobs, their start-up companies, and the constant push and pull between their work lives and the rest of their lives. I've talked to hundreds of experts, business executives, and entrepreneurs about the strategies that have helped them advance in their careers and how they've avoided sacrificing their own happiness in the process. I've learned strategies that have worked wonderfully, and I also found some approaches that absolutely didn't work, even though I hoped they would.

Through my research I learned thousands of tips and techniques and work style changes that could help, and I tried most of them myself, including everything I recommend in this book. And although many of those were extremely helpful, I mostly learned that building the life and career you really want is more about changing your overall approach, and the way that you value yourself, than it is about, say, learning a new time-management technique.

If you're like most people these days, you're struggling with too many things to do, read, watch, and listen to. *Career Self-Care* is meant to help, not add to the pressure. The chapters in this book can be read individually and in any order. Feel free to page through, find a topic or a chapter that appeals to you, and start there. Work your way forward or backward, or jump around if you like. You'll get just as much out of it in any order, so go ahead and start with chapter 22 if it makes you happy (which it might, since that chapter is all about happiness).

And please take the same approach with the insights and practical advice in this book. From spending one day a week doing no work whatsoever to starting conversations with strangers, I'm about to make a bunch of suggestions, some of which may seem ridiculous or impossible or irrelevant to you. Others may hit you between the eyes and make you think, "Huh. I wonder if that really would make a difference?" At least, that's how I tend to respond to career or life advice that resonates for me.

If something makes you go "Huh," please give it a try. It might help you move just a little closer to reaching your goals, whatever they may be. But it's also fine to simply read the book and leave it at that. It might help you work through your own ideas or beliefs about life, success, or your career. It could get you to take a look at the sources of support all around you that can help you in both your work life and your home life. It might get you thinking about self-care and how taking care of your own needs and desires could make you both happier and more successful. That's more than good enough. The book will have done its job, and so will you.

PART ONE

WHAT DOES SELF-CARE HAVE TO DO WITH YOUR CAREER?

Chapter 1

Taking Care of Yourself
Is a Radical Act

A few years ago, I interviewed Bhava Ram, who used to be named Brad Willis. Willis was once a war correspondent for NBC News. It was his dream career, and he'd climbed to the top of his chosen profession with a simple mantra: "I'm going to work harder and longer than anyone else."

That mantra sounded very familiar to me, and I bet it does to you too. Do you start every day with a mental to-do list that no human being could actually finish? Do you confront every obstacle by trying harder and studying more? Do you spend your working life, and your home life too, with your eye on the next goal, and then the next and the next? If the answer to all of that is yes, then welcome. You and I are both part of a very large and very overworked club.

Maybe you work for a boss or a company that expects unreasonable amounts of work from you, and maybe everyone in your organization uses that same bad mantra. Maybe you work for yourself in a profession where nearly everyone is striving to work harder and longer than everyone else. Maybe you have very big dreams about what you want to accomplish, and you worry about falling behind on your goals. Or maybe other people depend on you and the things you do, both at work and at home, and you live in fear of what might happen if you fail them.

All of that describes me. I've spent my entire adult life as a writer, which is to say that I work in an incredibly competitive profession where, among other things, there are legions of people who would happily do my job for free. For years I struggled along, making a living, sort of. Looking back, I was chipping away at an iceberg, establishing myself and building skills little by little. Finally, after a ridiculously long time, I gained the confidence I needed to take the next step and then the next.

I wish I could tell you that it all magically came together and that I was swept away to unimagined success like all those authors on the bestseller racks. Instead, it was an excruciatingly slow process. After many years of volunteering for the American Society of Journalists and Authors (ASJA), I got invited to run for the board, and after many more years on the board doing all sorts of jobs, I eventually became president. After years of writing for Inc.com, I wound up in the right place at the right time to have an online column of my own, and over time I built up a readership of more than a million page views a month. At some point, I finally started making a decent living, and around that time I also realized that if I could clone myself into two writers, there was enough demand for my work to keep both of us busy.

I wish I could tell you that on the day I had that realization I did something to celebrate it, such as plan a vacation or at least take my husband out for a nice dinner. Instead, I did what you probably do too: I worried about how to keep it all going. I took on almost every job I was offered. I fretted about how to increase my income since, even though my income had doubled over just a few years, it never seemed to be more than *almost* enough.

And, relentlessly, I compared myself to other people. One friend of mine completed a novel in six months. Why hadn't I done the same? Another built her expertise into a lucrative speaking business. Why hadn't I done that too? Everything I did, someone else had done more of or had done it better. Anything that I achieved seemed easy and unimportant the moment I achieved it. I just had to work harder and longer.

Let me tell you how the whole "harder and longer" thing came apart for Brad Willis. In 1986, when he was about to start a job with the big NBC affiliate in Boston, he went on vacation in the Bahamas with his girlfriend. He was trying to close a window near the ceiling of their rented cabin when the handles broke off in his hands and he fell twelve feet onto his back, cracking a vertebra. He was told he needed surgery, but he refused to take the time away from his brand-new job. Instead, he decided he could handle the incessant pain by wearing a back brace and taking painkillers and muscle relaxants. He hid his condition from his employers, first the NBC affiliate and later NBC itself "for fear the station will stop sending me on more rigorous assignments."

For seven years, he ignored the injury, becoming addicted to pain meds and alcohol while his career path continued upward, landing him the position he'd always wanted: network war correspondent. Then one day, while on assignment in the Philippines, he leaned over to look at some footage, and the bone snapped the rest of the way. Now in agony, he had no choice but to submit to surgery, but it failed to repair his badly worsened injury. Then he was diagnosed with throat cancer. He was told that he likely had a limited time to live.

Not wanting to end his life in a drugged haze, Willis decided to get clean. He wound up at an experimental pain clinic where he encountered yoga for the first time, and it restored him to both physical and mental health. Eventually, he beat the cancer and found a deeply fulfilling career as a yoga trainer and author. "Although years of physical pain and emotional anguish were nothing I ever would have wished for, I now realize that a broken back, failed surgery, cancer, and a lost career were my greatest teachers and biggest blessings," he wrote in his memoir, *Warrior Pose*. "They taught me more about the world than all my previous travels and experiences combined, compelled me to face myself, and made me a better human being."

There's a point to this story that you might have missed. The spinal injury was not what ended Willis's career as a war correspondent. Neither was the cancer or his addiction. What did it was the snap decision he made when he turned down the operation that could have spared him those years of pain. Here's what he wrote about his thought process at the time: "I have to push forward. In this business, the weak fall behind and most of them never catch up again. I'll never let that happen to me. *Never.*" In other words, a man who fearlessly walked among soldiers in Afghanistan and drug lords in Central America couldn't take four weeks away from his job for an operation he desperately needed *because he was afraid.*

When you're deeply committed to your career, as so many of us are, taking time away when you need it takes courage. Admitting that you're human — that you suffer sickness and injury and relationship breakups and family emergencies, and that all these things mean you sometimes can't fully concentrate on your work — is an act of real bravery. It might seem as if you're weak and can't simply take everything in stride. It might even seem as if you care less about your career than the Brad Willises of the world who simply push through the pain. You might fear negative consequences for your career, and depending on your job and the industry you work in, that fear could be justified. How can you risk giving up even a little of your dreamed-of success just because you need rest or healing or because someone you love needs more of your time?

Everything about Willis's case is extreme: the pressure he was under from his job and from his own ambitions and expectations, the depth of his denial, and the level of injury and suffering he finally had to face. And yet the values that went into his thinking seem very familiar, don't they? Just consider one tiny example: the often-seen cold medicine ad that promises to relieve your symptoms so you can keep right on working even when you're sick. That's a notion that seems horrifically wrong in a world that's been through Covid-19. But even before the pandemic, did it really make sense for people who were feeling too sick to do their jobs well — and were possibly contagious — to drag themselves to work?

Six years ago, about a year after my writing really started to take off and I started to have a solid income, my husband Bill and I both came down with a bad flu. I was nearing the end of my second term as president of ASJA, my column at Inc.com was gathering steam, and I was starting a large and lucrative project, managing a website for a big tech company. I was busier than I'd ever been, and getting sick just wasn't in my schedule. Bill went to the doctor and was diagnosed with bronchitis. Meanwhile, I pushed on until the morning I woke up feeling so awful that I knew I couldn't concentrate enough to do the interviews with several prominent executives I had scheduled for that day. So I sat down at my desk and sent out emails asking to reschedule. Only after that did I take my temperature, which turned out to be 102°.

Bill drove me to the doctor's office, where I was told I had pneumonia. A whole elaborate structure of meetings and deadlines and family obligations came crashing down with that one word. Over the next few days of rescheduling things, I discovered something that surprised me: Most deadlines, even in publishing, are a lot more flexible than you might think. And my clients were a lot more willing to accommodate my need to change plans than I had expected.

Except for one. There was a kickoff conference call planned for that website I was going to manage, and when I told the project manager that I couldn't do the call because I had pneumonia, he agreed to reschedule it — for the following day. When I objected that that might not be enough time for me to get better, he said if it wasn't, we could reschedule it again at that time. Faced with the prospect of having to reschedule every twenty-four hours till I got well, I dragged myself to the phone the next day and got it over with. He praised me for being a "trooper." But the moment I hung up, my sickness-addled brain forgot every single thing they had told me about the project.

With hindsight, I think I see his logic. The meeting's main purpose was to let the client know that the project was moving forward; he really didn't need me to contribute or remember much of anything. But that doesn't make his insistence that I could get over pneumonia in one day any less absurd. I wonder now what would have happened if I had simply said no, if I had explained that in order to get better, I needed at least a week with no work, no meetings, no email, and no rescheduling of meetings. I don't know how he would have reacted, but I wish I'd been brave enough back then to say what I knew I needed.

An unhealthy relationship to work like Willis's and mine, and maybe yours too, doesn't happen in a vacuum. We live in a society that idealizes the news reporter who self-medicates and pushes through the pain to get the job done, the entrepreneur who, like Elon Musk, sleeps a few hours a night in his office before going back to work and never actually goes out in the sunlight, and the athlete who ignores an injury and goes on to win the big prize. We're expected to be in love with our jobs, and I think that many of us are. But few of us would put up with a lover or spouse who made the kinds of outlandish demands on us that our jobs do. This nutty, work-obsessed culture of ours is what made it seem reasonable to an otherwise great project manager that I wouldn't mind taking part in an important conference call the day after being diagnosed with pneumonia.

This is why admitting that you're human and may need some time off takes courage in this work world of ours. It's why self-care is a radical act.

The Surprising Truth about Self-Care

I started to rethink the whole idea of "harder and longer" while doing research for my Inc.com column, which, ironically, was the very thing I was working hard and long to do. I'd begun writing about work-life balance, fulfillment, and mindfulness because my audience, voting with their clicks, had made it clear that these were topics they wanted to read about. The more I learned, the less sense it made to be working seven days a week and going years between vacations, as I'd been doing for a while by then.

Little by little, I began easing off and easing up. It started with a firm commitment to keep one day a week completely free of work. Next, I changed my relationship with email. Where I used to spend an hour or more a day going through my email and responding to everything that seemed important, I now started cherry-picking the things that seemed urgent and pretty much ignoring the rest. I slowly reset my priorities toward working fewer late nights and spending more time with friends or my husband or just digging in my garden. I kept making those kinds of gradual changes, and now, despite an intense work schedule, I take the time to go horseback riding twice a week.

It's far from a perfect balance. I wish I could say I always do it right, that I consistently quit work at a reasonable hour, or that I routinely take two-day weekends. None of that is as true as I would like it to be. But what I have managed is a mental shift that says it's OK if I occasionally miss a deadline or take longer than I should to answer an email or wait till tomorrow or next week to pitch one more project. It's OK to put my relationships and even myself ahead of my career and to get the rest and exercise and relaxation that I need, even if that relaxation consists of nothing more uplifting or better for me than binge-watching *Grace and Frankie*.

But here's what's most surprising: taking my career down a notch in my priorities list, and insisting on time off for myself even when it sometimes means dropping the ball on work obligations, has made me more successful, not less. And I'm not the only one to make this discovery. My friend Shelmina Babai Abji, who started life in a small town in Tanzania, became one of the top-ranked women of color at IBM, and is now a successful empowerment speaker and author of the new book *Show Your Worth: 8 Intentional Strategies for Women to Emerge as Leaders at Work*, told me that her career really took off after she became a single mom. It forced her to be ruthlessly efficient with her time, prioritizing what mattered, and leaving the rest undone. The famously driven Apple founder Steve Jobs used to quit work and get home in time for dinner at 5:30 every night. Amazon founder Jeff Bezos takes a similar approach to his schedule.

In this hard-driving age, at a time when technology means that no matter where you are, you're also always at the office, most of us think of work and life as either/or. You may think that a day you decide to take off and join a friend on a hike or at the beach is a day that's bad for your career. Or that if you decide to quit work early instead of answering those waiting emails, you've made a choice for self-care over excelling at your job. I certainly believed that for the longest time — but it turns out the opposite is true. Self-care and career are not either/or but and/and. You need to be good at the first if you want to excel at the second, especially over time. In the long run, "harder and longer" will not get you where you want to go.

There are two reasons why making sure you get the rest and

relaxation you need can actually be good for your career. The first is that if you take the time and space to take care of yourself, you are signaling to others that you are valuable. Just as people will unconsciously assume that a product is better if they have to pay more for it, they'll unconsciously assume that you are more highly skilled, more sought-after, and generally more worthy of respect if you insist on taking care of your own needs. More importantly, you'll be signaling that to yourself as well.

The second reason is that when you're happy and relaxed and well-rested, you're able to focus better on whatever needs doing, and you're better able to recognize and fulfill the needs of others. You're a better boss, a better employee, a better business owner, a better partner, and a better parent.

Too Many "Shoulds"

What does a healthy combination of career and self-care look like? Let's start with what it doesn't look like. It doesn't look like rushing from the office to the gym so you can force yourself through a workout that doesn't inspire you just so you can fit into that tight dress and look your best for that party when you'd rather be home eating popcorn with a good book and your cat. It doesn't mean cooking the perfect dinner when you're exhausted, or spending hours making homemade Halloween costumes because you think store-bought ones somehow mean you've failed.

There's not a thing wrong with any of those activities if you choose them for your own enjoyment or sense of fulfillment and if doing them makes you happy. But too many of us spend too much of our time trying to conform to too many "shoulds," and the shoulds in our society these days are simply too numerous for that to work. Just as we mercilessly compare ourselves to other people when we look at our careers, we perform the same self-torture when it comes to our weight, our clothes, our workout routines, our relationships, our kids, our homes, our vacations, and even our meals. It seems that Facebook and Instagram exist in large part to remind us of what other people are doing right that we're doing wrong.

Whatever "doing everything right" or even "doing everything well enough" looks like, I don't even come close. I'm decidedly overweight. My house is an embarrassing mess. I never succeeded in having children, which in my mind means I have no excuse for some of the things I've let slip. I don't spend as much time as I should keeping in touch with my distant friends and family members. I should exercise more than I do. I should weed the garden more often. I should give more to charity, volunteer more, and cook a meal once in a while. Not only that, but there's a carpenter ant infestation in a corner of the living room that I feel certain results from a moral failing of some kind on my part. And everywhere I look, there's somebody doing it better. A writer with more readers who earns twice as much as I do. A friend with a spotless house who runs 10Ks and goes on twenty-mile hikes every weekend. Another friend who lives in an old church with a magnificent English-style garden that she keeps up all on her own. Yet another friend who knows how to make her own soap.

Sometimes I let this stuff get to me. But then I stop and remind myself that I can never live up to my own expectations, and so maybe I should stop and give myself a break instead. So should you. You have to stop judging yourself against everyone who does any aspect of work or life better than you think you do. You have to find the courage and honesty to admit to yourself and other people that you can get tired and sick and burned out and distracted. That some days you are blindingly productive and other days making coffee is a monumental achievement, and that having both types of days is just fine. That any version of how you "should" work or live or look or keep your home that you may have seen on television or social media or in a magazine is completely irrelevant and has nothing to do with you.

Let go of all the shoulds, and little by little you can start to discover what true self-care means in your particular world, which is not the same as my world or your mother's world or anybody else's world. Once you've done that, you can experiment with different forms of self-care, from lying in bed reading mystery novels to training for a marathon to going to the movies alone to having a date night with your partner or spouse. Check in with yourself after each of these experiments and see how it made you feel. Did you feel good while you were doing it? How about afterward? Later when you got back to work? The more you can answer yes to these questions, the better you've succeeded at self-care.

Every human being needs certain things to thrive. These include adequate sleep (sleep experts say most people need eight hours whether they know it or not), nutritious food, exercise, sunlight, fresh air, time with people they love, interesting conversation, and unstructured empty time to think and reflect. Many of us also need time by ourselves, and that very much includes me. I was an only child and spent a lot of time on my own. My profession demands a fair amount of solitude. I suppose this explains why, if I go for too long constantly surrounded by other people, I start to get nervous and grumpy, and sometimes my digestive system goes haywire. I love being with my husband and my family and my friends — I really do. But there's a deep relaxation that comes from sprawling in front of the TV or reading a book or going for a hike or even sitting in a café, knowing that no one will interrupt me, at least not for anything more consequential than nodding as they walk by or asking if I'd like another cup of coffee. I can't get to that level of rest any other way. Spending time alone is important for my own self-care, and maybe it is for yours too. Or maybe not. We all need different things.

Once you learn what you need to truly take care of yourself, will you make sure to get it? Or will you wait and hope someone else will do that for you? In the 1980s, a generation of women learned the term *Cinderella complex*, which describes a woman's belief that she doesn't need to worry about her future finances because someday soon a man will marry her and take care of her material needs for the rest of her life.

In the 2020s, we know better than to expect that someone will come along and pay all our bills. But I think we're victims today of a different fallacy that's just as dangerous. We believe that if we keep on giving 110 percent all the time, someone will notice our hard work and fix it for us. Our boss will insist we take a day off. Our spouse or partner will see that we're exhausted and give us a spa day — and then do the laundry while we're out so we can slip into clean sheets when we get home.

But that's not how it works. You may have the world's kindest boss and most sensitive spouse, and it will still be true that giving yourself the care you need is your responsibility and no one else's. No one understands what you need as well as you do. No one can tell others what your needs are as well as you can. And no one else can give you what you need as well as you can yourself.

Staking that claim for yourself — skipping the gathering that you really don't want to attend, or going alone to the movie you've been wanting to see — sometimes requires a difficult negotiation with your loved ones and with your own guilty feelings. At work, that kind of negotiation can be even more frightening, especially when you know there's a Brad Willis in the next office who intends to get ahead by working harder and longer than you. Can you be braver than him or her? Can you lay claim to the time off you need or the more humane schedule or whatever will allow you to thrive both as a human being and as the bound-for-success person you also are?

I hope so, because I believe there is no definition of success that makes any sense at all unless it also includes the idea that you are happy and healthy and fulfilled in every possible way. I dream of a world where everyone shares that definition of success. In that alternate reality, the young Brad Willis called his new boss at the Boston NBC affiliate and said something like this: "Listen, I am beyond excited to start my job with you, but unfortunately I've just sustained an injury that requires surgery and four weeks to heal. I'm so sorry about that, but four weeks from now I will be there and raring to go and ready for you to send me to war zones in the far corners of the Earth. In the meantime, while I'm recovering, I'll learn everything there is to know about your station so when I get there I'll be ready for anything."

In that alternate reality of my imagination, Brad Willis is still a beloved figure at NBC News. And all of us are happy and healthy as well as successful.

EXERCISES TO TRY

This book is called *Career Self-Care*, and in later chapters there will be exercises to help you reach your goals at work, I promise. I'm starting here with personal self-care because I believe this business of learning how to take care of yourself is the foundation we all need for building a successful career and a successful life.

1. Meet Your Own Needs

Grab some paper or your journal. Write down this question: *What do I need that I'm not getting right now?*

Spend two to three minutes making a list of your answers. They could be things you need at work or at home – anything from more money to time to read a book to a bigger apartment to a night in a hotel with your partner away from your home and kids. Use your imagination, be honest, and write down whatever comes to mind.

When you're done, you may have a long list, which is great. Now spend a few moments thinking about what you really need the most to feel happy, healthy, and whole. Pick just three items from your list, circle them, and write each at the top of a new page. For each need you've selected, consider this question: *How do I make this happen?*

Now spend a little time writing an answer for each one. Maybe there's more than one answer because there are a few different ways to achieve what you need. Or perhaps getting what you need will require a few separate steps. For example, if you've written at the top of the page that you need to get out of your current job, your steps might include things like updating your résumé, going to industry events where you can network with people and learn about new opportunities, and responding to job listings.

Are you willing and able to take these steps? If so, make a commitment to yourself that you will. If you determine that achieving one of your needs requires something that you just can't do, then choose a different item from your original list. It would be better if you stuck with your first choices — after all, you chose them first for a reason. But if you can't, you can't. Either way, pick a date by which you'll have taken that first step.

Before you put away your journal or your paper, close your eyes for just a few moments and imagine how things will be and how you'll feel once you've taken the necessary steps to meet at least one of these important needs. I think it will be worth it. Don't you?

Chapter 2

The Disappearing Line between Life and Work

I get more than two hundred pitches a day from public relations people who want me to write about their clients. Having all these people desperate to get my attention makes me feel powerful and important, sometimes in stupid ways. Once when I was researching a story, I sent emails to a bunch of PR people on a Friday evening to set up interviews. Most of them answered me over the weekend, but a few didn't. "Humph!" I thought disdainfully. "I guess you don't *really* care about getting your client into my story after all." If I had a time machine, I'd go back and slap myself.

You've probably had the experience, one time or another, of sending off an email or chat message way outside of working hours, perhaps in the middle of the night, and getting an immediate answer. Maybe you thought, "What kind of nut answers email at this hour? Shouldn't you be sleeping or else doing something fun?" Then again, you were the late-night workaholic who started that email conversation in the first place.

One writer I know told me he wrote an article on his phone

while shopping at the mall with his family. I've never figured out how to write with any efficiency on my smartphone, which is probably the only reason I've never tried anything like this myself.

On Valentine's Day a couple of years ago, my musician husband got a gig playing in a local restaurant. I went with him, which meant I had to sit alone at a table for about four hours, and I admit that I very unromantically spent the first of those hours working on my tablet because I was behind on some deadlines.

I don't mean to suggest that any of this makes sense, I'm just saying that this kind of thing does happen, whether it should or not. My friend said he wrote the article at the mall "because I can," which is as good an explanation as any for why I spent time working in a restaurant on Valentine's Day.

What If Your Workplace Were Obliterated at 5 p.m.?

How we think about life versus work is evolving over time. Back in the 1980s, when I started my career, I used to fret about work all the time. A colleague of mine told me that at 5 p.m. each day, he would imagine that our company was obliterated by a bomb and would stay that way until the next morning. He advised me, for my own sanity, to adopt the same attitude. I thought that following this advice would be completely impossible. I was never done with my work at 5 p.m., and I hated leaving tasks unfinished. I wanted to be totally engaged in my job and think about it all the time. But I also understood that I and my colleagues who thought that way were the exception and not the rule.

In 2000, I remember reading an article about working at Microsoft that mentioned how engineers would often answer each other's emails in the middle of the night. It was seen as a good thing: they were devoted to their jobs. Just a couple of years later, I went on a dive trip with a group that included a very busy defense lawyer. The other divers joked that they would throw his phone into the ocean if he took one more work call. But when some acquaintances from out of town got arrested for having magic mushrooms in their car on their way to a music festival, my first thought was to call that lawyer. I knew he'd be easy to reach and would work hard for them, both of which proved to be true.

By 2014, though, I was horrified when I read an article by a busy advertising executive about how she had spent part of Thanksgiving Day. Sitting at the kitchen table in her mother's home, she held a conference call with her team and an important client while a pumpkin pie baked in the oven. I was so outraged by this that I wrote a whole column about it. It's one thing to take an idle moment when you're supposed to be off work to catch up on your own tasks, like I did at that Valentine's gig or my friend did at the mall. It's something else entirely to expect the people who work for you to drop whatever they're doing on a major holiday so they can take part in your conference call. Even asking them to do that is wrong because they might fear falling behind on the path to promotion if they refuse. If they're right to think that refusing could damage their careers, that's even worse.

Amazingly, this exec was presenting her Thanksgiving Day conference call as a *good* example of balancing life and work. She claimed that what she called an "always-on approach to work" wasn't at all a hardship, but instead a way of working smarter in the knowledge economy. She didn't seem to see any harm in asking her employees to interrupt their holiday activities to participate in a business meeting. As I read the rest of her article, I kept thinking that she just didn't get it.

In a growing number of places, a conference call on a major holiday is illegal. Increasingly, lawmakers and labor experts are advocating for and even legislating the "right to disconnect." The idea is that people both need and are entitled to forget about work during nonwork hours. Their employers and colleagues cannot reasonably expect them to, say, answer emails after hours or on weekends. The rules obviously are somewhat different for people whose jobs require them to be available outside normal hours, such as doctors on call, firefighters, or emergency plumbers. But whatever the schedule, each of us needs some time every day and every week when we don't have to think about work at all.

In most locations that have them, right-to-disconnect laws simply forbid employers from withholding promotions or otherwise disfavoring employees who don't respond to after-hours messages or phone calls. But some laws go further. In Germany and Portugal, for example, even sending an email to an employee after hours is illegal, whether or not you expect an immediate response.

The fact that protecting these rights by law seems both logical and necessary today tells you just how far our work lives have slipped beyond what used to be their normal boundaries. And that's not good. A 2018 study from Virginia Tech called "Killing Me Softly" revealed that the mere expectation that employees check their email outside of work hours is enough to raise stress levels for both them and their families.

To turn this bad trend around, you need more than just the right to disconnect. You also need the desire to disconnect. Most of us secretly like feeling tethered to our email as though it were an umbilical cord. It's not just because we believe our boss or our customers expect that from us, and it's not because we believe some disaster will happen if no one can reach us for a couple of hours. Or — I take that back — we do believe some disaster will happen if we disconnect for a couple of hours. That disaster is that we will miss something. You've probably heard the term *FOMO*, an acronym for "fear of missing out." It's a universal affliction in our digitally driven age.

Discovering the Joy of Missing Out

I'm guessing you didn't need psychology researchers to tell you that all of this attention to work outside work hours isn't good for you. I'm also guessing you check your email on your days off, several times during the day, just like I do. But then there are the occasional days when, say, I go for a hike in the woods and I don't check my email or text messages or chat messages for a long while, mostly because I can't.

And you know what? Those are really good days. It's not that I stop thinking about work when I'm away from it. I'm not wired to do that, and you probably aren't either. But I do stop thinking about work in terms of immediate problems to solve or short-term successes or failures. Instead, I start thinking about my bigger dreams and goals and challenges. You need that separation from the day-to-day of work in order to think those big strategic thoughts or come up with those creative ideas that can really make a difference. This is why people go on retreat, and it's why you so often come up with great ideas while doing something completely disconnected from work, such as boating or hiking or even standing in the shower.

In the fall of 2019, I spent five days at Breitenbush retreat center in Oregon, a place so completely off the grid that it makes its own geothermal electricity from the hot springs around and beneath its buildings. There's no internet of any kind. The only way to get a cell signal is to drive five miles down the road. Breitenbush does have an email account, and the office staff will relay a message to you, but only if there's a dire emergency. When you spend time there, you are truly disconnected.

In spite of this, or more probably because of it, Breitenbush is one of my favorite places in the world. Every time I go there, deprived of email, text, Slack, and Facebook, unable to check how much traffic my columns are getting or whether they're being shared on social media, I feel...different. And I am different. I slowly turn into someone calmer, more introspective, more like my thoughtful and serious younger self. I walk the trails and soak in the hot springs and spend hours and hours reading and writing in my journal. Without my usual occupations and preoccupations, I become more open-minded and openhearted and more willing to be vulnerable and try new things. On my last visit, on a whim, I went to a spirit guide workshop, which is the kind of thing I don't really believe in, would never do at home, and will probably never do again. Yet I'm glad I tried it.

I recently discovered a wonderful TEDx Talk by Caroline McHugh called "The Art of Being Yourself." Toward the end of the talk, she gives this priceless piece of advice: "With every passing year your job is to be better and better at being who you already are. This is not a cosmetic exercise. You're already different. Your job is to figure out how, and then to be more of that."

For me, being off the grid and away from all my technological connections and especially my work life makes me more like myself. I believe disconnecting can do that for all of us, which is why it's so important that we have that right. Some people talk about JOMO — the joy of missing out. That's what Breitenbush does for me. You might consider giving JOMO a try.

There's another reason that many of us are so bad at drawing a line between at-work and not-at-work. These days, many of us work for ourselves. The rise of the solopreneur and the gig economy has transformed work life for a huge swath of the American population. According to the Pew Research Center, there are more than 15 million self-employed people in the United States. I'm one of them. If you work for yourself, you have customers rather than an employer, and some people believe that the customer is always right. Customers, in particular, usually believe that.

That throws a whole different spin on things because now, if you work all night to meet an impossible deadline or if you skip an important life event because you're needed at some meeting, you're not giving in to the absurd demands of an unreasonable boss; you're providing stellar customer service, which is what you're supposed to do. Put the customer first. Be obsessed with the customer. Delight the customer. How many times have you heard those phrases in ads, articles, and business books?

Even if you're not an entrepreneur, the rise of the gig economy and the fact that entrepreneurs are lionized in today's world seem to have led to the odd expectation that everyone should act like a business owner even if they're just an employee. Amazon, for one, has enshrined that idea in one of its famous leadership principles: "Leaders are owners. They think long term and don't sacrifice long-term value for short-term results. They act on behalf of the entire company, beyond just their own team. They never say 'that's not my job.'"

That principle, named "Ownership," is number two on Amazon's list, second only to "Customer Obsession." No wonder those of us who are self-employed seem to think that it's normal to let work take precedence over personal life, and everyone else seems to agree. Sitting up late answering emails, working on weekends, missing parties and school plays — all of that seems normal. The other day my husband got very mad at me because he'd made a nice dinner for us, but I didn't come out of my office till nearly eleven o'clock at night. If I hadn't been yelled at for it, that would have seemed normal too.

How do we change all this? Can we rewrite the rules and create a new normal, within our own lives if not society at large? I think the answer is ... maybe. We live in a world where Amazon's principles are held up as examples of how to be successful. So are those of Apple CEO Tim Cook, who says he gets up at 3:45 every morning so he can start reading customers' emails. If you insist, for example, that you need a full eight hours of sleep to function at your best (which, by the way, sleep experts say is true), you will definitely be outside the norm.

Who's Really Making You Work Late?

What would happen if you started setting boundaries past which your work is not allowed to go? My guess is that you'd be negotiating those boundaries only with yourself and that no one else expects you to still be at your desk at 9 p.m.

Of course, what's actually dictating your late hours is probably your workload, and you may be at your desk late into the evening because whatever it is you're working on absolutely, positively needs to be done the next day. I don't mean to suggest you start missing all your deadlines, but I am suggesting that if you limit your working time to a reasonable number of hours, you will find you don't get any less done.

Actually, that's not just a suggestion; it's a scientific finding. Researchers at Stanford found that people who work sixty hours a week get less done than those who work forty hours a week, and multiple other studies have had similar results. So if you miss a deadline or two on your way to achieving a more humane work schedule that will improve your mood and retention and likely the quality of your work as well, does that sound like a worthwhile trade-off?

Is it actually possible to tell your boss or your customer — or whoever you're trying to please — that your workload is too great or your deadlines are too tight or you need some extra time or some extra help? The answer to that will depend a lot on where you are, how dependent you are on your job or on that particular customer, what the competition is or isn't for your role, and how easy it would be for you to find another job and for your boss or customer to replace you. All of these are questions only you can answer.

But here's something to keep in mind. Most of us, whether we work for bosses or customers, feel helpless to control our own work lives. But it's rarely true that we're as helpless as we feel. So please at least consider setting some boundaries, what those would be, and how you would tell others about them — even if it's just a thought exercise for now.

Combining Home Life and Work

There's a flip side to the disappearing boundary between work and home life, and that's the disappearing boundary between home life and work. For years, the trend toward people working from home or from coworking spaces or even while traveling the globe has been growing. Things like document-sharing software, video-conferencing, and chat for work teams made a physical presence in a specific location less and less necessary for most people. For some companies, having people on site is more a matter of philosophy than necessity. Many business leaders prefer to disallow remote work because they believe there's a value to people sharing a workspace every day. And, depending on the work in question, they may be right. But the Covid-19 pandemic rewrote the rules for even the most remote work–averse bosses. When your state is under social distancing orders, having employees work from home is a whole lot better than not having them work at all.

Working from home may or may not increase your efficiency. Either way, it means, for instance, that you can often schedule your day around picking up your kids from school or taking a short daytime hike or even, in my case, going horseback riding. It means you can dress however you like and eat whatever you want for lunch and take your dogs for a walk whenever they need to go.

Increasingly, though, you can do those things at the office too, especially if you work for a tech company in an urban area. At Amazon, for example, about seven thousand dogs are registered to accompany their owners to work, not as service dogs, but because Amazon leads the growing trend toward dog-friendly offices. It's true that welcoming dogs to the office is a relatively low-cost perk that helps Amazon and other companies recruit skilled employees and make them feel more at home. It's also true that it encourages people to stay in the office longer because they don't have to worry about a pooch at home needing to be walked.

The same two motives apply to pretty much all the perks that tech companies offer employees: meals, showers, childcare, recreation areas, gyms, sleep pods, hairdressers, and on and on. And even companies that don't offer homelike perks are relaxing their policies about things like making personal calls at work and wearing casual clothes.

Thus, not only can people increasingly work from home, but they can also increasingly conduct what would normally be their home lives while at work. No wonder the line between at-work and not-at-work has turned into a blur.

This blurring of a once-clear boundary is bad if it causes you to give up too much of your personal life in favor of your work life or if it strains your relationships or messes with your physical or emotional health. But it can be good if it allows you to combine work and life in interesting new ways that help you be better at both. For that to happen, though, you need to be in charge of your own work-life combination, and you need to know that you are.

A few years ago, I interviewed a career coach named Wendy Capland, and she became my coach. Somewhere along the line, I asked her about work-life balance. "Everybody struggles with work-life balance who works," she said. "I've coached thousands of people, and it's on everybody's list. Now they call it 'work-life integration.' I laugh at that, but in some ways it really is about having an integrated life and less about balance."

Capland said she thinks of the "balance" between work and life as a seesaw. Most of the time one side is up and the other is down, and you're constantly moving back and forth between the two. "There are periods of time when we all have to work our asses off," she said. "We have a deadline; we have a commitment. We choose to do that for all the good reasons. And then there are times when it's not a heavy push, and we can integrate more of our personal lives into our day. So it's about feeling satisfied with where you are at the moment."

Her comment made me think about one August a few years ago when my cousins in France sent their fourteen-year-old son to stay with us for a couple of weeks. I was, and am, a work-obsessed person. But when I found that my husband and I were completely responsible for an adolescent who had never been to the United States and didn't know much about it, all thoughts of work flew right out of my head. Although I managed to perform the bare minimum that I absolutely had to do over the next fourteen days, my heart wasn't in it.

My lack of interest in work was so complete, and so unusual for me, that it scared me. Was my all-about-work self gone for good? Was I going to be a slacker from here on out? That was a ridiculous worry. After two weeks of baseball games and outdoor concerts and tubing in the local creek and making him virgin mojitos while Bill and I had real ones, we drove my cousin back to JFK. He flew home to France, and everything, including my work obsession, went back to normal. The seesaw had tipped back the other way again.

I still think that ad exec's Thanksgiving Day conference call was a ridiculous thing to do. But maybe she's onto something with her insistence that the ever-blurrier line between our work lives and our real lives is something to be embraced and celebrated rather than resisted and feared. It only works, though, if we're the ones to decide which side of that line we're on.

EXERCISES TO TRY

1. Set a Boundary

Pick one boundary that you would like to set between your work life and your real life. It should be a boundary that is meaningful to you, perhaps taking a full hour for lunch outside the office every day or leaving work early enough to make dinner at home. Or it might be something as simple as not opening your email after 8 p.m.

Try to abide by that boundary every working day for three weeks. Use your journal, if you're keeping one, to keep track of which days you succeed at doing this, but please don't beat yourself up when you fail. I have been trying to set the boundary that I stop working every evening at 9 p.m., and I've missed that curfew more often than I've met it. But I'm still glad to be trying because even when I fail, I do get done with work earlier than I would have otherwise. And I can always try again the next day.

On the days that you do succeed in keeping to your boundary, write down how it made you feel. Did work go well? Were you better able to relax in your off time? If the boundary made things better, maybe that's a good reason to keep it. If it didn't, consider trying a different one.

2. Eliminate the Nonessential

If you're going to set better boundaries with work, it will help to eliminate anything you're spending time on that isn't really meaningful to your job. For a few days, keep track of how you spend your time. You can jot down what you're doing in your notebook or use an online tracking tool or app. For each task that you perform, ask yourself:

- Is this a valuable part of my job? (Examples might be making a sales pitch or solving a problem that is keeping a colleague from doing their job.)
- Is this nonvaluable but still necessary? (Examples might include filling out an expense report.)
- Is this a task I can put off till later with no serious consequences? (If yes, then consider putting it off.)
- Is this a task I can hand off to someone else? (If yes, then please, please do that.)

After a few days, see if this approach has helped you reduce your work hours enough to stick with your boundary, whatever it is.

3. Discuss Better Work-Life Balance with Your Boss

If you're struggling to do your job and still have a personal life, could it be that you're pushing yourself to do too much? Would anyone really mind if you left some of the work undone? If you aren't sure, then give it a try and see if anyone notices or objects when you abandon some less-crucial tasks.

If it's really true that your job expects too much of you, is there something you can do to change that? Consider bringing this up with your boss. Can you get additional help? Can you give some of your work to someone else or perhaps just leave it undone? Even if you don't feel safe having this conversation with your boss, try to imagine what you would say. Try to imagine getting a positive response. Ask yourself if it would really be out of the question to just broach the subject and see what happens.

Chapter 3

What If You Showed Up at Work as Yourself?

A few years ago, when I served on the board of a small nonprofit, one of the other board members became a source of frustration to the rest of us. She volunteered for projects but then let them drop. She missed board meetings, even though we met by conference call. The rules said she could be removed from the board for missing so many meetings. But she was also extremely bright and very successful, and she had done great work in the past.

We had a talk with her, letting her know that her absences were a problem and asking if she could do better in the future. And then the truth came out. Over the previous few months, she'd had a difficult pregnancy, given birth, and nearly died from post-delivery complications. She just hadn't told us about it.

I hope you find this as appalling as I do. Unfortunately, I also kind of understood it. She and I both worked in the fast-paced world of technology, and we spent much of our time dealing with people in Silicon Valley. And in this world of tech start-ups, optimistic venture capitalists, and big-dreaming founders, bad stuff isn't supposed to happen. You're invited to bring your whole self to work, including your child and perhaps your dog. But you're supposed to leave your medical problems at home. The same goes for your heartbreak, depression, and marriage difficulties.

In 2015, the *New York Times* published a scathing exposé about what it was like to work at Amazon. Multiple sources, both named and anonymous, described being put on a "performance improvement plan" — that is, probation — for letting things like cancer interfere with their job performance. One woman who'd given birth to a stillborn child said she'd been through the most devastating experience of her life, but her manager told her she would be closely monitored to make sure she stayed focused on her job.

Although Amazon denied many of the assertions in the story, it did not deny that events like this had taken place, although it did say such treatment of employees was at odds with its policies. But the company was frankly proud of its hard-driving culture, where managers were encouraged and at times required to fire anyone not giving 110 percent to the job. Amazon founder Jeff Bezos was known for saying that Amazon's culture was friendly and intense, but if necessary, he would settle for just intense.

Things at Amazon have changed somewhat since that story was published. In 2021, the company added "Strive to Be Earth's Best Employer" to its famous list of leadership principles. However, this was mostly a response to reports of tough working conditions at its warehouses at a time when the pandemic had made the general public suddenly aware of how important these workers were to their daily lives. It was also a response to the first serious effort to unionize one of Amazon's warehouses, although that effort failed. Amazon may have lightened up, but it remains an intense place to work.

As demanding employers go, Amazon may be an extreme case. But it's far from the only company to expect employees to be upbeat and efficient at all times, whatever they might be feeling inside. That's a challenge, because it's impossible to bring your whole self to work, or be yourself at work, if you are never allowed to show fear or sadness, frustration or anger.

Bad things happen at every job. Even if you have your dream job and the best boss in the world, something will happen at some point to frustrate, infuriate, or depress you because workplaces are made up of human beings, and it's human nature to sometimes upset each other. Dealing with those moments is always difficult, more so if you're in a low- or entry-level position and hoping to work your way up, and even more so if your gender, race, sexual orientation, religion, or anything else makes you different from the rest of your organization or from its leaders.

No matter who you are, it's always tempting to hide your feelings and keep your mouth shut when upsetting things happen at work. And if your biggest concern is to keep your job or advance in your company or retain an important client, the truth is that hiding your emotions may be the safest thing to do. But every time you do it, you make both yourself and your workplace just a little less human — and you make it just a little bit harder for you to be happy there.

A year into my first job at a magazine publishing company, things were going very well, or so I thought, and I suggested that my boyfriend also apply for a job there. He was hired for the same job that I had, but in a different area. We kept our relationship secret. And in less than six months, he was given a raise that put his salary well above mine.

It's been decades, but I still remember how it felt to hear that news. I congratulated him and struggled to smile while my whole body was going into shock. I had been working extremely hard, traveling on weekends, doing everything that was asked of me and more. I loved my job, and I'd thought my job loved me. Apparently, though, our relationship had been one-sided.

I stewed about it for a week, and then I started looking at ads for other jobs. I went on half a dozen interviews but didn't get any offers, which was just as well, since all the jobs I applied for seemed a lot less fun than the one I already had.

Finally, I did what I should have done in the first place. I went to my boss and, my voice quavering, asked him why someone with so much less seniority was making so much more than I was.

My boss, bless him, gave me a straightforward answer. Basically, my problem was timing. At annual review time several months earlier, I had been new to the company, and I was still figuring out how to be good at my job. Because I hadn't proved myself yet, he'd given me a minimal raise and a noncommittal performance review. It actually included the phrase "The jury is still out," but I was so completely clueless I didn't see that as anything to worry about.

By the time I asked my boss about my boyfriend's salary a few months later, the jury was no longer out. I was being given additional responsibilities. And so, even though we were between the usual times for raises, he said he would arrange for an increase right away and that there would be a much bigger one when annual reviews came around. I was hugely relieved to learn that my relationship with my job wasn't one-sided after all. And yes, I was happy that I'd once again be making more than my boyfriend was.

I can't imagine how much harder it would have been if I had faced a real problem, such as sexual harassment or illegalities, or if I'd had a boss I trusted less. I do know that, at least in my career, every time I've found a way to show up as myself at least a little, or found an acceptable way to say what I was really thinking, it's always been difficult, but it's always worked in my favor.

Showing up as yourself is exponentially harder when there is trouble in your personal life, and most of us get so accustomed to hiding those feelings we hardly even know we're doing it. In 2020,

Meghan McCain, a conservative TV personality and daughter of the late senator John McCain, went public with the news that she'd had an early-stage miscarriage months earlier and then gone back to work a few days later, acting as if nothing were wrong. My first reaction was surprise, not that she'd had a miscarriage but that she felt she could tell the world about it. "You're allowed to talk about that?" I thought. I'd had that experience twice, and I'd never told anyone I worked with.

A few days after my first miscarriage, I flew off to a conference where I knew I might land some new clients. I never seriously considered not going. That was tough, but the second time was worse. I was forty-five, and I'd clearly lost my last chance to have a baby of my own. Less than a month later, I was in New York City, cochairing the annual conference of the American Society of Journalists and Authors. The conference draws several hundred people, and besides being a professional event, it's also a gathering of hundreds of writer friends and acquaintances who only meet in person once a year. There I was, surrounded by scores of people who cared about me, who had known me for many years, who would have been sympathetic and supportive, and I said nothing. As if to add a little extra torment, there was also a fertility conference at our hotel that weekend.

At the time, I thought my only choice was to keep going and pretend everything was fine. With hindsight, I see that I could have at least told a few of my close friends what was going on with me. They might or might not have known what to say, but at least it would have stopped me from feeling like I was hiding a shameful secret.

A few years later, I attended a different organization's board meeting. There was a high-profile executive on that board whose wife had died of cancer only a few days earlier. None of us expected him to show up, but then word reached us through an intermediary. He was coming to the meeting, but he absolutely did not want to talk about his loss.

"I just want to say, I heard and I am so sorry, and I won't say anything else about it," I told him when I first saw him. And I didn't. But at a dinner that evening, the conversation turned to talk of places to live, and I told my board colleagues that my husband and I planned to move from Woodstock, New York, where we'd lived for more than twenty years, to Snohomish, north of Seattle. When they asked why we were making the move, I explained that it was for Bill, who had fallen in love with the area and the community of fellow musicians he'd found there, and that even though I loved Woodstock, I was moving because I wanted him to be happy and to fulfill some of his dreams. As I said it, I happened to look across the table at that widowed executive. He hadn't said a word, but he was looking back at me with an expression of such profound sadness that I've never forgotten it.

Why are we so determined to wall off the human part of ourselves when we're at work? We even do it over things that are relatively trivial. Last year, I was interviewing a CEO I'd never met before, and he said in passing that I seemed like an ex-hippie. I'm too young to have lived through the true hippie era, but his guess as to my tastes and my politics was on target. But instead of feeling happy that I was known and understood, I felt mortified because I hadn't done a good enough job of hiding who I was. I asked him how he knew, although, really, it wouldn't have been hard to guess. I had shoulder-length gray hair that I left to its natural ways. I was wearing flats. And on my wrist were delicate rubber bracelets that I'd bought in a funky store in downtown Austin; they were made by women in Africa out of flip-flops washed up from the ocean.

I was also wearing a bracelet that said "J-35." That may not mean anything to you if you don't live in the Pacific Northwest, but it's the designation of an orca (or "killer whale") who captured the public imagination in 2018. She's one of the Southern Resident orcas in Puget Sound, a community of orcas that is listed as endangered and is gradually dying out because of declining salmon populations, pollution, and increased boating in the sound. Orcas seem to be as intelligent as humans and to care for their family members as much as we do, and when she had a calf who died shortly after birth, J-35 carried that calf's lifeless body in her fins for seventeen days, sometimes assisted by other members of her pod who seemed concerned for her. The story spread, inspiring a debate about whether it was right or wrong to approach and observe her during her grief, as well as calls to breach some of Washington's hydroelectric dams that interfere with the salmon. So, yes, I suppose "J-35" did give me away.

It's daunting in these days when seemingly innocuous things like an affinity for wildlife, a religious affiliation, a liking for international travel, or even a preference for watching tennis as opposed to NASCAR can be construed as taking a political position. We live in a nation and a world that are filled with political divisions and acrimony. Deeply felt political convictions probably *should* go unexpressed in the workplace. It's both wrong and self-defeating to make people you work with uncomfortable because they disagree with your politics, opinions, or religious beliefs.

But for most of us, it goes way beyond concerns such as these. The less people know who we are, we believe, the safer we are. If someone turns down your pitch, passes you over for promotion, rejects you, or even fires you, it might hurt less if you can tell yourself that they don't really know who you are. And if you show up to work wearing standard-issue dress-for-success attire and only display generic family pictures, not, say, pictures of yourself with your belly-dancing troupe or listening to hip-hop at a downtown club, then no one will ever criticize anything about who you are because there won't be anything to criticize. If you never seem upset or angry or even overly joyous at work, then no one will know how much you care and how easily you can be hurt. The more we keep our true selves hidden, the less vulnerable we feel.

That kind of safety comes at a cost, though. A few years ago, I interviewed an image consultant, author, and coach named David McKnight, who has a lot to say about the importance of being yourself at work. Fresh from an Ivy League education, he went to work at a venerable consulting firm. His clients were Fortune 500 companies. "I was coming out as a gay Black man in corporate America, and it was very difficult," he told me. So he hid his true self behind navy blue suits and white shirts and a serious and stiff demeanor. "It came through in one of my reviews," he recalled. "'David performs very well, but his team doesn't really know who he is.'"

"There are so many ways that we cover," he continued. "A working mother may not be inclined to say, 'I can't work late tonight because the babysitter can't make it.' An African American woman may choose to straighten her hair because it makes her look a little more European. People from different backgrounds may choose to make a concerted effort to hide their accents."

McKnight acknowledged that people who hide their true selves because they fear it will hurt their careers might have a valid concern. A working mother could indeed risk being passed over for a promotion if she says she must go home to her kids.

Sometimes it's a delicate balance, he acknowledged. You might have to conceal some aspects of who you are to foster your own advancement and try to be your authentic self in other ways, he said. But if you truly don't feel that you can be your real self around your colleagues or customers, then in the long run this workplace is probably not a good fit for you. That's for two reasons. First, concealing who you are sucks up a lot of energy that would be better spent on your job and on achieving your career goals. And second, other people are rarely drawn to those who conceal their true selves.

"If I don't feel comfortable or I pretend to be someone else, a lot of times people can feel it," he explained. Think about the people you yourself have encountered at work and elsewhere. I'm willing to bet that the ones who made the biggest positive impression were those who seemed the most genuine.

McKnight now makes presentations to LGBTQ groups and has given up his strict regimen of navy blue in favor of more vivid colors that better reflect his true self. He says his signature now is "big bold glasses." He has coached many professionals to be truer to themselves in both their interactions with others and their business attire, and he's watched them blossom as a result.

"When you are very comfortable and you show people who you really are, that's typically when they warm up to you," he explained. "If customers feel they can connect with you, they're more likely to do business with you. On the most fundamental level, people do business with people that they like. If you're trying to cover up aspects of who you are, people will feel like there's an invisible veil between you and them." On the other hand, if you have the courage to be your true self, "People will either love you or they won't. But it won't be because of something you're hiding."

Take crying in the workplace, a prospect that would horrify many people, including me. If you're a woman in a leadership position or in a male-dominated industry, you may rightly fear that if you let yourself cry at work, you'll be labeled as not tough enough, even though legendary Apple founder Steve Jobs, who was as tough and as driven as anyone has ever been, cried in the workplace all the time.

Consider, just for a moment, a world where someone crying at work might be seen as a good thing and not a bad one, because that would mean it was a place where people were free to express their emotions. They might laugh as well as cry, shout or sing as it suited them, arrive at work with their kids and their dogs, and surround their workspaces with the things they love best. Consider a world where you could be your complete, weird, temperamental, happy, sad, and dazzling self. Wouldn't you want to work in a place like that? I know I would.

EXERCISES TO TRY

1. Have an Anti-stress Tool Kit

Sometime or other, or maybe more often than you'd like, something will happen to upset you or stress you out while you're at work. It's best to be ready with a few tactics to help you deal with those emotions. Over the years I've interviewed many experts and gotten a lot of advice about how to manage stress and upset at work. Here are some things you can try in the moment, or you can even combine them into an at-work emotional tool kit. Experiment and see what works for you.

- **Do thirty to sixty seconds of vigorous exercise.** This could be doing a few lunges or jumping jacks or running up a flight or two of stairs. If an upsetting event has released the stress hormone cortisol and perhaps adrenaline into your system, this is a good way to start clearing them away again. It's also what you evolved to do — those hormones are there for the precise purpose of helping you run faster or fight harder in a crisis, so a little movement should feel right.
- **Observe the effect stress or upset is having on your body.** Chade-Meng Tan, who developed Search Inside Yourself, Google's popular mindfulness program, says that failure and upset produce physical sensations, and you can start getting past those emotions when you recognize their physical effects. "Consider emotions as simply physiological sensations, that is all," he says. "They may be pleasant or unpleasant, but they are simply experiences. Just let them come and go as they wish." If you can do that and be kind and generous with yourself as you experience these emotions, "you can be more resilient," he says.
- **Take a few long, deep breaths, or even just one breath.** Sometimes when you're upset or frustrated at work, simply sitting in your chair, with your feet on the floor, and taking two or three deep breaths can be enough to restore some of your

calm. (There's more advice from Chade-Meng Tan, and also more detailed breathing exercises, in chapter 20.)

2. Start Thinking about Being More Like Yourself at Work

It's a frightening proposition, I realize. But use a piece of paper or your journal and write the answer to this question: *What would you do if you could be your real self at work?* Would you dress differently? Behave differently? Decorate your workspace? Laugh louder? Ask to use flex time? Pick one day a week when you attend no meetings? Let your imagination run free – this is your wish list.

When you've got your list, look for one thing you can try. Can you make one small step toward being your real self, whether it's wearing that "unprofessional" shade of nail polish that you really love or saying what you really think, just once, instead of telling your colleagues or bosses what you think they want to hear?

Just try it as an experiment. Take a tiny step toward being your true self at work. See how it makes you feel and how others react. You can always change back if you don't like it. But unless you're an ax murderer with bodies buried in your basement, I can almost guarantee that your coworkers or customers won't judge you as much as you think they will.

Chapter 4

The Power of Journaling

What if I told you that the most effective tool I've ever found for self-motivation and advancing your career can be purchased at any office supply store for around $6.99? Writing in my journal lets me work out my frustrations, dream big dreams, and then figure out how to move toward those dreams in real life. My career would be very different without it.

I told you in the beginning to use this book any way you want. If you know for sure that journal writing is not your thing, feel free to ignore what I'm about to say or even to skip this entire chapter. But before you go, just consider for a moment that what I'm calling a "journal" can take many different forms. For me, it's a fountain pen and a notebook with lined pages. For you, it could be typing or speech-to-text. In the series *Grace and Frankie*, Jane Fonda's character uses video blogging to figure out what she truly wants (to reconnect with an old boyfriend) exactly the same way I do it with pen and paper.

You can use a journal in all kinds of different ways. Here's how I use mine:

1. To set intentions and goals
2. To make specific plans
3. To track my progress toward my goals
4. To create a record that I can refer to in the future
5. To give myself free rein to privately express my thoughts and feelings and fears and joys so that afterward I can give my full focus to what's most important
6. And finally, to acknowledge my own accomplishments because, for me and perhaps for you too, it's much too easy to forget about them

I've always kept a journal, even as an adolescent. For most of my life, my journal has been a paper version of a therapist, a place for me to dump out my emotions so I could work through them. The night I learned that nearly everything my first husband told me about himself was a lie, I wrote down every word of our conversation, not because I thought I'd forget it, but simply as a way to process it. When my beloved aunt, my favorite traveling companion, died unexpectedly of a brain hemorrhage, I didn't write in my journal for an entire week, because I knew that writing those words down would finally make the news feel real.

That form of journaling served me well for many years. It was mostly a stream-of-consciousness version of my day-to-day moods. But then, a few years ago, I watched a four-minute video by digital product designer Ryder Carroll describing his invention: the bullet journal. It's a way of keeping track of your tasks, plans, and daily activities. I was initially skeptical. I already used note-taking software to keep track of daily tasks and goals, and an online calendar to track appointments. I figured I was pretty damned organized. Did I need yet another tool?

I did, or rather I needed a new way of looking at something I'd been doing for a very long time. For people like me who love scribbling in a notebook, Carroll's brilliantly simple innovation is this: if you number the pages of your notebook and create an index where you list what you've written on each page, then you will always be able to find anything you've written down any time you want to. You can safely use your journal to keep track of important things because nothing will ever be lost. While my journal is still where I pour out my thoughts in a near-daily act of self-therapy, it's now also where I make plans for pitching ideas, write down my goals, and make sure I'm moving toward those goals.

Carroll's video "How to Bullet Journal" on YouTube or at the Bullet Journal website will give you the basics of bullet journaling in a visual way that's easy to understand. But the bullet journal is only part of the picture. It's the combination of tasks and plans with hopes and dreams that makes journaling so powerful.

Here's how I've developed a power journal for my own use over the last couple of years. Please feel free to use this as a blueprint for your own power journal, or adapt it in any way that makes sense. Experiment and try different approaches or combine approaches until you find what works for you.

1. The Index

Once again, thank you, Ryder Carroll, for this simple, genius innovation. When you first start your new journal, set aside the first few pages of your notebook to be your index. Write "Index" at the top of each page. This is where you'll keep track of everything else you put into your journal. In my current journal, the index looks like this:

September 2021	6–7
August 22	8–9
Week of August 26	10–11
August 26	12–13
August 27	14–16
August 28	17–18
GeekWire meeting	19

As you can see, I use my journal to record my plans for each week and my thoughts on each day, but I also use it to take notes about things that I want to remember, especially when I'm meeting someone face to face. For me, writing in a notebook is much more graceful than typing on a laptop or taking notes on a smartphone.

I've learned the hard way that it can be difficult to guess when you start a notebook how many pages you'll need for the index. But it doesn't matter if you guess wrong. If you set aside too many pages, you'll have a couple of empty index pages at the beginning of your notebook that you can leave blank or perhaps fill with doodles. If you set aside too few, you can just continue the index elsewhere in the notebook. (Since you have an index, you'll always know where to find your continuation.) Because you use the index every time you write in your journal to record what went where, you have to turn to it frequently. I've found that if I run out of room for the index in the first few pages of a notebook, it's best to put the rest of the index in the last few pages, making it easy to flip to.

2. Future Tasks

There are always a lot of projects that are on my horizon, but I may not be working on them in the coming week or month. So I use a few pages after the index to list tasks, such as pitching new pieces to magazines or arranging to meet new people. I also write down target dates for when I want to have these tasks done, and I check back on them periodically.

3. Books Read

This is something I recently added to my journals, and it works well for me because I read so many books. Every time I finish a book, I write down a paragraph or so about it, both to solidify my memory of it and so that I have a written record I can refer to if I need to remember what I thought of the book or roughly what was in it. I imagine a similar approach could work for movies, television or video series, places you've visited, restaurants, or anything else of the sort where you want to keep track of your opinions and reactions.

4. The Coming Month

This step is optional. At the start of the month, number the lines of one or two pages for each day of the month, from 1 to 30 or 31. This is the first step in Carroll's bullet journal method, but truthfully I've gone back and forth on whether I need it. You will definitely need it if you (like Carroll) use your paper journal as your calendar. But if you use Google Calendar or Outlook or another online calendar, it may be unnecessary. I use this monthly calendar to keep track of things that I want to refer to quickly and that don't belong on my work calendar. For example, about a year ago, our cat Hamlin got badly dehydrated, so we bought him a water fountain for cats to encourage him to drink. It works well but needs to be disassembled and cleaned every two weeks, so the days-of-the-month page is a handy place to keep track of the last time I did it. Do you need something like that? Up to you.

This next step is not optional. On the next page, write a list of the things that you want to accomplish this month. This will help you tap into your journal's power as a motivational tool because the simple act of planning what you hope to accomplish over a whole month forces you to think beyond the day-to-day and start considering your overall goals and the steps you must take to reach them.

For example, you know the next step toward reaching your career ambitions would be a promotion. You know the job you want, but you aren't sure how to get it. You could take steps toward that goal by asking someone who has the job for advice, perhaps over coffee, and for tips about how to do the job effectively. Another step might be to sit down with your mentor or sponsor (see chapter 9) and ask for advice about how to be considered for that position.

It's very easy to plan to do these things and then not get around to them. You can't be sure if your colleague or mentor will have the time to talk to you. And maybe they'll tell you that you wouldn't be a good fit for a job like that, and maybe they're right and you wouldn't be. Besides, you're pretty busy already. Maybe you'll get to it later.

Later can easily turn into never. Believe me, I know. But once you write something in your list of tasks for the coming month, you've made a commitment to yourself to take that first step, and you have a reminder of that commitment.

When you're planning your month's tasks, it can be a good time to look at your list of future projects. Move items you're ready to start work on into your monthly task list.

5. The Coming Week

Use one or two pages in your notebook to lay out the seven days of the week, with at least three or four lines for each. Carroll uses a ruler to draw lines between the days; I usually do it free hand. In any case, create a calendar week — you're basically turning these pages of your notebook into a date book to track a single week. Enter appointments on the appropriate days of the week. As the week goes along, you can also enter notes on each day for things you want to keep track of or remember later. For example, "Took the day off to help Joe move." I use this weekly calendar to note whether I got any exercise on a particular day, and if so what it was. Not wanting to write "No ex" in my weekly log helps motivate me to get out and get moving.

On the next blank page, make a list of tasks you plan to get done in the coming week. You can pull some of these from the list you made for the month, and you should, otherwise you might get to the end of the month and have nothing to cross off your list. I don't usually include my day-to-day work responsibilities since they're a given. I do include things I'm afraid I might forget, such as emails and pitches I've been meaning to send, and also things like conferences I've been meaning to check out and possibly sign up for. I also include projects I need to work on that don't have a deadline because otherwise they could get forgotten or put off indefinitely.

My list of tasks for the week nearly always falls between six and ten items. I don't plan it that way; that just seems to be how it always works out. Fewer than six would be fine. More than ten would be too many. You don't want to feel overwhelmed every time you look at your weekly task list.

This process is much more powerful than the task lists or to-do lists you and I have been using our whole lives. By attaching a task to a particular month or week, you are implicitly giving it a deadline. You are also forcing yourself to review your list of tasks on a weekly and monthly basis.

When the week is over, create a new spread of calendar pages for the coming week, and a new list of tasks for that week. Now is your time to go back to the previous week's list. Cross off or check off any tasks that you got done.

What about the tasks you didn't get done? For each one, ask yourself whether it's a task that really matters and whether it needs to be done by you. If the answer to both questions is yes, then migrate it over to your new week's task list. If it isn't really essential, or if events have rendered it irrelevant, then just cross it out. At the end of the month, use the same process to review, cross out, or migrate the tasks you had listed for the month.

This approach keeps you honest, both about which tasks are really important and about which tasks you've been repeatedly putting off and need to just get done. Once you've moved the same task from one week to the next, or from one month to the next, three or four times, you will naturally start asking yourself if this is something really important for you to do and, if so, why you keep putting it off.

A couple of years ago, I applied this process to writing the proposal for this book and then to following up over weeks and months with my agent until we found the right publisher for it. If I hadn't, I really don't know whether I'd have had the persistence to make it happen, especially given the daily grind of deadlines and urgent projects. Without my power journal, you truly might not be reading this book right now.

6. Your Daily Thoughts

Now that you've dealt with your tasks and reminders, you get to use your journal as a place to dump out whatever is going on in your mind, your life, your emotions, your job, or anything else that's currently occupying your brain cells. If you had a dream the previous night, this is a great time to write it down. If you had a fight with a friend or you're worried about losing a customer or your child made the honor roll and you want to crow about it, write it down. I've written down what I was planting in my vegetable garden when that was taking up excessive brain space. I rarely journal on vacation, but the day after I return from a trip, I like writing down a day-by-day account of what I did while I was away.

The best way to approach this is to just start writing and not stop until you've filled up at least a page or two. Ideally, this should be fun. It's one of my favorite times of the day. For me, part of the pleasure is writing in a well-made journal with my favorite fountain pen and some bright-colored ink — it feels like my illegible handwriting gets to fly over the paper. For you, it will likely be something completely different. Maybe it's turning on your smartphone camera and talking into it, recording yourself speaking, or typing into an app.

When you have a difficult decision to make or a new opportunity to pursue, or when something unexpected happens, good or bad, in your work or life, the most important conversation you need to have is with yourself. That's also true when you're trying to figure out what your next step should be and what you really want most from your career and your life.

Your journal can be the place where this important conversation happens, whatever form it might take. I always find that the few minutes I spend writing in my journal are a good investment because they make me feel calmer and more able to focus for the rest of the day.

7. Everything Else

When I go to conferences and meetings with potential clients and when I have a coaching session, I've learned that the best place to take notes is my power journal. Research shows that for retention and comprehension, handwritten notes are better than typed ones. And typing notes isn't always easy or practical at a conference or an in-person meeting. Because I have the index, as long as I can remember more or less what year the meeting took place (so I know which journal to look in), I'll forever be able to find those notes when I need them.

When I read self-help books like this one, my power journal is my favorite place to do any written exercises that may come up. That makes it easy to find them again, and I just naturally find myself flipping to those pages and thinking more about those exercises over the following months.

Throughout this book, I suggest exercises to help you with your own career and self-care process. As always, use them any way you like — or not at all. But if you at all like the idea of writing in a journal, then please grab one and use it for those exercises, if nothing else. That way, you'll have them all in one place, and you'll be able to look back at them in the future. That's one of the best self-motivating tricks I know: to look back on where you were six months or a year or five years ago. That will help you see how far you've come and where you might want to go next.

EXERCISES TO TRY

1. Experiment!

What kind of journal is right for you? A beautifully crafted notebook with handmade paper? A composition notebook from school? Or maybe not even a notebook but just a sheaf of papers you keep in a folder or box? I've tried all these options and many more, and here's what works for me: a variety of nice journals, roughly five by seven inches in size, with lined paper. I write on them using a fountain pen and a variety of colorful inks.

I invite you to take your experimentation even further than I have. Write on your smartphone with a stylus. Record your voice and use speech-to-text. Make a video of yourself. Instead of writing about your day, draw about it. Or paste things into your journal to remember events, like the stub from that concert you attended. To find out what works best for you, try as many different things as you can think of.

2. Keep a One-Sentence Journal

If the ideas in this chapter sound too complicated and time-consuming for you to manage, here's an approach to journaling that absolutely everyone has time for: write a single sentence at the end of every day. Most people who do this use it as a quick record of what happened that day that they can look back on later – one person I know says that the days she doesn't write her one sentence don't feel complete. But you can use your one sentence for anything you want. I usually write a single sentence reminding myself of what I accomplished that day. (More about this at the end of chapter 11.) The idea was popularized by

The Happiness Project author Gretchen Rubin, who also sells a special notebook designed for one-sentence journaling.

3. Ignore All These Instructions

If you like the idea of journaling but none of the suggestions here appeal to you, there's one more thing you can try. Grab a journal or mobile device or a scrap of paper or anything else you like, and just start something. It can be anything you like – a single word, a scribble, a doodle, a letter to yourself or a letter, perhaps imaginary, to someone else. Your journal is yours and no one else's. And there's no way to do it that's wrong.

PART TWO

THE PEOPLE IN YOUR WORK AND LIFE

Chapter 5

Who's Your Tribe?

In 2005, *National Geographic*'s Dan Buettner did some fascinating research on what he called Blue Zones, places where a surprisingly large percentage of the population lives to be over one hundred years old. These places seemed to be quite dissimilar. They included Okinawa in Japan, a Seventh Day Adventist enclave in California, and Sardinia, an Italian island northwest of Sicily. What did these disparate places have in common?

Actually, quite a lot. Some of their similarities are things the medical profession has been telling us for many decades will help us live longer. For example, people in all these communities do a lot of walking and eat a lot of vegetables. But this may be Buettner's most unexpected finding: the people in these places all live in tight-knit communities. The Okinawans actually organize themselves into small groups called *moais*. *Moai* translates as "a group for common interest." The concept of the moai began as a way for the residents of a village to pool resources for the common good. More modern moais have five members who are grouped together as young children and usually remain friends for life. If a member of the moai receives a windfall, they all share. If a member of the moai suffers an unexpected setback, the other members help out. That sense of belonging and help and protection supports Okinawans for their entire lives, and it's one explanation why Okinawan women — most of whom belong to a moai — live eight years longer than American women on average, even though Okinawa is Japan's poorest prefecture, with lower incomes and higher unemployment than the rest of the nation.

The opposite is also true. If being in a tight-knit community lengthens your life, being isolated shortens it. According to the National Institutes of Health, social isolation and loneliness increase your risk of high blood pressure, heart disease, obesity, a weakened immune system, anxiety, depression, and cognitive decline. It's as if we evolved as a species to live longer when we're in a community, and maybe that's just what we did. According to the famed sociobiologist Edward O. Wilson, early humans who lived in groups and cooperated to get things done had a huge advantage over noncooperating humans and were thus much likelier to pass their genes along.

It's only in recent times that many of us have formed the new habit of living alone and doing our own thing, and while that fits well with our ideals of individuality and self-reliance, it may not be good for our bodies or our souls. My mother came from the Philippines, leaving behind a large extended family of siblings, aunts and uncles, and innumerable cousins. When one of her brothers died, another family member seemed to see it as a natural result of living alone since his wife had died and his children were grown, noting, "Nobody to greet him when he came home, only the dog."

We All Need Our Own Tribe

Community is deeply important for your physical and mental well-being. Depending on the community, it can also be really,

really good for your career. In my own life and career, the most important community is the American Society of Journalists and Authors, a group of about a thousand freelance nonfiction writers who are spread out all over the United States and even in other countries yet manage to work together on projects and have both friendships and business relationships that span geographies and decades.

I'll never forget the first time I walked into the ballroom at a members-only ASJA meeting. There were hundreds of people in the room, and in some way they all reminded me of me. They were all smart and articulate. They weren't shy about jumping in and talking to new people, and by that time neither was I — it's what self-employed entrepreneurs have to do. Most of them didn't look especially athletic (I wasn't either), and most were somewhat frumpily dressed in baggy jackets and comfortable shoes of the sort that I was wearing too. "I've found my tribe," I thought. It was a feeling I'd never had before.

I'd have been very surprised if someone had told me that day that, in time, I would join the board of ASJA, serving there for sixteen years, and that I would eventually become president of the whole group. Or that nearly every good thing to happen in my career from that time on would come about either directly or indirectly through ASJA. But that's what happened, mainly because ASJA members are incredibly generous about sharing both contacts and inside information and helping each other succeed.

It didn't really hit me until I started writing this chapter, but in its own non-Okinawan way, ASJA functions like a moai. Even though we all work in a very challenging industry where too many writers are chasing too few decently paying jobs, we share work opportunities with each other for the common good. ASJA members volunteer hundreds of hours putting on our conferences, serving on our committees or on our board, and doing mundane things like handing out conference badges and stuffing tote bags. We even have an emergency fund, which many of us contribute to, that provides small bailout grants to professional writers who've fallen on hard times.

As much as I love ASJA, I know it's not unique. In every profession and every industry, in every geographic region, and often within companies, groups like this exist where people help each other solve problems, find better jobs, and provide each other with advice and moral support. It could be a trade group, a union, a professional association, or an alumni group. It could be organized around a shared ethnic background or sexual identity or religious affiliation. Groups for common interest exist everywhere in many different forms, and I absolutely guarantee there's at least one out there for you. It's well worth making the effort to find it.

Should You Create a Mastermind Group?

Your group could even be a private club that you create for yourself. Not long ago, my coach, Wendy Capland, told me about something she calls *mastermind groups*. The concept is simple but powerful: You join or create a small group of people who are in the same profession and have some of the same objectives that you do. You meet once or on a regular basis to talk and share information and support each other's goals.

Capland has been using mastermind groups as part of her own career since the 1980s, when she worked as a human resources executive. Wanting to learn more about her profession, she found five other HR executives in the tech industry, each of whom had at least five years' experience. They met at each of their workplaces, and whoever was hosting would either make a presentation or elicit the group's help to solve a thorny problem. Later, when she started her own business as a coach, she created a mastermind group of other independent coaches.

When she described the concept to me, I realized that I've belonged to a few mastermind groups over the years, even though nobody called them that. The most important, most beneficial, and longest running was my writing group, the Glaring Omissions. We were all serious writers who met once every three weeks or so at each other's houses to critique the work of other members and to support their publishing dreams; we also held occasional public readings. Members were carefully chosen, based on their writing and on an in-person meeting with existing group members. The group's size fluctuated over the years but was usually around eight to ten members. The Glaring Omissions met regularly during the twenty-two years that I lived in Woodstock, New York, and it kept right on meeting after I moved away. Many published books and long-lasting friendships resulted from that group.

I've loved every mastermind group I've been in. And yet that doesn't make it easier to start one. I know, for example, that I could benefit from a mastermind group of successful public speakers, which is something I need to do more of and at a higher level. I know several very successful public speakers who could doubtless give me lots of good advice and might also enjoy sharing ideas with each other, and I've wondered if some of them would agree to join a mastermind meeting if I invited them. I've even made a list of potential mastermind members in my journal and put it in my planned tasks to invite them.

And that is as far as I've gotten. One issue is that it's been a few years since I've done any serious speaking, and I wonder if I have anything useful to share. But that's a common worry, Capland says. In fact, when she started her mastermind group for executive coaches, she'd had her coaching business for three years, but she only invited others who'd been doing it for five years or longer. How did she make that work? "Everybody knew I had the least amount of experience," she said. "They didn't care."

But a bigger part of the problem is the same thing that so often prevents us from doing things we want to do. It's hard — really, really hard — to reach out to someone, even someone you know, let alone a stranger, and ask them to join you in an endeavor. A kind of squirmy shyness overtakes me every time I think about asking other people for help or participation, even people who've already shown themselves quite willing to help me, and even though they might benefit too.

This may be why the members of Capland's coaching mastermind group were so willing to meet with her even though she was less experienced than they were. They were probably flattered to be invited, but also glad to have someone else do the difficult work of asking people to join, figuring out who would be in the group, and finding a mutually agreeable time for everyone.

You may never have heard of the concept of mastermind groups, but I'm guessing there have been times when you wanted to ask those more experienced than you for guidance. Maybe you did it, or maybe you didn't because of fear. What if they said no? What if they said no in a hurtful way that made you want to curl up and die? Very few people actually do this, but when it does happen, we remember it forever and never stop fearing it will happen again. It's way too easy to let worries like these paralyze you. And if you do, you're missing out on one of the most powerful boosts you can give to your career and to the quality of your life.

Creating a mastermind group is also a valuable opportunity to broaden your horizons. We so often tend to congregate with people who resemble ourselves in terms of age, ethnicity, background, political viewpoints, and sometimes gender. When you create your own mastermind group, you have the chance to change this dynamic and bring in people who are different from you and from each other. And there's plenty of research that clearly shows that having these more diverse viewpoints will increase your odds of success.

The Value of Community

I spend a lot of time thinking about how to form a group or find a tribe because of the roles that solitude and isolation — and community and connection — have played in my own life. My parents were both immigrants, and although each had a large extended family, those families lived thousands of miles away. I grew up in a Manhattan apartment building where we didn't have any kind of neighborhood community. My father was Jewish, and my mother was raised Catholic, but there was no religious community in our lives either. You can see why joining ASJA, more than a decade later, felt like such a revelation.

Five years ago, my husband Bill and I decided to move all the way across the country from Woodstock to Snohomish, Washington. There were several reasons for this move, but community was one of the biggest. Snohomish was the central gathering point for a happy, jumbled, informal collective of more than a hundred professional and semiprofessional musicians who gathered several nights a week to play music, talk, hang out, and — this being the Pacific Northwest — drink craft beer. It was like some combination of a giant club, an extended family, and an extra-large band. Bill, an accomplished songwriter and guitarist, fit right in. Pretty soon we were spending most of our free evenings with this group, at open mics, performances, parties, and recording sessions. I remember more than once looking around at all these people, many of whom had become dear friends, and thinking that hanging out among them was much like being in a warm and wonderful bath.

Then came the summer of 2016. The farmhouse we'd rented since we first arrived in Snohomish was put up for sale, along with its land, at an exorbitant price only a developer could pay. We bought a more modestly priced house a bit farther out of town and prepared to move. At the same time, Bill's closest friend, whom he had known for more than thirty years, was dying of cancer, so we were spending most of our time in the hospital with him. Then I came down with a raging gum infection. I was told I needed surgery that would put me more or less out of commission for three days. I sensibly decided to delay this until after moving day, but that plan proved unworkable because soon my mouth hurt so much that I couldn't think clearly enough to do much of anything. Meanwhile we already owned the new house, along with its mortgage payments, and our rental was rapidly coming to an end.

"I don't know what to do," I told Bill. "If I have the surgery now, we'll never be able to move in time."

"We have friends," Bill said, and he put out a call for help. And so it was that a few days later, as I lay on a sofa recuperating, a group of people came over, put all of our things in boxes, piled them into pickup trucks and vans, and drove them to our new home. Once I'd recovered, we threw the mother of all parties to thank everyone. Being part of a community can serve you in so many ways, some of which you may never have expected.

If you follow only one piece of advice in this book, please let it be this. You need community to support you in both your career and your life. That need is literally encoded in your DNA.

If you're already part of a community of like-minded professionals who help sustain and encourage you, then great! You're probably a lot better off than you would be without them. But if you're not, do what you have to do to find a community that can nurture you and your ambitions for the future. Online communities are great, but ones that meet face-to-face, or at least by video chat, are better. You may not gel with the first one you try, or the second, but please don't give up. Keep trying until you discover or create a group that's the right fit. There's a moai out there for you. You just have to find it.

EXERCISES TO TRY

1. Find a Community That Fits

Think about the role community plays, has played, or could play in your career and your life. What communities have you belonged to so far, and what have you gotten out of being in them?

What community would you like to belong to? Do a little research online and by asking around among your peers to learn what communities might be available to you that you don't know about. Consider trying different communities on for size by attending a meeting or two and seeing if it feels right.

2. Try a Mastermind Group

As a first step, grab some paper or your journal and make a list of at least four people you would like to learn from. These can be people you already know or people you would like to get to know.

Can you make a commitment to yourself to reach out to just two of these people? Ask them if they'd agree to a single meeting in person, perhaps over coffee, or by video chat to talk about their work and yours. It's wise to start with just two or three people in case they have contacts they want to invite as well. And inviting someone to a single meeting is asking for a smaller commitment than inviting them to join an ongoing group. Besides, you won't know until that first meeting whether the group is a congenial mix of personalities or not. If it is, it will feel natural to make plans to meet again.

Chapter 6

How to Have a Conversation
with Anyone, Anywhere, Anytime

In chapter 1, I mentioned my friend Shelmina Babai Abji, an author, women's empowerment speaker, philanthropist, and former vice president at IBM, all of which is remarkable, considering that she started life in a small town in Tanzania. Professionally, we've exchanged all kinds of useful information, and I like her a lot.

We met at a cocktail party after the TEDxSeattleWomen conference, and recently she said to me, "It's so lucky that you happened to sit down next to me that day."

"Yes, it is," I agreed.

That was a big fat lie. I was certainly glad that I'd met her, but luck had nothing to do with it.

I'd arrived at the cocktail party and meandered through the crowd with my ears wide open, wondering who I might like to meet. As I walked by, I overheard Shelmina deep in conversation with two other women. She was talking about her work with women's groups overseas and she seemed fascinating, so I decided to get to know her. I sat down on the same bench as Shelmina and the other two women, bided my time for a bit, and then glided smoothly into their conversation without interrupting it. At the end of the cocktail party, Shelmina and I were walking out side by side, the other two people having vanished long ago. We were still chatting, and she drove me to my car, which was parked somewhat far away.

That's one of the thousands of times that being good at starting conversations with strangers has helped me get what I wanted. It's a skill anyone can learn, and if you don't already have it, I recommend acquiring it because you'll find that, for the rest of your life, you'll have a huge advantage over those who haven't developed this skill.

The Gentle Art of Starting a Conversation

You may think that starting conversations with strangers comes naturally to some people and not to others, but I guarantee that at least some of those "naturally" gregarious people have worked hard to make it look easy. Let's start with some basic principles.

Find Your Confidence

This is the only hard part — overcoming your own shyness and fear. Everyone, including me, feels some amount of reluctance at the prospect of talking to a stranger, especially if we have to initiate the conversation. There isn't anything you can do to magically make that reluctance go away, but there are a few things that may help if you keep them in mind.

The first is what feeling shy about talking to strangers says about you: you're a human being. Just as it's deep in our DNA to want to live in tribes (see chapter 5), our very nature causes us to fear and mistrust those who are not of our tribe, especially if we've never met them. There's a reason so many parents keep telling their children not to talk to strangers, even though statistics show they're in greater danger of abuse from someone they know than from someone they don't. That human quality of distrusting strangers leads us to war, gang battles, racism, and acts of unspeakable violence, and it also makes us afraid to engage with people from outside our own communities.

The second thing to keep in mind is that most of us tend to attach disproportionate fear to social situations, sometimes to an absurd degree. Consider that several surveys have shown that for many people, public speaking is their number one fear, outranking even death. This too, believe it or not, is baked into our DNA; for early humans, getting kicked out of one's tribe often led to death, so the terror of being ostracized lives deep inside each of us.

But we are modern humans with rational minds, and those minds can recognize that while embarrassment may be highly unpleasant, it definitely won't be lethal. You may or may not like the results of starting a conversation with a stranger, but there's usually no actual danger.

The other thing to remember is that, since fear of talking to strangers is pretty much universal, the person you start a conversation with may be just as frightened as you are — or perhaps more so. If that person wasn't afraid, they might have been the one to start the conversation with you. The fact that you're starting the conversation suggests that you are the braver one.

Put the Focus on the Other Person

One of the most powerful words a marketer can use to get you to pay attention to something or click on something is *you*. I read this a long time ago when I was trying to learn how to make my headlines more clickable and my copy more appealing, and it does work. The reason is that it puts the focus on the reader rather than on me.

The same strategy works for starting a conversation. If you

want to engage someone's attention, you might be able to do it by telling that person something surprising about yourself — that you recently won the lottery, for example. But an easier and more reliable way to engage people's full attention is to invite them to talk about themselves. This is why I most often start a conversation by asking a question.

Besides being the best way to capture another person's attention, having someone talk to you rather than doing the talking yourself has multiple advantages, starting with the most obvious: when you're talking, you're not learning anything. When you listen to someone else talk, there's a decent chance you'll learn something useful. The very first thing you're likely to learn is whether this is someone you want to get to know better, either because you like the person and might want to be friends or because this is someone with useful knowledge or connections who could possibly help you — or better yet, you could help each other.

Sometimes it's both: you like your new acquaintance and want to spend more time with them, and you also could be professionally useful to each other. Those are the very best encounters, and they're why being able to talk to strangers is a sort of superpower. Sometimes it's neither — you have no particular desire to deal with the person socially or professionally. When that's the case, it's simple enough to find an appropriate gap in the conversation, say something like "It's been nice talking with you" (even if this is a lie), and gracefully move on.

Find Common Ground

There's another advantage to getting your conversational partners to talk to you about themselves. It's the quickest way to find out what you have in common. You're almost certain to have *something* in common with anyone you meet, even if it might not be immediately obvious. If you get the other person to talk, you may be able to tease it out. Finding common ground is the best way to keep a conversation going beyond the first few moments of introducing yourselves. So home in on whatever shared interests, opinions, or experiences you may have as quickly as you can.

There's a flip side to this search for shared interests. You also need to be careful of areas where the two of you may violently disagree. Sadly, this is particularly important these days because of the polarized nature of both politics and discourse in general. The person you're speaking with may express deeply felt political, social, religious, or anti-religious views. If they fit with your own, then great! You've found some common ground. If they don't fit with your views, either remain noncommittal or express disagreement as neutrally as you can. Think of it as an opportunity to learn about a point of view you may not agree with. In today's world, most of us don't do that often enough.

If your conversational partner doesn't come out with a viewpoint on any of the day's divisive issues, then for pity's sake don't volunteer one yourself. It may be true that if the two of you are to become friends or colleagues, you'll need to talk about this stuff at some point. But don't do it when you've just met.

You may argue that you can't be friends with, and wouldn't want to associate with, anyone who holds certain beliefs that are fundamentally at odds with yours. Most of us feel that way about some things. I myself have a hard time associating with anyone who believes women are less fit for positions of responsibility than men are. If someone disagrees with you on something you fundamentally believe, then you don't have to talk to that person. Just find a graceful way to slip out of the conversation, and go find someone else to talk with.

Never-Fail Conversation Starters

Now that we've got the basic principles down, what should you actually say when you want to start a conversation? Here are three openings that pretty much always work.

1. Ask for Information or Help

Once when I was walking west across 42nd Street in New York City during a protest that was happening all around town, a man heading east stopped and asked me if I knew what was going on at the United Nations. I had just come from there, so I told him that nothing much was happening. I'd heard a rumor that there were pacifists lying down and blocking traffic in Times Square, so I was on my way to check that out. He told me he had just come from Times Square and that nothing was happening there either. We fell into step together and wound up chatting, and then dating, and a few months later, we were married. By that time, I'd found out that he didn't really care that much about the protest at the United Nations; he'd simply used the question to meet me. The marriage turned out to be a disaster, but his conversation starter was stellar.

Asking someone for information or a favor may be the best way there is to get that person to want to engage with you. I realize this is counterintuitive. In fact, when I mentioned this phenomenon to my current (and much better) husband, he misunderstood and thought that I'd said that if you want someone to like you, you should do *them* a favor. That certainly seems more logical.

The reason the opposite is true is something called the *Ben Franklin effect*, so named because of this quote from Ben Franklin's autobiography: "He that has once done you a kindness will be more ready to do you another, than he whom you yourself have obliged." Franklin had used this knowledge to solve a problem he was having with a fellow member of the Pennsylvania legislature who seemed to dislike him intensely. Franklin learned that his nemesis had a rare and interesting book in his possession. So Franklin courteously asked if he could borrow it for a few days. Not only did his enemy lend him the book, but it changed their entire relationship, Franklin wrote. "When we next met in the House, he spoke to me (which he had never done before), and with great civility; and he ever after manifested a readiness to serve me on all occasions, so that we became great friends, and our friendship continued to his death."

In modern times, psychologists say that the Ben Franklin effect is a result of cognitive dissonance, the distress we all feel when we hold two conflicting beliefs at once. Most of us instinctively try to resolve this dissonance by changing one of our conflicting beliefs. The willingness of Franklin's antagonist to lend the rare book meant Franklin must be deserving of a favor, even though the other man might only have done it because courtesy wouldn't allow him to refuse. That was dissonant with the thought that Franklin was hateful. Since the loan of the book had already happened and couldn't be changed, the only thing that man could do to resolve the dissonance was change his opinion of Franklin.

If you use the Ben Franklin effect as a conversational starter, it's best to ask for something that the other person can give you right away and without too much thought, which is why requesting a small piece of useful information is such a good approach. But you can also ask someone to hand you something, save your seat for a few moments, or do any number of other small favors. You can even ask for something you don't really want or need. My Inc.com colleague Jeff Haden observed a very clever car salesman do exactly that, asking prospective customers to hold his day planner for him while he cleaned up a spill that he had surreptitiously made himself. He told Haden that it worked "every time" to get people talking with him. The Ben Franklin effect is so powerful that it's often my go-to for starting conversations.

2. Mention a Shared Experience

Talking about the weather is such an overused element of small talk that Dave Matthews lampooned it in his song "So Much to Say." But there's a reason that discussing the weather is such a well-worn conversational tactic: it's something everyone experiences, and we mostly all feel the same way about it. If it's 95° out, everyone will feel hot. If there have been two solid weeks of rain and now the sun is out, that will make nearly everyone happy. (I have one childhood friend who says he dislikes sunny days and stays home with the shades drawn, but he is truly an outlier.) So something like "Man, it's really coming down!" is a pretty reliable conversation starter.

But there are many different shared experiences you can use to forge a quick connection with someone you want to talk with. If I'm at a conference, one conversation starter I use often is "Are you having a good conference?" That's open-ended and invites others to respond pretty much any way they choose. If the local team just won — or lost — an important game, that may be another shared experience that you can use as a conversational opening. The construction of a new Costco became a reliable conversation starter for many people in my neighborhood.

In nearly any group setting, there's some aspect of the experience that's the same for everyone and worthy of comment. Use it to get a conversation going.

3. Give a Compliment

You might think smart people can easily tell when they're being flattered and therefore won't be affected by a compliment. But a fascinating study conducted in Hong Kong in 2010 showed that even when people know perfectly well that they're being insincerely praised, that praise still affects them on an unconscious level. In this case, the flattery came in the form of an advertisement for a department store that complimented the reader on their fine fashion sense. As praise goes, that was pretty obviously insincere, and the subjects of the study readily identified it as such. But they still turned out to be more favorably disposed toward the store than those who hadn't been praised by an ad.

This is why finding a reason to compliment someone is often a highly effective way to start a conversation with a stranger. If the other person is wearing an unusual item of clothing or jewelry or carrying an unusual bag or briefcase, those are all good targets for a compliment. (Do not compliment the person's physical attributes, though, as "You have lovely eyes" could be seen as intrusive and borderline creepy.)

If possible, you're even better off complimenting something the other person said or did. You could say, for example, "I thought the way you handled that difficult customer was very effective." If the other person made a speech or taught a class, then praising them for that is a no-brainer.

If you really want to use the power of this technique, plan ahead the next time you are going to attend a function where there's someone you know you want to meet. These days, nearly everyone has a forum where they express their thoughts and opinions or share their expertise. It could be a blog, LinkedIn, Twitter, online videos, articles for websites or trade magazines, or maybe even a book they've written. Spend a little prep time reading some of what your target person has written or watching their videos or listening to their podcasts. Then when you meet that person, you'll have a perfectly targeted compliment at the ready that will make them feel doubly good, first because you liked whatever they had to say, and second because you took the time to read or watch or listen. This works even on famous people and high-profile business leaders.

What If You Get Rejected?

This is the most terrifying part of starting a conversation with someone you don't know. You're afraid they might get up and walk away in a huff or say something like "Get away from me!" And there's no way to shield yourself from the possibility that this might happen.

People in general are more open to conversations with strangers than you might think. But that doesn't mean everyone, and it doesn't mean all the time. If you go around initiating conversations with strangers, which I really hope you do, you will inevitably come upon some who don't want to talk to you.

Most people in that situation will try to be polite about it. That's why it's important for you to keep your eyes and ears open during conversations with strangers so that you can spot clues that tell you whether they want the conversation to continue. If they're saying little beyond blandly agreeing with you, that's a clue that they would rather not keep talking. Their feet are another clue. People unconsciously point their feet toward what they like or are interested in, so take a quick glance down to see if the other person's feet are pointed toward you or away from you. If one or both are pointed away, it's probably a good idea to politely end the conversation and move on.

Sometimes people will be fairly direct in letting you know they don't want to talk. Once when I was visiting my mother and my ninety-something-year-old stepfather in Florida, we pulled into a stranger's driveway by mistake while looking for an unfamiliar address. A man came out of the house to find out what we wanted. After we'd established that we were at the wrong place, my stepfather tried a random conversational gambit. It was the middle of Wimbledon, and so, with no preamble about tennis or even sports, he inquired, "Are you in love with the Williams sisters?"

Looking a bit surprised and unmistakably disdainful, the other man simply answered no and went back inside his house. It was the kind of social rejection that I believe would have smarted for most people, but I doubt my stepfather was particularly bothered. He had spent many decades as a salesman, starting conversations and getting people to talk to him and making friends with all sorts of folks. I suspect he'd been through more failed attempts at starting conversations than you or I ever will.

When people rebuff your attempt to start a conversation, it really should be no more a big deal than the Williams sisters question was for my stepfather. The problem is that most of us tend to dwell on these rejections. This, again, is in our DNA; our brains are hardwired to focus on negative information and ignore positive information. That's an obvious survival skill because if you're, say, in the jungle, it's a lot more important to notice the poisonous snake lying in your path than the beautiful flower growing next to it.

The best antidote for this that I know of is repetition. The more often you try starting conversations with strangers, the easier it will be. First of all, with practice you'll get better at saying the right things and reading the signals quickly. But even more important, you'll succeed more often than you fail. Most people in most situations are more willing to talk to you than you might think. Talking to strangers, and doing it again and again, is the best way to find that out for yourself.

Not only that but talking to strangers will make the world a better place. There's actual research that shows this. In 2014, researchers at the University of Chicago tried a fascinating experiment in which they instructed some commuters who rode trains or buses every day to initiate conversations with strangers. Then the researchers compared those subjects' mood with other commuters who just followed their normal routine. It turned out that commuters who'd been instructed to chat generally enjoyed their commute more than those who kept to themselves.

Humans are social creatures, so it's no surprise that talking to people, even people we don't know, tends to elevate our mood. But what was more surprising — and sad — about the Chicago experiment is that the people in it expected the opposite. They thought talking to strangers during the ride to work or home would make them unhappy instead of happy, and if the experiment hadn't required them to converse, they would have kept to themselves. They also expected that other people would not want to talk with them, which made them reluctant to start conversations. But they were wrong on both counts. Most people did welcome the chance to converse, and based on other research it seems likely that having someone to talk to made the commute more pleasant for them as well as for the experiment participants.

This experiment reminds me of one of the longest airplane trips of my life, a flight home to Seattle from Chicago in November 2017. I'd been at an ASJA board meeting and conference, where I was scheduled to stay for an extra few days. I abruptly cut my trip short when my husband had a heart attack. I managed to grab a seat on the last Southwest nonstop from Midway to SeaTac that night, a four-and-a-half-hour flight. Like the commuters in the experiment, I typically keep to myself while traveling, and on airplane flights I usually stick anti-pressure earplugs in my ears and sink into a cocoon of work, reading, and playing games on my tablet.

But this time was different. Before I got on board, I already knew that Bill had had emergency surgery and had stents newly installed in his heart. I'd even talked to him in the recovery room, but I had no idea what would happen next or what our future might look like. And so, as I walked up the aisle of that crowded flight, a woman met my gaze and nodded at the empty middle seat next to her, and I took it. I thought talking to a stranger would be the best way to settle my addled mind that night, and it was. I told her what was going on. It turned out she was a widow and had been through a heart attack with her own husband.

"What's your husband's name?" she asked me.

"Bill," I said.

"Bill is going to be just fine," she said firmly. And it turned out she was right.

Talking to strangers is more than just a powerful career-boosting skill. And it's more than a way to make yourself happier or to calm yourself in the middle of a crisis. Most of us, in today's world, don't spend enough time talking to strangers, or at least not randomly selected ones. We may talk to people on social media, but these are people we already know or people who already agree with our opinions and views: like-minded people who join us in groups or message boards, or perhaps the friends of our friends.

But if this horribly divided world we're living in is ever to be whole again, then all of us are going to have to get better at talking with people when we don't already know that they agree with our beliefs and views. In other words, random strangers. So knowing how to start conversations with people we don't know is a lot more important than it first appears. Not only will it boost your career but it could make the world a better place.

EXERCISES TO TRY

1. Repeat the Chicago Experiment

If you commute to work or travel often, break whatever habit you have of reading the news or listening to a podcast or scrolling through social media on your smartphone. Instead, make a point of starting a conversation with a stranger. If you don't commute by public transportation, try it in the grocery store, at the playground, or wherever strangers happen to be. Take a stroll around your neighborhood and chat with any neighbors you come upon whom you don't yet know.

2. Do Your Homework before Meeting a Bigwig

If you know you have a conference or other event coming up where a prominent person or executive you hope to impress will be in attendance, take some time in the week before to do a little research. Track down your target's blog posts or other writings, or see if there are any interviews with him or her available online. Think ahead about what you'll say when you meet. Perhaps you agree with their position on some current issue, or maybe you like their idea for a new innovation. Then try out your approach and see how it goes.

3. Plan Some Conversational Openers for Your Next Event

This can be especially helpful if you feel shy or nervous about talking to people you don't know. Think ahead about how you might open a conversation with a stranger using any of the strategies in this chapter. In fact, if you want to use the Ben Franklin effect, you can try something like this: "I'm reading this book, and there's a chapter on starting a conversation with a stranger. I'm trying to learn how to do that. Do you mind if I practice on you for a minute or two?" Most people will say yes.

Chapter 7

Dealing with Toxic People

Years ago, Bill and I moved to rural Massachusetts, far away from all my writer friends. I loved the area and I was happy to be there for my husband's new job, but I missed the social atmosphere I'd left behind. Then I found what seemed like a perfect solution: a fun-looking magazine for the food and wine industry was located in a neighboring town. I didn't know much about the restaurant business, but I was willing to learn; it turned out, the magazine needed a business writer. I didn't know anything about wine either, but I really wanted to learn about that! On my first visit, the managing editor kindly invited me to the magazine's impressive wine cellar and picked out two wines that he said would be educational for me to take home. I was ecstatic.

Then I met the editor in chief. He was suave and invited me into his large office for a chat. There was some talk about the magazine and how my work would fit in. Then he mentioned, almost in passing, that he thought the managing editor was not very good at his job.

My radar went up immediately. I was about to start working with that managing editor — why bad-mouth him to me? It was an obvious red flag, but I was in love with the idea of working at the magazine, so I ignored my misgivings and headed back to my home office with several assignments to complete.

I hit trouble on the very first one, which was an overview of how restaurants handled desserts. Since I wasn't an industry expert, the magazine had promised to provide sources for the story. They did — after several reminders from me — four days before the deadline. I sprang into action and completed the piece just in time, but it wasn't the best piece of writing I'd ever done.

I didn't hear from the magazine for several days, but I didn't worry about it because I'd been invited to join their weekly Friday morning meeting. Hanging around drinking coffee and discussing ideas with a bunch of writers and editors sounded like just what I'd been missing, so I showed up promptly at 10 a.m. I waited and waited for the editor in chief to start the meeting, which he delayed to 10:30, then 11. I hung around awkwardly, making occasional small talk, but mostly keeping to myself because the people at the magazine were busy doing their jobs. No one seemed particularly bothered or surprised that the meeting had been delayed, which told me this was something that happened often.

While I was waiting, the managing editor handed me a printout of my story, saying simply, "This is for you." In the margin of the first page, the editor in chief had written, "Not very good. Rewrite." And that was all.

I had expected to rework the story — it was my first time writing for this magazine and about this industry. But to tell me my work was subpar without any suggestions for improving it was insulting and unprofessional. Worse, it left me to figure out with no guidance at all how to make the piece better match what the editor was looking for. Just as I was digesting this, word came that the editor had canceled the meeting after all. It was now completely clear that I was dealing with a toxic person.

I took my article and went home. Now that I knew the deadline didn't matter, I took another week to rewrite it, using the time to do additional research. I knew the piece was much stronger when I emailed in the second draft. I also knew I should stay away from the office, thus forcing the editor in chief to interact with me by email. With email, I figured, it would be harder for him to just scrawl, "Not very good," and send something back. He'd have to be more specific and make himself clearer. I sighed as my lovely vision of collegial conversations with other writers over glasses of fine wine evaporated.

Four Types of Toxic People

Toxic people are everywhere, and like the editor in chief at the restaurant magazine, most will do something to let you know how toxic they are within minutes after you meet them. But because they're everywhere, they can be hard to avoid, and unfortunately they can sometimes cast a big shadow over your work life. It's a near certainty that, at some point in your career, you'll have to deal with a toxic colleague or — worse — boss. If you work for yourself, you'll encounter a toxic customer at some point, or you may be forced to work with a toxic person because they have skills that you need. Even if you're extraordinarily lucky and there are no toxic people in your work life, you're pretty much guaranteed to have at least one somewhere in your family. Unless you're a hermit living alone on a remote island, you can never completely avoid toxic people, which is why we all have to learn how to deal with them.

There are many different types of toxic people in the world, and most display more than one type of toxic behavior. But let's look at some general types to help you recognize them when you encounter them.

Narcissists

One evening many years ago, my then boyfriend and I tried to stop at an Italian café for a drink after an evening out. It was a popular place, the only one like it in the neighborhood, and there were no available tables. As we walked away, my boyfriend turned to me and said angrily, "I would like to be so famous, so beloved, that if I arrive at a café and all the tables are full, they'll get some wood and build one rather than turn me away!"

I said nothing. At the time, we were both aspiring young writers, both at the beginning of our careers. The only response I could think of was to ask, "Don't you think I want that too? Don't you think we all do?" But I was pretty sure saying that out loud would only spoil the mood even more. Anyway, he wasn't capable of considering other people's desires or viewpoints. All he could see was himself.

Most of us have encountered narcissists at one time or another, and we're particularly likely to encounter them in the workplace because, narcissism experts say, they tend to end up in leadership roles. Their high self-regard comes across as extreme self-confidence, and in our Western culture most of us are drawn to self-confidence because we can't help believing that it's backed up by superior knowledge or ability. Since narcissists are obsessed with how they come across, most of them look great — they dress for success — and they tend to be well-spoken too. Put it all together, and you have a recipe for achieving high positions. "Narcissists are running the world," UCLA psychiatrist and author Judith Orloff told me when I interviewed her about difficult personalities a few years ago.

It's easy to fall for a narcissist — I've done it more than once — for the same reasons that people are likely to hire them, promote them, and invest in their start-ups. But over time, having a narcissist in your life or your workplace tends to be an unpleasant experience because most narcissists are incapable of considering any point of view but their own, and they act only out of self-interest. In a clinical study, participants were paired up in two-person teams and then given a task at which, unbeknownst to them, they were certain to fail. Afterward, most participants shared the blame equally with their partners, but not the narcissists — they quickly blamed the other person. When things go wrong, you can pretty much count on a narcissist to throw you under a bus.

Narcissists want you to respect them, but they may not care too much whether you like them. "Studies have shown narcissists are willing to sacrifice being liked if they think it's necessary to be admired," Roy Baumeister, a social psychologist at Florida State University in Tallahassee, told *Psychology Today*. Of course, most management experts say leaders *shouldn't* care about being liked. It's management orthodoxy that if you worry about whether people like you, it will make you an ineffective boss. I have no idea whether this is really true, but it's easy to see why so many narcissists wind up in leadership roles.

Manipulators

A few years ago, I was having coffee with a friend who was extremely busy, highly popular, and rarely available to socialize. She had made time for me on this rare occasion because I was moving across the country soon, and she knew we'd be seeing little of each other in the future. We were happily ensconced in a quiet corner of a Woodstock café with hot drinks in front of us when my mobile phone rang. It was a friend of mine calling from an electronics store, where he was shopping for his mother, one of the most manipulative people I've ever met. He wanted to buy her a tablet or e-reader to use in bed, but she had told him it had to be ever so light as she would tire easily holding it. Because he viewed me as an expert on technology in general and electronic reading in particular, he was seeking my advice. And just like that, I got sucked in. I wound up wasting half my time with my rarely available friend in a struggle to come up with an e-reader solution this demanding person might like.

It's uncanny how manipulators — even working second hand — can get you jumping through hoops to try to please them. In this case, the manipulator was controlling not only her son, but through him, me as well. Looking back, it would have been so simple to avoid. I could have said that I was unavailable and if he needed my help, he would have to call at another time. Even better, I could have let the call go to voicemail in the first place, which would have been both smarter and politer than answering. Once I picked up the phone, I was probably a goner. They made me feel needed, like I was uniquely wise about technology and thus the only person in the universe who could help them!

Manipulation takes many different forms, but often it comes as gossip or a confidence. Whenever someone tells you something that's supposed to be a secret, watch out — there could be manipulation at hand. Years ago, a particularly manipulative friend of mine went through a bitter divorce. My husband Bill and I still liked her ex-husband, who seemed to have few friends. "I should reach out to him," said Bill, who tends to be gregarious. And he did. He left a message on the ex-husband's answering machine, inviting him to get together for coffee or drinks.

When my friend heard about this, she took me aside to tell me that her husband had never much liked Bill. I didn't respond, and after a few beats she added, "You can tell Bill if you want."

This time, the manipulation was so obvious I nearly laughed out loud. If I told Bill that her husband didn't like him, any chance of their becoming friends or talking to each other would be erased. As it worked out, they did not become friends, but I avoided passing on a message that would only have hurt Bill's feelings and ensured that the friendship never developed, which of course was what my friend wanted.

The thing about manipulation is that it works best when you're unaware of it. So keeping an ear out for possible hidden motivations behind the things people say or do is your first line of defense.

Passive-Aggressives

When I was sixteen, my uncle died of pancreatic cancer. He had been the head of the family, the husband of my father's older sister, and a wealthy and successful man. My aunt and uncle had always been a big presence in my life, and my father and I lived in an apartment one floor down from theirs. My uncle's death was a tough loss for the family, made worse because my grandmother, my father's mother, had died just a month earlier.

My father didn't discuss his feelings about either death (or any death). Both his parents were now dead, and the rest of his family was in Europe, except for my aunt. She was his last connection.

On the day of my uncle's funeral, as the family gathered at my aunt's apartment, my father lingered downstairs in our apartment attempting to fix a malfunctioning vacuum cleaner. Looking back, I can recognize this for what it was: an inarticulate man struggling to manage his grief and the burden of family responsibility that had just landed on his shoulders. But the teenage me could only see his selfishness. His sister needed him and so did I, but here we were on our own, playing hostess to a passel of random relatives, most of whom I barely knew.

The plan was for the funeral party to travel together to the service and the gravesite in cars hired for the occasion. I suspected that my father thought I would phone downstairs to tell him when the cars arrived, so that he could join us at the very last minute. But he hadn't come out and said so, perhaps because he knew what I would answer: Your place is not downstairs, it's upstairs with your sister. She needs you. *I* need you. The damned vacuum cleaner can wait.

And so, when the cars arrived and the relatives asked me where my father was, I just shrugged. We waited for a bit, but the cars were double-parked outside on a narrow Manhattan street, and so soon enough we all trooped downstairs and sped away.

At some point, my father discovered that we'd left without him. Calculating that it was too late to find us and catch up with us, he asked the doorman to alert him as soon as we returned, and he hurried upstairs as soon as we did. My aunt was so furious that she turned on her heel and walked away, refusing to speak to him or look at him. My father was furious too — at me. He lit into me right there in front of the rest of the family. This was, of course, a tactical error, as they all came to my defense and told him in no uncertain terms that missing his brother-in-law's funeral was his fault and not mine.

When I told my husband this story recently, he said the same thing: it wasn't my fault. Maybe he's right, but even at sixteen I realized that by swallowing my anger and making a ten-second phone call, I could have averted the pain and hurt feelings that lasted for years between my father and his sister. Or I could have accomplished the same thing by *not* swallowing my anger, by calling him and telling him exactly how big a jerk he was for staying away.

Instead, I turned a bit of bad judgment into a very big mess. And like most passive-aggressive people, I came out of it all looking completely innocent.

How should you deal with passive-aggressive behavior? As with manipulation, your first line of defense is recognizing it when it happens. What you do next depends on the nature of your relationship. With the people you're close to, calling out the behavior and asking them to be more overt with their negative emotions can be helpful. But in many cases, calling out someone's passive-aggressive behavior will result in a display of wide-eyed innocence. It's likely a better strategy to treat passive-aggressives as though they were children: tell them precisely what you need from them and when you need it. If my father had done this, he could have avoided the entire mess — I'd have either had to call him or tell him up front that I wasn't going to.

Anger-Mongers

Anger-mongers are the opposite of passive-aggressives — they're all aggression, all the time. You know the type of people I mean. They're the ones you censor yourself around, trying your best not to be the target of their wrath.

Years ago, I served on the board of a nonprofit with a fellow member who was a true anger-monger. I often suspected that was his real reason for serving on the board — he rarely volunteered to lead board initiatives or take on tasks, but he clearly loved a good debate. It gave him the opportunity to pound the table with his fists while making some passionate point or other. And if anyone dared interrupt his tirade, he would insist loudly, "Let me finish!" On the other hand, he often interrupted other people himself.

The rest of us board members never confronted the anger-monger. It was easier to just let him rage on till he wound himself down, then continue with whatever we were doing. But a few months later, a different board member quit the board because she couldn't stand the anger-monger.

Confronting an anger-monger is never easy, especially if you're as conflict-averse as I am. My experience on the board taught me a valuable lesson about the dangers of just letting this behavior go, and yet I still struggle to react appropriately when confronted with someone who trades in unreasonable anger.

Things get even tougher when the anger-monger is your boss or a valued customer — which is highly possible since people often feel comfortable dumping their anger on those who can't easily walk away. If so, keep reminding yourself that irrational or excessive anger is inappropriate and that the problem is the anger-monger's and not yours.

Orloff recommends confronting overly angry people. As unpleasant as it is, that probably is the wisest approach. You can do this in a calm way, in private, after the angry person's outburst, letting them know that you will not put up with the behavior and making clear what the consequences will be — you might leave for a different position, report the behavior to Human Resources, or whatever else makes sense. Be prepared to make good on your ultimatum if the anger-monger attacks again.

One other thing: you may be tempted to simply walk away from an anger-monger in the middle of an outburst. I've done that myself. What I discovered is that if you're going to do that, be prepared to keep on walking. Walking away will make the anger-monger exponentially angrier, and it will escalate the conflict between you. You could wind up destroying the relationship for good.

Long-Term Solutions

Up to now, I've offered mostly short-term tactics for dealing with toxic people. It could be that's all you'll need. A manipulator who tries to manipulate you and fails a few times may very well give up trying, for example. But most of the time, you also need a long-term approach to dealing with the toxic people in your life. You basically have two choices: get farther away or get closer.

Getting farther away by getting the toxic person out of your life is often the simplest and best thing to do. Find a different boss or customer or friend. Let's face it — life is too short for you to spend a large amount of your time with someone who makes you miserable.

That's what I did with the editor in chief from the food and wine magazine. I finished out my first set of assignments for the trial period. Then I sent an email explaining that because the work took more time than expected, I regretfully needed to raise my rates to nearly twice what they'd originally offered. In case that didn't work for them, I could recommend a different writer who would likely be available at my original rate. (That's a handy thing about being a writer: if you have work you don't want to do, you can almost always find someone else who does.)

Dramatically raising my rates, if I can find a reasonable explanation for it, is my favorite way to "fire" an undesirable client. It allows them to reject me, rather than me rejecting them, which makes them feel better and leads to fewer hurt feelings. It makes me feel better too because — damn! — I *am* worth that much! And every once in a while, someone says yes to the higher rate, which is a nice incentive for putting up with whatever they're doing to annoy me.

However you do it, it's always a good idea to avoid burning bridges if you possibly can. In most industries and most communities, people know each other, and word gets around, usually with surprising rapidity. Even if you know you never want to work with or even talk to the toxic person again, making an enemy of them won't help you. It could, in fact, harm you.

There's another approach to dealing with a toxic person that is much more challenging but ultimately might be more rewarding: befriending that person.

I know, I know — you would rather be set on fire. But hear me out. Toxic people are never born that way. They become that way, either because they believe it makes them safer or because they believe it will help them get what they want. And many toxic people are toxic in some situations but not others. We've all known people who are sweet and mild-mannered to all their friends and neighbors but turn into anger-mongers in the privacy of their homes. (Both my father and Bill's father fell into this category.) We've seen business executives who are wonderful at charming customers but act like ogres to the people who work for them. We've even known parents who are helpful and supportive to one child and belittling to another, or people who are toxic during one portion of their lives and become someone completely different later on. Bill Gates is a great example of that last phenomenon. He was once known for the belittling way he berated his employees. Now he's a warm and fuzzy philanthropist who's widely beloved and seems to regret his former churlish ways.

With that in mind, can you set aside your resentment of the toxic person long enough to get to know them a little better? Your move to make friends may surprise the toxic person, who is most likely accustomed to being avoided. Whatever else happens, it will almost certainly change the dynamic of your relationship. As you come to understand the toxic person, their behavior may start bothering you less, and you may see that there are effective ways to defuse it. And as the toxic person comes to trust you and feel comfortable with you, their behavior may change for the better.

If I'm honest, I have to admit that I haven't managed to befriend very many toxic people. I'm much better at the other strategy — walking away and never looking back. But the few times I've managed to make a friend of a toxic person, it's always been worthwhile, and I've wound up with a more fulfilling relationship than I'd have thought possible. Remember the Ben Franklin effect described in chapter 6? Befriending a toxic person was the strategy Franklin used to transform his enemy in the Pennsylvania legislature into a lifelong friend. It can work for you too.

The Toxic Person in the Mirror

Finally, consider the possibility that you yourself could be a toxic person on some occasions or in certain situations. Before you dismiss this idea, keep in mind that most of us can and do engage in bad behavior at times, even if we're mostly nontoxic. I wish I could say that the day of my uncle's funeral was the last time I behaved like a toxic person, but it wouldn't be true.

Social psychology expert and writer Jeremy E. Sherman has identified some habits he says are common to toxic people. Ask yourself these questions, and don't freak out if you answer yes to some or even all of them. That just tells you that you have some behavioral bad habits you need to change. And now is a perfect time to start changing them.

1. **Do I tell people how honest, trustworthy, or generous I am?** If you do, that may be a sign that you're a toxic person because most people who are trustworthy and generous don't say so. They know that others will judge them by what they do, not by what they say they are. I'm reminded of a new housing development that was being built down the road from us when we first rented a house in Snohomish, Washington. The developer put up a sign that said the homes were "Built with Integrity." To me that seemed like a signal that the opposite was true.

2. **Do I justify my actions by pointing out that others do the same?** Believing you're not so bad because you're no worse than someone else is a likely sign that you need to re-examine your behavior. No matter how evil something is, you can always find someone else who's already done it. But shouldn't you try to be better than the worst people you can think of?

3. **Do I believe that just because I hate a behavior in others, I would never do it myself?** If so, you're probably way off base because the fact is most of us do things that infuriate us when others do them. Take interrupting, for instance. I loathe being interrupted, but does that mean I never interrupt anyone else? Sadly, it does not. Most of us are guilty of doing at least some of the things that annoy us the most, and having the self-awareness to know that is a big step toward being less toxic.

Learning to see ourselves as others see us is one of the most difficult things we can do, and most of us fall short of this most of the time. But especially if you're in a leadership role, it's essential that you find out how others perceive you. Asking friends and colleagues whom you trust to (gently) tell you the truth about how you come across is one way to do this, and I highly recommend it, though it can be unpleasant. Getting a view of yourself from the outside can help you be a better boss, mentor, parent, partner, or friend. And it might give you better insight into the toxic people you have to deal with as well.

EXERCISES TO TRY

1. List the Toxic People in Your Life

Just writing down a list of the people in your life who frequently make you uncomfortable or angry or unhappy can help you feel better all by itself. But take it a step further by drawing a line down the middle of the page (or using both sides of a notebook). On one side, write the person's name. On the other side, write a strategy for dealing with that person. It might be avoiding them, requesting a transfer to another department or location, or looking for a new job. In the case of a toxic family member, it might mean making the difficult decision not to show up to holiday dinners anymore.

Another approach might be making sure not to do the one thing that pushes the toxic person's buttons. (If tardiness reliably sends them over the edge, can you make sure to be early to every meeting?) Or it might be trying to get to know them better and seeing if – like Ben Franklin – you can get the person to stop being toxic, at least when you're around. When you're done with your list, you'll have some strategies you can try for dealing with the toxic people in your life.

2. Write Your Own Toxicity Confession

Think back to a time when you behaved badly, when you engaged in toxic behavior. (You say you never have? I don't believe you.) Write an account of what you did, who was affected, and what was going on with you to make you behave that way. I did that myself in this chapter when I described the day I caused my father to miss my uncle's funeral. It had been many years since I thought about why I did it or how much harm I caused. It was really good for me to remember that time and also to forgive myself for it.

So please do the same. Write a full and openhearted account of whatever you did wrong. And then forgive yourself. Next time, you'll do better.

Chapter 8

How to Thrive (or at Least Survive) in an Unequal World

On the day I turned twenty-nine, I happened to mention my birthday to my boss. "Your biological clock is ticking!" he told me.

I had never discussed my personal life with him, or whether I even wanted children. Looking back, I realize how offended and annoyed I was. But I was barely aware of it at the time. Instead, I forgot it quickly. For one thing, he was my boss at a job I loved at a time when jobs, especially in publishing, were hard to come by. Besides, that kind of thing happened — and continues to happen — all the time. Like some sort of awful lava lamp, if you start paying attention to the sexism, racism, homophobia, ageism, and ableism all around you, it becomes difficult to see anything else. Without really thinking about it, I had trained myself not to notice. Maybe you've done that too.

In the 1982 movie *Tootsie*, Dustin Hoffman plays out-of-work actor Michael Dorsey, who's so desperate for a part that he disguises himself as a woman and lands a role in a soap opera.

Experiencing gender bias and sexual harassment for the first time, he chafes at things that most women just accept as part of normal life. In the scene that gave the movie its title, Michael, in his female persona of Dorothy, is told by the director, "Tootsie, take ten."

"My name is Dorothy," she (he) responds. "It's not Tootsie, or Toots, or Sweetie, or Honey, or Doll." The men in the cast are always addressed by their names, she says. "I have a name too. It's Dorothy. Capital D-o-r-o-t-h-y. Dorothy."

A couple of years after the movie came out, I ordered business cards for myself for the first time. But when I went to pick them up, I discovered an error. The words *Freelance Writer* were written in the kind of script you'd expect on a wedding invitation, rather than the more professional serif font I'd selected. A male store employee who presumably never saw *Tootsie* argued that I should just accept the cards as they were, apparently believing that a patronizing tone, peppered with endearments like "Honey" and "Sweetie" would somehow cow me into giving in.

After about the fourth one of those, I finally turned it back on him. "Sweetheart, Deary, Darling, Honey-Pie — you're going to have to fix it," I said. It's a moment I remember clearly decades later only because it was so damned satisfying. I had called him out on his demeaning language and his shoddy service and let him know I wouldn't be patronized, all in a single sentence. He redid the order without further objection.

While writing this chapter, I came across an interview Dustin Hoffman gave about *Tootsie* years later to the American Film Institute. He said he hadn't wanted to make the movie unless he could convincingly pass as female, so he asked the studio to do some makeup tests and see. When he saw himself done up as Dorothy on screen, he said, "I was shocked that I wasn't more attractive. And I said, 'Now that you have me looking like a woman, now make me a beautiful woman.'"

That's as good as it gets, the makeup artists told him. "It was at that moment that I had an epiphany," Hoffman recalls. "I went home and started crying, talking to my wife." He realized that if he had met Dorothy at a party, he wouldn't have bothered talking to her because she wasn't beautiful. "There are too many interesting women I have not had the experience to know in this life because I have been brainwashed," he said, tearing up right there in the interview. "That was never a comedy for me."

Not much has changed since then. The presumption that a woman must be beautiful or else she's worthless is still very much with us. In Michelle and Barack Obama's twin memoirs about their time in the White House, both relate that on the day of a public appearance, Michelle would have to wake up hours earlier than her husband so she could undergo the lengthy process of having her hair and makeup done. And, she wrote, the same was true for every woman in public life.

At the time I was reading Michelle Obama's book, then British prime minister Theresa May was struggling to navigate Brexit, the United Kingdom's withdrawal from the European Union, something no nation had ever done before. The news was full of images of May seated behind the prime minister's desk, writing letters to EU leaders or talking to the press outside 10 Downing Street. She was always perfectly made up, stylishly but conservatively dressed, her graying hair coiffed just so. You might think the leader of a nation with the sixth biggest economy and the eighth mightiest military on Earth might have better things to worry about than making sure her hair and makeup were perfect before starting work in the morning.

Being judged on our appearance, and considered worthless if unattractive, is just one way the mere fact of being female puts women at a disadvantage. Here's another: unpaid labor. *Unpaid labor* refers to all the things we do without pay because they need to get done, such as childcare, housecleaning, cooking, yard work, caring for sick relatives, and so on. Studies show that unpaid labor falls disproportionately on women in every nation in the world — there's not a single one where such work is evenly divided between men and women.

Women do the biggest share of unpaid labor in the poorest countries, so you might think they'd do the least in the richest one — the United States — but that's not true. The progressive nations of Scandinavia have the closest thing to parity. In Norway, men spend an average of three hours a day on unpaid labor while women spend an average of three and a half. In the United States, men spend two and a half hours a day on unpaid labor, while women spend more than four. "This means, on average, women do seven years more of unpaid work than men over their lifetimes," Melinda Gates wrote in her book *The Moment of Lift: How Empowering Women Changes the World*. "That's about the time it takes to complete a bachelor's *and* a master's degree."

All these statistics were compiled before the Covid-19 pandemic, however. Since then, social scientists report, the disproportionate burden on women has worsened. You don't need statistics to tell you that, though; it's been obvious in Zoom meetings where women working from home have struggled to keep up while simultaneously homeschooling the kids. It's also been obvious in the way the pandemic disproportionately drove women from the workforce, not only because the high-touch service jobs we tend to do have disappeared in larger numbers but also because so many women simply couldn't continue working when there was no school and no daycare. One surprising analysis by the National Women's Law Center found that the number of jobs lost by women was equal to 100 percent of the net US jobs lost in December 2020.

For those of us who still have jobs, the workplace is an unlevel playing field, just as it's always been. Take the gender wage gap, a phenomenon that's been recorded since the 1960s. In 2010, women earned just over 77 cents for every dollar earned by men in the United States, according to the National Committee on Pay Equity. In the years since then, women's pay has risen…all the way to 82 cents on the dollar. At that rate, it would take more than fifty years to achieve equal pay, but it will probably be longer because the gap is shrinking more and more slowly over time.

However much white women may be held back by gender bias in the work world, that inequality is exponentially worse for Black women and other women of color. Women overall may earn 82 cents for every dollar earned by men, but for Black women, that number is a depressing 63 cents. This may not sound like a lot of money. But over a forty-year career, on average, Black women will earn nearly a million dollars less than white men by the time they retire. For Hispanic and Native American women, the gap is even larger. There's a Black Women's Equal Pay Day every year, the symbolic date until which Black women must keep working in order to be paid what white men made in the previous calendar year. In 2021, that day was August 3.

An even bigger problem than the pay gap is how women are seen, and how we see ourselves, in the workplace. In 2017, Google engineer James Damore started a furor in the tech world with a memo questioning the company's — badly needed — diversity effort and opining that the absence of women in high-paying tech jobs resulted from hormones rather than bias. "I'm simply stating that the distribution of preferences and abilities of men and women differ in part due to biological causes and that these differences may explain why we don't see equal representation of women in tech and leadership," he wrote.

Four years later, well after Damore was fired for his memo, it still fills me with fury for the way it stupidly or willfully ignores the many ways, both subtle and overt, women are told that we belong in the workplace, but always in a secondary role. Just how companies communicate this became painfully clear when some clever researchers at Stanford University decided to test their theory that women weren't being welcomed into high-tech jobs by the simple method of attending recruiting sessions aimed at the university's STEM graduates. Stanford graduates with technology degrees are some of the most sought-after college graduates in the world. At the time of the study, unemployment was at a historical low, and companies reported that a lack of employees with the skills they needed was the primary obstacle to their growth. So these recruiters had good reason to want every single graduate they met to apply for a job. And they acted like it! They handed out gifts. They promised lavish salaries and perks. And yet they still made the female students unwelcome.

In most of these sessions, the researchers observed, men made the presentations. Women, often introduced by their first names only, stood in the back and handed out the gifts or snacks. Sometimes a female engineer from the company would be present at the recruiting session, but if so, she never gave a presentation. In one session, the lone female engineer repeatedly attempted to answer a question from the audience, but she was cut off each time by a male engineer who talked over her. And as the researchers watched, many female students in those sessions got up and left before the end. The message that they weren't wanted had been received loud and clear.

This is the sort of reason I and so many women like me have spent our careers being careful not to look at that awful lava lamp. Once you do, it's impossible to stop seeing gender bias everywhere. There's emotional labor — the work of organizing meals, planning get-togethers, and giving gifts, the things that make workplaces, and families, feel livable and connected — which is mostly performed by women. There's the pink tax — the average 7 percent higher price tag on products marketed to women compared to the same products marketed to men. And I recently came across a *Consumer Reports* study that found women are more likely than men to be seriously injured in a car accident because automobile safety features are designed with men's bodies in mind. There's not a tiny corner of the world anywhere, not even behind the wheel of her own car, where a woman can expect equal treatment.

But this is a book about solving problems and making both your work life and your actual life more successful and happier. So what can you do about all this? I've struggled with that question quite a bit because there are no really good answers. We shouldn't have to live in a world where our lives and our careers take on extra layers of difficulty and danger because of our gender, race, sexual orientation, age, accent, religion, background, or physical ability. But this is the world we're in, and there aren't any others to choose from. So while I can't tell you how to fix our unequal world, it may help if you avoid doing a few specific things.

Don't Assume You're Getting Fair Treatment

In chapter 3, I wrote about how upset I was when my then boyfriend got a raise that made his salary much higher than mine. Here's the question I would ask my younger self if I could: *You were a proud feminist who marched for women's rights. Why did it never occur to you that the explanation for his getting a higher salary than you, when you'd worked for the company a year longer, was simply this: he was a man, and you were not?*

Back then, the owners of the company and its most senior executives were male. Women ran Human Resources and managed the office, the same job my mother had at her company. Everything else was overseen by men. Years later, I would learn the distinction between line areas and staff areas in a company. Line areas were those that produced or sold the company's actual products, such as sales, marketing, operations, and so on. Staff areas were the functions a company needs to stay open, things like HR and legal and facilities. Staff functions would always be subservient because they were only there to support the line functions, where all the power was. Staff areas in the company where I worked, as well as most other companies I encountered, were more frequently headed by women than line areas.

Why didn't I see all this back then? Why didn't I even consider the possibility that gender bias was behind our respective salaries? Probably because I was emotionally tied up in my work: I couldn't bear the thought that the company I loved was paying me unfairly for the job I loved. Instead, I wore blinders that I put on myself. Don't make the same mistake.

Don't Blame Yourself

A few years ago, when I learned that a male colleague was being paid more than me for regular articles when, once again, I'd been doing the work longer than he had, I didn't let myself think about gender bias, or at least not in the usual way. Instead, here's what I told myself: *He did a better job of negotiating the contract than I did. He's better at that because he's a man, and men are good at understanding and demanding what they're worth. I allowed them to pay me less than I'm worth, and therefore it's my fault.*

Now that I've written it out, I'm amazed at the mental acrobatics I went through to convince myself that my being underpaid was not a matter of gender bias — even though I knew the statistics about unequal pay. And yet my reasoning was true, as far as it went. In my experience, men do indeed do a better job of negotiating on their own behalf, especially when it comes to money. But why is that? It's easy to assume that the culprit is our upbringing, in which girls are often taught to avoid being overly assertive. We're also discouraged from talking about money and are encouraged to assume that the men we marry will do the lion's share of the earning.

But while it's easy to assume this is the problem, the evidence shows otherwise. Research on 4,600 randomly chosen employees in Australia — which keeps better records than the United States of who asks for raises and whether they get them — found that women ask for raises just as often as men do. But women get the raises they ask for 15 percent of the time, compared with 20 percent of the time for men. In other words, when women ask for a raise, they're more likely to be turned down.

And that's not all. Academics who've studied the issue in depth told the *New York Times* that when women ask for more money, the person they ask is likely to view them negatively, as demanding and therefore unfeminine.

In other words, there's just no way to get it right. Asking for what you know you're worth means you'll be seen as unfeminine or brash. Not asking means being paid less than you deserve and continuing to live with the gender wage gap forever. Meanwhile, the ugly truth is that most companies depend on the gender wage gap to stay profitable. Most employers don't have it in their budgets to give their female employees a 20 percent raise.

All of this sucks. Don't make it worse by blaming yourself for it like I did.

Don't Hold Yourself Back

A frequently quoted internal study at HP found that women only apply for a job when they meet 100 percent of the stated qualifications, whereas men will apply if they meet 60 percent. Considering that it's from an internal study at one high-tech company and not necessarily representative of the workforce overall, why does this statistic get talked about so much? Because it's one of those numbers that feels both significant and true. When I encounter a statistic that shows women are deliberately holding themselves back in the workplace, I think, "Of course we are!"

When the study came out, women's leadership expert Tara Mohr decided to dig in further. She asked more than a thousand women and men this question: "If you decided not to apply for a job because you didn't meet all the qualifications, why didn't you apply?" By a wide margin, the most common answer for all respondents was that they thought they wouldn't get the job.

That's revealing, Mohr wrote in an article for the *Harvard Business Review*. First, it shows it's not a lack of confidence in their own abilities that's holding women back. In fact, only 10 percent of women said they chose not to apply because they thought they couldn't do the job well. What's holding them back is the belief that they can't get the job in the first place, so why waste their time and set themselves up for rejection?

"They thought that the required qualifications were...well, required qualifications," Mohr wrote. "They didn't see the hiring process as one where advocacy, relationships, or a creative approach to framing one's expertise could overcome not having the skills and experiences outlined in the job qualifications. What held them back from applying was not a mistaken perception about themselves, but a mistaken perception about the hiring process."

Well, maybe. There are two different ways to interpret this statistic. One is that women are indeed holding themselves back by not applying for jobs that they could very possibly get. Another is that women accurately expect that if they apply for a job, they'll be held to a very high standard, and so they'd better be perfectly qualified or maybe overqualified if they expect to get hired.

Which interpretation is true? LinkedIn shed some light on this question by performing a statistical analysis on the billions of hiring interactions that take place on its platform and conducting follow-up surveys. Consistent with the HP report, LinkedIn found that women applied to 20 percent fewer jobs than men did and were 16 percent less likely to apply to a job after viewing it. But it also found women may be right to assume there's gender bias in hiring. Recruiters who search LinkedIn profiles when they have a job to fill are 13 percent more likely to click on a man's profile than a woman's when it comes up in their search results.

Once they've reviewed a profile, they're also slightly less likely to contact a woman than a man and invite them to apply.

On the other hand, women who apply for a job are 16 percent more likely to be hired and 18 percent more likely if the job is in senior management. This might sound like pro-female gender bias, but of course it only makes sense when you consider, at least based on the HP study, that the female applicants for any given job are more likely to be 100 percent qualified than the male ones.

Then again, you may want to ignore all this research and just go after the jobs you want. In 2018, Seattle journalist Jody Allard wondered what would happen if a woman were to "job hunt like a man." She decided to find out by conducting the experiment on herself. She hoped to leave her current job quickly and had been spending long hours on the search for new employment. But, she realized, her own behavior matched HP's findings. "Despite my eagerness to find a new position, I found myself applying only to jobs I was extremely qualified for (and in some cases, overqualified)," she wrote in an article for The Lily, which is published by the *Washington Post*.

So she decided to change that. She couldn't quite bring herself to apply for a job if she was only 60 percent qualified, but if she was 70 or 80 percent, she would go for it, "regardless of title or level," she wrote.

At first, she felt elated. There were so many more jobs out there that she could try for! Almost as quickly, emotional discomfort set in. "I found myself battling a monster-sized case of impostor syndrome," she wrote. "I sent psychic apologies as I applied for jobs that weren't 100 percent up my alley (barely restraining myself from emailing actual apologies)."

But to Allard's surprise, the strategy worked. She soon had phone interviews lined up with twelve different companies. One was for a director-level job, the most senior role she'd applied for. Partway through that interview, the recruiter said, "I'm not sure you have the skills I'm hiring for." Allard thought the jig was up, but then the recruiter continued, "But maybe that's not the most important thing." The recruiter invited Allard in to meet the rest of the team and then offered her the job.

That may be the most important lesson here. There's bias out there — of course there is. But if you decide not to let your own insecurity or your negative expectations slow you down, really good things can happen.

Don't Hide Who You Are
(At Least, No More Than You Have To)

A member of *Inc.* magazine's solopreneur community, and a former member of the military, was assigned to teach a leadership lesson to military supervisors. Before the class began, an experienced female teacher warned her about "the penalty for being nice" and advised her to start out the course with a very strict response to any sort of disruption in the classroom. She was warned that if she didn't immediately get the class in hand, a handful of students would disrupt the class for the entire course. Our future solopreneur decided to follow that advice, and she started out her course being very tough and quickly correcting anyone who was at all disrespectful. The course went well, she got great feedback, and she built lasting relationships with some of her students. Later on, she passed the same advice along to a new female instructor, who didn't take the suggestion and was "too nice." Her classroom was constantly disrupted, and she received negative feedback because of it.

Being a woman in the workplace, especially in a leadership role, means constantly wondering how you're coming across. Are you too much of a pushover? Or do others think of you as "a bitch" — an insult that can only be leveled at women — because you're being too pushy? Women are constantly striving to find the appropriate middle ground between pushover and bitch. Like fretting over your looks, that sucks up energy that could be better spent elsewhere.

Like the pay gap, this business of not being able to be yourself is a problem that's exponentially worse for women of color. A couple of years ago, I interviewed a Black entrepreneur named Jessica Eggert who, when her first child was born, was working as an executive at a company in Florida.

"I was always told that I'd have to work twice as hard as a Black woman to get anywhere close to what others had, so I'd make sure to be the first one in and last one out, answer emails at all hours of the night, and get more work done than anyone else," she said. "When I had Oliver, I knew I still wanted to work and be an amazing parent. But figuring out how to balance that was extremely difficult."

Eggert was working for a fast-growing company, and she knew she had a lot of potential for advancement there. At the same time, she said, "I knew I was going to have to work hard to be seen as someone who belonged there, especially in leadership."

She had observed the company's attitude toward working mothers. "It was clear from our interactions with clients and with other employees that there wasn't a lot of respect for women in the workplace, especially moms. They weren't given opportunities to move up, and I would hear, 'Oh, she needs to go home early for the kids.'"

So when she returned from maternity leave, she became a stealth mom. She displayed no pictures of her son anywhere around her workspace. She put fictitious meetings on her calendar to hide the fact that she had to spend a few minutes pumping breast milk, which she would do sitting on the floor of the ladies' room because there was nowhere else. All this was extremely stressful, and her milk dried up within a few weeks.

By the time her second child was born, Eggert had left that company, moved to a different state, and started a business of her own where she could decide what was and wasn't acceptable for a mother with a new baby.

And what about those male executives who disapproved of working mothers and disparaged women who had to pick their kids up at daycare or school? I'm willing to bet that many of them had children of their own. And the only reason they themselves didn't leave early to care for those children was that they had women in their lives who did it for them, women who were part of the $10.9 trillion unpaid labor economy.

Eggert felt that hiding her true self was the price she had to pay to succeed at her job, and she was likely right. But there's something very, very wrong with this picture. Why should someone who is doing her job well have to pretend having a child doesn't matter in order to prove that she belongs there? Why isn't her work proof enough?

In the start-up world where I spend much of my work life, a lot depends on the decisions of VCs — venture capitalists — who pick which start-ups to bless with their millions, their advice, and, perhaps most valuable of all, their connections. VC funding is notoriously biased. In 2019, the percentage of VC investments that went to women-led start-ups reached an all-time high. That high was 2.8 percent. In 2020, thanks to the pandemic and the resulting economic crisis, VCs cut back on funding, at least where female founders were concerned, so the percentage of funding to women-owned businesses went back down to 2 percent. That's bad enough, but then consider that Black female founders got 0.27 percent of VC funding in 2018 and 2019, and Latina founders got 0.37 percent.

VC investors often say that they bet on the founder, rather than the product or company they are building. On the surface, this seems wise. Often in business, great execution trumps a great idea, and a founder who's already started a successful company is much more likely to succeed again. But look below the surface, and you'll see this as a convenient excuse for VCs to give funds to people they feel more comfortable with or like better. Investing in start-ups is such a crapshoot to begin with — many more fail than succeed — that it's easy to imagine there's some sort of alchemy to it, and that alchemy is known to wizards who resemble, say, Mark Zuckerberg or Bill Gates.

Think I'm exaggerating about this? There's a *New York Times* interview with Y Combinator founder Paul Graham that shows how literally true this is. Graham is to VCs as Eric Clapton is to rock guitarists. The interview described Y Combinator's efforts to figure out why it invested in some companies that it shouldn't have. "I can be tricked by anyone who looks like Mark Zuckerberg," Graham said. "There was a guy once who we funded who was terrible. I said: 'How could he be bad? He looks like Zuckerberg!'"

It's particularly galling that VCs operate this way when their industry claims to be data driven. If only that were true, they'd be doing the opposite. A Boston Consulting Group study from 2018 found that investors who backed start-ups led by women did better than those who backed those led by men; in fact, female-led start-ups returned twice as much on the dollar as their male-led counterparts.

Why don't they seem to see that? For one thing, most VCs get into that line of work because they've been successful founders in their own right. They're likely tempted to invest in people who remind them of themselves, which means this is a perpetually repeating cycle: young white men investing in young white men, who, if they're successful, come back to invest in more young white men.

If you're a woman, chances are you can't walk into a meeting with a potential investor or employer and convince anyone that you look like Mark Zuckerberg. But can you push back against bias at home and at work and perhaps change it, just a little bit?

What if you called out bias when you saw it? What if you demanded that the man in your life start doing half the unpaid labor around your home? What would happen if you simply stopped doing more than your fair share?

I'm dreaming here. I realize that. None of this can change overnight, and maybe it never will. In the meantime, if you're earning less than a male colleague, if a man gets promoted over you, or if someone fails to take you seriously — or makes an inappropriate comment about your biological clock — don't do what I did. Don't sweep it out of your mind, don't ignore it, and whatever else you do, don't blame yourself.

In September 2021, a former intern at the Pentagon named Maya Guzdar published an essay in the *New York Times* describing a highly unpleasant incident at a cocktail party in which a senior employee cornered her, asking inappropriate questions about her ethnicity and partying habits, and finally lunged at her, until a male officer pushed him away. She believed that reporting the incident to the higher-ups would only wind up hurting her, and so she decided to let it go.

"That night when I returned home, I began to downplay the incident in my mind," she wrote. "I watched with almost clinical detachment as I began gaslighting myself. 'I'm overreacting,' I told myself. 'It wasn't that big of a deal.'" Fortunately for Guzdar, there had been over a dozen witnesses to the event, some of whom were in positions of authority and assured her that it was indeed a very big deal.

Too many of us have spent too much time assuring ourselves that words or acts of sexism or racism or hate, things that reduce our own humanity, really are no big deal. We tell ourselves this because we want to stay in places we love, in jobs we love, with people we love. We want to earn money for ourselves and for our loved ones. We want our career dreams to come true. From love, we tell ourselves whatever we need to in order to stay. We do these things because we have to, because this is the world we live in.

Maybe someday our daughters or granddaughters will change it into a better one.

EXERCISES TO TRY

1. Speak Up for Your Female Colleagues

Women working in the Obama White House often found themselves ignored or talked over in meetings; their ideas were overlooked, only to be proposed later by men to great approval. When that kind of thing happens, there's no way to say, "You mean that thing I just said ten minutes ago?" without sounding peevish. But, they realized, others can do it for you. So several of them formed a pact, agreeing that whenever any of them proposed an idea or a solution in a meeting, the others would repeat and validate it, making it harder for anyone present to forget who said it first. You can try this too, with or without a formal agreement with the other women who work with you.

2. Don't Accept Unacceptable Behavior

Just because bad behavior is common, that doesn't mean you have to put up with it. In 2017, software engineer Susan Fowler set the stage for the #MeToo movement when she published a lengthy account of being sexually harassed on the job, titled "Reflecting on One Very, Very Strange Year at Uber." The following day, another female Uber engineer, Aimee Lucido, wrote a response, titled "Reflecting on Susan Fowler's Reflections." The main point of this response was that sexual harassment in Silicon Valley was commonplace and not restricted to Uber. Lucido recounted an incident that occurred when she was a twenty-year-old intern at Google and a thirty-year-old manager at a party tried to corner her in a bedroom, supposedly so they could play go. She wrote that she forced him back out into the common area, where he proceeded to follow her around, saying mushy and inappropriate things while getting extremely drunk.

"At the time, we thought it was hilarious," she said. "In fact, we thought this was so funny that we spent weeks joking about it." In retrospect, she no longer found it amusing.

In a weird way, Lucido's reaction to Fowler and others speaking out about harassment and bias reminds me of my own. Not that I ever thought any of this stuff was funny – not my boss's comment about my biological clock, not his offhand remark that you could never really trust a woman to return from maternity leave, and not any of the other daily reminders that a woman in the workplace could never be on the same footing as a man. All of this felt like a normal part of being in the work world, part of the air around us, and not worth remarking on. So when Fowler and others spoke up, I kept thinking, *Wait a minute! You mean we're allowed to object to this?* We certainly are, and moreover, inappropriate behavior will only change when more of us object to it. With that in mind, I'm asking you to look right at the lava lamp. Look for gender bias, harassment, racism, homophobia, and all other forms of prejudice wherever you are, even though that will mean seeing it everywhere, all the time.

And then – this is the really hard part – call attention to it, as often as you can. People will roll their eyes. They may accuse you of not focusing on what's important. In these uncivil times, they might even make fun of you. Do it anyway. It's the only way to move the needle, even if it's just a tiny bit.

Chapter 9

How to Get Mentored — and Sponsored (Which Is Just as Important)

What image comes to mind when you hear the word *mentor*? For me, it was always Lou Grant in *The Mary Tyler Moore Show*, a kindly, grizzled executive who was happy to pour you a Scotch from the bottle he kept in his desk drawer. Whenever Mary faced a problem, from a difficult coworker to a challenge in her love life, she would walk into Lou's office, close the door, drop into a chair, and tell him all about it. He'd dispense some gruff bit of wisdom that would make everything much clearer. When she had a massive bout of insomnia, he went to her apartment and sang her lullabies until she fell asleep with her head on his shoulder. *That is what a mentor is supposed to be*, I thought. Someone older and wiser who's there for you no matter what you need.

Real life doesn't much resemble *The Mary Tyler Moore Show*. I've never had a mentor, at least not one who ever reminded me of kindly old Lou Grant. Maybe you haven't either. And yet, you know you really need mentoring. Having someone who's seen it all to help you figure out your next career move can speed you along on whatever career path you've chosen.

There's actual research that says so: 97 percent of people with a mentor say their mentor is valuable, while 75 percent of executives in Fortune 500 companies credit their mentors with helping advance their careers. Some years back, Sun Microsystems decided to measure the effects of mentoring on its employees. It followed one thousand employees from different areas of the company over five years to see if participating in a mentoring program made a difference to their advancement. It found that those who took part in the mentoring program as mentees were five times more likely to get a promotion than those who didn't. The mentors benefited too — they were promoted six times more often. And mentoring may be even more useful if you're running your own company. Research by UPS found that 70 percent of new companies that had mentors survived for five years, which is twice the five-year survival rate of new companies overall.

You may be convinced that mentoring really is valuable, but how do you get mentored? Begin, if necessary, by letting go of Lou Grant or any other fantasy of what a mentor should be. Mentoring may not look at all the way you think it should. But you can still get the guidance you need to get where you want to go.

More Than One Mentor

It may not be realistic to think that a single mentor can answer every question and solve every problem you have. Years ago, I interviewed Lyle Stevens, a successful entrepreneur whose software company, Mavrck, had just graduated from the prestigious incubator Techstars. He told me he and Mavrck had four different mentors. One was a technological expert. A second knew a lot about marketing and suggested a whole new area where the company could find customers. The third gave advice about recruiting and employee retention, always a challenge in the tight labor market of the software industry. The fourth provided general guidance about how to run a business and helped Stevens, who had young children, navigate work-life balance issues.

All were experienced executives who had agreed to be mentors for the company. How did Stevens find them all? Some were execs who'd signed up as potential mentors with Techstars. He also asked around among his entrepreneur friends to find out who'd mentored them in specific areas where he knew he needed help. What these two approaches have in common is that they led him to people who had already displayed a willingness to mentor. You can try picking someone you admire or would like to emulate and asking that person to mentor you, but the odds that they'll say yes are a lot lower.

Using a Formal Mentoring Program
(Inside or Outside Your Organization)

If you work for a company that has a formal mentoring program, it's a good idea to participate, the Sun Microsystems research suggests. Participation in a mentoring program turned out to be a great idea for Paola Doebel, senior vice president and managing director of North America for IT service provider Ensono. Before joining Ensono, she held executive positions at Dell and then became a vice president at Hewlett Packard Enterprise. At Dell, she took advantage of a formal mentorship program that allowed employees to request mentors with specific skill sets. She asked for a mentor from Human Resources. "I was trying to figure out what it took to get promoted to director. Good work's not enough — what else did I need to be thinking about?"

Doebel and her mentor met regularly for six months, and during that time she learned a lot about how high-level promotion decisions get made. "At that point, it's not just an individual leader's decision," she says. A whole group of leaders must agree. "The death of a promotion or the death of advancement is when only one person in the room knows your name."

With her mentor's guidance, Doebel stepped up her networking game, introducing herself to key executives in her area and in other company departments who could influence her advancement. She got the promotion she was seeking, but even if she hadn't, the mentoring still would have been valuable, she says. "It provided me a lot of guidance and counsel and insight."

If your company doesn't have a formal mentoring program, consider looking for mentoring programs at the trade organizations in your industry. If that doesn't work, consider the different business groups you belong to — or could belong to. Is there a chamber of commerce or a local business group in the town where you live or work? How about women's or identity-based organizations within your profession that you could join? These are all great places to find people more experienced than you who might be willing to become your mentors.

If none of these groups has a formal mentoring program that appeals to you, consider making up your own personal program. You don't need anyone's permission to go looking for the career support you need. Identify a few people who you think might be effective mentors for you, and then reach out to them. Let them know you're looking for business advice, and ask if they have five minutes to answer a few quick questions. Stevens says it's smart to test-drive a potential mentor in this way because not everyone will have the right insights or experience to help you. Describe a specific problem you're having and ask for suggestions, or give a quick description of your goals and ask if there are threats or opportunities you haven't thought of. You'll be able to tell quickly whether a potential mentor will be able to help you. Someone who fully understands your industry or problem will have specific ideas and suggestions, while someone who doesn't have that expertise (but might not want to admit it) will answer with generalities.

Once you've determined that someone could be an effective mentor for you, take the next step. Ask if they would be willing to become your mentor and — this is important, Stevens says — lay out very specifically what that will entail. You'll have the best chance of getting a yes if it's a fairly limited commitment. Stevens asks his company's mentors to promise only one hour of counseling twice a month, and possibly a full-day visit once or twice a year.

Unofficial Mentoring

The preceding suggestions will help you develop a formal mentoring relationship with one or preferably several official mentors. But that's just one approach to getting mentored. When Stevens was recruiting executives to be Mavrck's official mentors, he tried finding people through his college's alumni association. In one way, he struck out since none of the alumni he asked agreed to a formal mentoring relationship. But, he said, two of them became informal advisers that he called once a quarter or so while the company was getting started.

This is where Stevens's experience of mentorship intersects with mine. I've never had a single capital-M mentor, and I've never been a mentee in a formal mentoring program. But I've been informally mentored probably hundreds of times. And I've informally mentored others many, many times too.

I first learned how important informal mentoring can be many years ago when I decided to quit my job at a trade magazine company and strike out on my own as an independent writer. I'd known for a long time that's what I wanted to be. I was working at my more-than-full-time job and climbing the company's hierarchy pretty quickly, having gone from trainee to senior associate editor in two and a half years. But I would see those freelance writers in the hallways or at borrowed desks, looking happy and relaxed, masters of their own fate. I remember them as tanned, but that's probably my imagination. Their work was mostly writing, whereas in my job I would write less and less the more senior

I got, occupied instead with editing and planning and all the other tasks that go into putting out a magazine.

I wanted to do what they did, so I began asking nearly every freelance writer I knew if I could buy them lunch or an after-work drink in exchange for some advice about how to become a freelance writer myself. Several of them agreed, and they became my teachers. They shared what had and hadn't worked for them. One whom I'll never forget sat me down in the dark back booth of an almost-empty midtown bar and laid out for me, step-by-step, how to write a pitch for an article. He remained a helpful adviser on any number of issues for decades after, both in my writing career and in my career at ASJA, where he served on the board for years before I did.

I've used this informal approach repeatedly over the years, and I've almost always gotten useful guidance. The fact that there's no commitment for either party makes it easy for you to ask and for the other person to say yes. It also can help avoid a potentially awkward problem if you start a long-term mentoring relationship and then discover that you and your mentor aren't a good fit after all. You're asking only for a one-off meeting, so if you see no need to meet again, you can just leave it at that. Although all the writers I met with provided useful advice, I didn't have any further lunches with any of them, and that was fine for everyone involved.

What Can a Mentor Do for You?

On the most basic level, a good mentor can help you figure out how to do your job better and how to impress bosses and/or customers. They can help you set priorities and figure out which of your tasks will make the most impact, which can be a mystery in many work situations.

To use a really silly hypothetical, let's say someone gives you a bucket of stones, tells you to polish them, and walks away. You know your promotion to some other, less tedious, job depends on excelling at this task. But would that mean polishing each stone perfectly until it shined all over? Or getting the entire bucket of stones polished in less than an hour? Or polishing all the stones using as little polish as possible?

It can be hard to get straight answers to questions like these, but a good mentor should know the answers or help you find them. In the same way, a good mentor can keep you from making costly mistakes, such as transferring into a troubled department within your company or taking on customers who create more aggravation than they're worth. They can lift the veil on a complex company or industry, letting you know what's going on below the surface when you may not be able to find out any other way. This can be especially valuable if, like me, you're not particularly good at sniffing out company gossip.

Even more important, a good mentor can help you with something that just about everyone is bad at: seeing yourself the way other people see you. In my early days as ASJA president, I led a day-long meeting where we had several matters to discuss. None were urgent, so I decided it made sense to let everyone's opinions be heard. When there was disagreement on an issue, rather than try to impose my will or call a divisive vote, I put it off so we could discuss it again at a later time. I thought I was being thoughtful and not rushing into decisions when it wasn't necessary. But some of the board members felt I'd wasted their time since so few decisions were made. In retrospect, this seems stupidly obvious, but at the time I didn't get it.

Luckily for me, another board member, who'd been president before me and who'd been an informal mentor, took it upon himself to let me know what some others were saying. It was an upsetting conversation. I remember feeling deeply embarrassed, but he did me a huge favor because it was exactly what I needed to hear. From then on, I tried to make sure that decisions were made at every board meeting and that concrete actions came out of them.

While I still worked to make sure everyone had a say, I stopped putting off decisions just because I could.

I believe mentors are most valuable when they either disagree with you or disagree with the prevailing opinions in your organization or industry. You wouldn't want someone who always disagrees with prevailing wisdom to be your only mentor, but this is exactly the sort of reason you should have more than one. A mentor with a contrarian viewpoint will always stretch your thinking on a given question, even if you don't wind up taking their advice. This is one reason why organizations with more diverse management tend to perform better than their peers. In any group, there's always a danger that group thinking will set in — that's human nature. Having a contrarian mentor is one way to fight that.

Stevens told me that Mavrck's multiple mentors often contradicted each other, which makes sense when you consider that each was focused on a different aspect of the business and so they had different priorities. That's exactly how he wanted it, he said. "We want someone to always poke holes in what we're thinking," he explained. "The worst thing is folks who all think the same way."

But, I asked, if you're given two or more pieces of advice that contradict each other, how do you know which advice to follow? "You make a decision knowing what the alternatives are," he said. A mentor may be able to guide and advise you, but it's your job, your career, or your company that will be affected by whatever you decide. That means any advice you get, from a mentor or anyone else, must be filtered through your own plans and desires, and the decisions you make must come from your own best judgment. No one else can do that for you.

A good mentor will make you consider dangers and especially opportunities you might never have seen for yourself. I'd been on the board of ASJA for a few years without ever thinking I could run the place, but a former president who thought I had a lot of potential began telling me that she thought I could be and should be president and that she'd be happy to support me if I went after the job. I didn't take her up on it at the time. It was a few more years before I actually ran for president. But I'm not sure I'd ever have gotten there if she hadn't gotten me to think about it.

A good mentor can widen your view of what's possible for you, by guidance, by example, or both. It's way too easy for most of us, women especially, to place limits on ourselves without even realizing we're doing it. A good mentor can show you what's outside the box you may have put yourself into.

This is also why, Lou Grant notwithstanding, it's smart to get some mentoring from at least one person who is not your boss. A good boss will mentor you, of course. But your boss also has a stake in whatever decisions you make. If it's to your advantage to move to a different department or even a different company, your boss may not tell you that. If your boss's job is your next logical step on the career ladder, your boss may not be honest about how long they intend to remain in that job.

Mentors and Sponsors

In addition to needing people to mentor you in your career, you also need sponsors. That term was first explained to me by leadership coach and author Daina Middleton. What's the difference between a sponsor and a mentor? A mentor is someone who provides useful career advice and guidance and may teach you new skills or help you improve existing ones. Your relationship with your mentor is just between the two of you. A sponsor, on the other hand, may or may not give you guidance but will be your advocate within an organization or in the marketplace at large. A good sponsor will speak up for you when you're not around. They will put your name forward for attractive opportunities and support you if you're going after a particular project or position.

"As you get more senior, a sponsor is super critical," Doebel says. "This is somebody who's willing to go to bat for you. Ultimately, to get to that next level in your career, it's required."

It's especially important, she said, if you're aiming to get to the VP level or above in a large organization. This requires the support of everyone you work with, "not just straight up but also diagonally," she says.

"That's when you start getting into, who in that room is a promoter, who's a detractor, and who's neutral? Who can you get from detractor to neutral, and who's never going to get there? Who can you get from neutral to promoter? Having a sponsor who's influential in that room is unbelievably important."

You can't find a sponsor via a formal mentoring program, Doebel says, because you're asking that person to vouch for you. So how do you find a sponsor?

"That's something you earn," she says. "As you get more senior, you need to start looking at the people around you as potential sponsors. A great way to do that is to reach out and create a connection, but also just do great work. And be transparent about what you want to become. No one's going to step up and vouch for you if they don't know what you're asking for."

When it comes to both mentors and sponsors, remember that the relationship should be as even as you can make it. That doesn't mean there has to be a quid pro quo every time someone does you a kindness, but it does mean that you should have an idea of what the other person is getting out of it. There could be many different answers to that question. Mentors or sponsors could be hoping you'll support their initiatives in the future, especially as you advance within the organization or industry. They may be hoping you will work with them on their own pet projects, which you absolutely should do if you can. They may need to tap your expertise in an area they don't know well. A typical example of this might be an older mentor who helps out a young mentee with guidance or advice, but also needs the mentee to help them use social media more effectively. (This is sometimes called *reverse mentoring*.)

In many organizations, managers are partly judged on how often and how effectively they've mentored less-senior employees. In that case, mentors may be advancing their own careers by helping you. Or they may simply be getting what one expert I interviewed called "mentoring warm fuzzies" — helping others along on their career paths makes them happy in itself. If you know exactly what your mentors and sponsors want to get out of helping you, you can make sure they get it, whatever it is. This simple principle is why I so often ask people to give me advice over meals or drinks that are my treat. It's not that I think a steak or a couple of cocktails is adequate payment for advice that can help my career, but this small way of showing my gratitude acknowledges that they are doing me a favor.

How to Mentor

What if you yourself want to mentor someone, or someone has asked you for mentoring? First of all, congratulations! You must be doing something right. The most important thing to remember about mentoring or advising someone is this: it's never about you; it's always about them. That's incredibly easy to say but incredibly difficult to do. If someone asks you how to get ahead in their job as, say, a circus clown, and you've seen them perform and they're just about the worst clown you've ever had the displeasure of watching, you can't just tell them they're bad at the job. You also can't tell them that they'd be happier and more successful if they took up computer programming instead.

No, your job is to make this person into the very best clown it's possible for them to be. And the way to do that is not to overwhelm them by listing the ten different areas of their clown performance that need improvement. Instead, focus on one or two areas and give them some helpful advice that will make their performance incrementally better — for example, how to paint on a more appealing clown smile and properly place their red nose.

Whatever you do, stay positive and encouraging. No matter how bad things are, do not make them want to give up. What if you're absolutely sure they're terrible at the job and there's no future for them in it? No matter how sure you are, I believe you could possibly be wrong. I base this on the many, many times I've watched someone go from being hopelessly bad at something to really good at it after many hours of hard work. You can't know for sure that someone will fail at a job because you don't know how willing they are to work hard and improve. Your role is just to point them in the right direction so that the work they do is as effective as possible and to be generally encouraging so that they don't give up in despair. That may not sound like fun, but once again, it's about them, not you.

There's one other thing to remember, something that goes way beyond individual mentoring and mentors. No matter who you are, nearly everyone you meet will have something that they can teach you, and you will have something that you can teach them. We are all each other's mentors, or at least, we have the potential to be. The challenge is in seeing what the people you encounter can teach you. It requires an open heart and an open mind, what many people call a *learning mind*. It means understanding that lessons can come from unexpected places and in unexpected forms. If you can do that, chances are you will get all the mentoring you need.

EXERCISES TO TRY

1. Make Two Lists

The first list, your wish list, should include things like the next job or promotion you'd like to have, projects you want to propose or join, and new responsibilities you'd like to take on. It should also include the skills you want to acquire or improve, such as leading a team or becoming proficient at social media marketing or creating a new product. It's fine to have lots of items on this list.

Now go back to the list and pick your top five items. For each of those, add the name of one or more people who could help you get there. They might be people you know, people you know through a friend, or people you just know of. Who can help you learn a new skill, guide you through the corporate hierarchy, or introduce you to the right people? You now have a list of at least five people who can help you get where you want to go.

2. Ask for Mentoring

Now it's time to put your list to use. Pick three names, and reach out to each of them. The best way to make contact will vary depending on the person and the industry, but email is sometimes the most straightforward way to start a conversation. You can also use social media to send that person a message. LinkedIn is particularly good since it's focused on professional relationships. On the other hand, these days, when most communications are emailed, texted, or posted, a phone call can sometimes be an effective way to cut through the clutter and reach someone.

The more specific you can be with your request, the more likely you are to get what you want. Ask if the person would be willing to spend ten minutes on the phone or meet you for coffee to give you some advice about the particular skill or opportunity you're after. It's usually smart to say you're asking for advice, since most people will be flattered, and flattery can be a very effective way to get what you want (see chapter 6).

Once you're satisfied with the wording of your request, treat it as a template and use it to reach out to each of the potential mentors on your list until you have as many as you need. Most likely, some will say yes. Others won't respond, in which case you should follow up at least twice. You may occasionally encounter someone who says no and is nasty about it, either because that person is having a bad day or is just unfriendly in general. Try not to take it personally.

Whatever response you get, the fact that you made the request means you have completed the exercise. Give yourself a pat on the back because reaching out and asking for favors is never easy.

3. Make Yourself a Mentor

As the Sun Microsystems research showed, mentoring usually benefits the mentor as much as the mentee, and though I don't know of any specific research about this, I believe it's as true if you're self-employed as it is if you work in a big corporation. If you're not already a mentor, find or create mentoring opportunities for yourself. If your company has a mentoring program, see if you can join as a mentor. Put it out there in your company and/or LinkedIn profile that you enjoy advising young people in your profession or industry. If you feel like you're not ready to do this, try contacting local colleges or high schools. They're often seeking people to help students figure out their opportunities after graduation. Mentoring and advising others is an important skill to master in almost any profession. The sooner you start doing it, the better you'll get.

PART THREE

HOW TO GET WHERE
YOU WANT TO GO

Chapter 10

Why You Should Make Sure to Do What You Love

Years ago, an acquaintance of mine opened a restaurant. That's one of the hardest businesses there is, and he was forced to close after about six months. Determined not to suffer financial ruin again, he headed in an entirely different direction. He got an MBA and went to work in an investment company. He bought a house in an upscale suburb, where he lived with his wife and kids and mortgage payments that he could just barely afford. It worked for many years, but in time, the investment company fell apart and his job evaporated, leaving him with huge bills to pay and no income with which to pay them. Eventually, the bank foreclosed on his house. He'd traded in his passion for financial stability but wound up with no job, no home, and a mountain of unpayable debt.

The most frightening example I ever encountered of someone heading for a career they didn't love happened when I taught an undergraduate creative writing class at NYU. I had about a dozen students, a varied group from many different majors. Most weren't English majors; they were just taking the class to fulfill a core requirement. They varied in interests, tastes, and writing skill. One of them was a young man who sat at the far end of the table from me. He seemed to be trying to call as little attention to himself as possible. I think he would have gone through the whole semester without saying a word, except that wasn't possible in my class. Each session, we would review two of the students' pieces, and I went around the table each time, asking every student to give their opinion of the work. Thus forced to speak, this reticent student came out with some of the most insightful comments of the whole group.

Toward the end of the semester, the students had to hand in a longer work that I would then discuss with them in a private conference. When this student handed in his piece, it was handwritten in big letters on lined paper as if he'd rushed to get it all down. It turned out to be a short story about a college student majoring in premed at his parents' insistence. The protagonist struggles to keep up with his science courses but falls further and further behind. At the end of the story, feeling miserable and trapped, he commits suicide.

The information I had about my students included their declared majors, which is how I knew that the student who wrote this piece was taking prelaw — preparing for a profession that seemed as bad a fit for him as being a doctor was for his protagonist. The parallels were impossible to miss.

I pointed this out to him during our one-on-one conference, concerned for him but also conscious of the limits of the teacher-student relationship. "You need to think about this," I told him. "I know," he answered, in a way that told me that he already had and might now be ready to make some changes. I don't know what happened after that. I don't know if he showed the story to his parents, although I hope he did. I do know that letting yourself get stuck in a job that's wrong for you can literally kill you.

In his now-famous 2014 commencement speech at Maharishi University, comedian and actor Jim Carrey talked about how all

of us make decisions based on either love or fear. Fear is sometimes disguised as practicality, he said. His own father "could have
been a great comedian, but he didn't believe that that was possible
for him," Carrey explained. "So he made a conservative choice
and instead he got a safe job as an accountant, and when I was
twelve years old, he was let go from that safe job. And our family
had to do whatever we could to survive." That included a period
of homelessness during which the family lived in a van. "I learned
many great lessons from my father, not the least of which is that
you can fail at what you don't want, so you might as well take a
chance on doing what you love," he said.

As a teenager, Jim Carrey had to work overnight as a janitor
in the tire factory that eventually provided his family with a home
and his father with a job. Even so, he managed to start a stand-up
comedy career around Toronto. He got his first lucky break at
nineteen, in the form of a front-page story in the entertainment
section of the *Toronto Star*. His career grew from there, with more
appearances around Toronto and a starring role in a TV movie
that was renamed *Rubberface* just for him. Then he was invited
to tour with Rodney Dangerfield, which led to a move to LA and
stardom.

So Carrey, at a young age, followed the advice he would later
give to that audience of graduating students. He took a chance on
doing what he loved, and it worked out spectacularly well. Was
his success guaranteed? Sure, Carrey is phenomenally talented,
but there are plenty of phenomenally talented people who spend
their days managing retail stores or writing computer code and
only use their talents in their spare time. What if Carrey had been
like them, incredibly good at comedy but not able to make a living
at it?

We happen to know the answer to this question, because
Carrey said it himself in a 2007 interview with the *Hamilton Spectator*. "If my career in show business hadn't panned out I would

probably be working today in Hamilton, Ontario, at the Dofasco steel mill," he said. As a young man, he often thought that the steel mill was "where the great jobs were." That was probably true, especially compared to the tire company where he, his father, and his brother all worked when he was young.

That makes me think about my husband's cousin Thaddeus Klingman, known to all as Teddy, who spent almost his entire working life at Orange & Rockland, the electric utility for Middletown, New York. Teddy died of cancer at fifty-seven. His title at the company was senior systems operator, and he monitored electricity usage in the counties the company served.

When Teddy was a child and people asked him what he wanted to be when he grew up, I'm pretty sure that senior systems operator at Orange & Rockland was not his answer. And yet Teddy loved that job. It had a good salary and even better benefits, particularly for someone with no college degree. His good salary meant that he could not only support his family but also travel the world during his generous vacation time. Most of all, he enjoyed the camaraderie of his colleagues and the chance to indulge his love of practical jokes, something he did frequently. When he got sick, that good job meant he didn't have to worry about paying his medical bills or losing his income.

Doing what you love doesn't necessarily mean having a job that puts your name up in lights or that offers a fancy office. It's not necessarily about earning more than anyone you know. It may not be whatever you dreamed of when you were a child (ballet dancer, in my case). It might not be about people being impressed when you tell them what you do, or having people look up to you or wish they could be you. It's not even about using all your talents to the fullest — very few jobs do that, if any. It's certainly not about doing what your parents or your friends or your college roommates would most approve of.

It may not even be about changing the world for the better.

It could be about any of those things, or a combination of them. But really, it's about doing work that makes you happy, that feels meaningful to you, that pays at least as much as you need, and that "feels like you." Your job should be something that, to you, is worth getting out of bed for in the morning.

One Passion per Person?

"Find your passion." This career advice has been repeated frequently for decades. Then, a few years ago, there was a backlash. For example, the 2018 *Atlantic* article titled "'Find Your Passion' Is Awful Advice" quotes research by the revered psychologist Carol Dweck. The problem with "find your passion" is two-fold, passion skeptics argue. First, there's the frequently repeated corollary that if you find work you love, "you'll never work a day in your life." As they rightly point out, this is nonsense. Any job, no matter how beloved, is a grind sometimes. There will be setbacks, frustrations, and many, many days where you would rather be doing literally anything else. None of this means that you haven't found your passion or that you need to go looking for a different employer. It just means that nearly anything worth doing still sucks some days.

The second objection is more nuanced. It argues that your passions are not a fixed, inborn thing. Instead, depending on your peers, circumstances, influences, and experiences, you could potentially become passionate about many different things. To prove it, Dweck and her colleagues conducted a series of experiments. In one of them, students (none of whom were astronomy majors) watched an interesting and engaging documentary about Stephen Hawking in which his concepts were explained in an easily understandable way. After watching this video, many of the students said they were fascinated by black holes. Then the researchers had them read a technical and challenging *Science* article about black holes. After that, many of the students said they weren't too interested in black holes after all. Here's the point of the study:

The students who gave up their black hole fascination had earlier been taught that our interests and abilities are unchangeable and innate, the "fixed theory." Those who had been taught that interests and abilities can change with practice and exposure — the "growth theory" — were willing to stick with that confusing article longer and try harder to learn from it before giving up their interest in black holes.

The truth is, when it comes to interests and abilities, the growth theory is right. Neuroscientists report that people can and do develop different interests and passions throughout their lives, depending on their circumstances and the influences around them. This is something I've pondered quite a bit because I was born in 1960, right at the end of an era when women were expected to devote their lives to cooking, keeping house, and child-rearing. I've often wondered how things would have gone if I'd been born just a few years earlier. I've never raised children, I'm a lousy housekeeper, I'm hopeless at interior decorating, and while I am a pretty good cook, for the past several years I've handed that job over to my husband almost completely because that's what works best for our partnership.

I like to fantasize that if I had been born at an earlier time, I would have been one of those mold-breaking women, dismissed during her lifetime but revered afterward, who insisted on her own career and ignored the world's expectations. But I suspect the truth is I would have learned to love sewing curtains for the children's bedrooms and baking a perfect apple pie. And maybe those things would have made me just as happy as my writing career does now.

I think the search for a perfect career or a perfect job has a lot in common with the search for the perfect partner or spouse:

1. **There's more than just one.** Some people believe that there's one perfect love out there for each of us. But that idea doesn't stand up to scrutiny. First of all, in a planet with 7.8 billion people

on it, the chances of meeting your one right partner are virtually nil. But even if you believe that a greater power will bring the two of you together, what about the many widows and widowers who lose a beloved spouse but go on to marry someone else that they love just as much?

Just as there isn't one perfect partner out there, there isn't one perfect career for you either. This means you can feel free to experiment with different jobs and professions. The more different things you try, the more you can be sure you've found the right one when it happens.

2. **It might not be love at first sight.** When my husband and I first met, he knew right away that we belonged together. I was not convinced. For one thing, he wasn't exactly my type. I'd always been drawn to thin, dark, brooding guys, and he's pretty much the opposite of that. But he was persistent. Eventually, I got to know him and came to see that he was in fact the perfect person to spend my life with.

A job might not seem like the perfect fit at first either. That doesn't necessarily mean it's wrong for you. It could be wrong for you, or you might need to get to know the work the same way I needed to get to know my future husband. If you're not sure, it may be worth taking the time to find out.

3. **It won't always be fun.** No matter who you are and no matter how much you love your partner or spouse, I guarantee that if you spend any time at all together, you will eventually wish (at least momentarily) that person would go far, far away and never come back. There will be times when you doubt whether you really belong together. There will be times when your relationship drives you crazy or, worse, bores you. The magic of a committed relationship is when you can see those moments as the temporary blips they are and when you can tell the difference between the normal ups and downs of any long-term relationship and the serious problems that mean a relationship won't work.

Even the best job in the world will still have its boring moments and its aggravations. (I'm using the term *job* to mean work you do for a living, even though you may be doing it as a self-employed business owner or contractor.) You will have good days and bad days and days when you wish you could be anywhere else. Only you can know whether those are just the ups and downs of any job or a sign that you should be looking to make a change.

4. It's all about values. A wise ex-boyfriend of mine once said that the most important question in any relationship is whether the people involved share the same values. (We didn't.) The more I think about that, the more right it seems. You and your partner don't have to have exactly the same priorities or even the same political views. But if what you value and what your partner values don't sync, it's going to be very hard to have a satisfying relationship in the long run.

In the same way, there's a lot you can put up with or work around in a job. But if the work doesn't align with your values, you're never really going to be happy. That applies to a job that pays well but requires you to do things that go against your conscience. But it might also apply to a job that you enjoy but that pays badly if one of your primary values is to earn enough money to give your child the best possible education. Your values are yours and no one else's, and no one can tell you what those values should be.

5. You may have to let love find you. I'm always perplexed by the way dating apps ask users to determine how many miles away they're willing to look for their perfect mate, or how old a partner they're willing to consider. What if the perfect person for you lives one mile outside your maximum radius or is six months older than your maximum age? Setting such criteria could possibly eliminate the love of your life. But if you don't set any criteria, you're left with a muddle of possible dates that's too confusing to be useful.

So maybe the logical thing to do is to set some criteria but be flexible, remaining open to all kinds of possibilities and to finding potential dates wherever they might appear, which could include the grocery store, the playground, or a cooking class. Maybe you should even consider the person you call to repair your laptop after you've tripped over the cord and knocked it off the table, which is how I got together with Bill.

It would be a mistake to wait and hope for the right job or profession to find you. You should always be the driver, not the passenger, in your career, and if you wait for the right job to come along, you are basically putting someone else's priorities ahead of your own. It doesn't make sense to do the job-hunting equivalent of standing around the produce department, waiting for someone good-looking and single to come along. But it does make sense to stay open and willing to sometimes try things you might not have thought would be a good fit. Your career is a journey, not a destination, and it most likely won't be a straight line. The best careers almost always include a few twists and turns and side trips along the way.

Help! I Hate My Job!

What if, right now, you're in a job that you hate, that doesn't inspire you, or that makes you so crazy that you dread Monday mornings and you feel like it's eating you up inside? What should you do?

First of all, whatever you do, don't do nothing. Don't just tough it out, figuring that you're lucky to have a job at all. Maybe you are and maybe you aren't, but either way, it's your responsibility to make yourself happy if you can — if only because the happier you are, the better you'll be at your job and the better you'll be as a partner, spouse, parent, or friend.

If you hate your job, your first task is to figure out exactly why you hate it. If you're in a stew about how miserable you are, it might be a challenge to step back and analyze exactly what you aren't getting that you need or what you are getting that you don't want. But that's exactly what you need to do.

Let's start with the single most common reason people quit a full-time job, according to research by Payscale: money. Leaving a lower-paying job for a better-paying one is hard to resist for most people. If your job isn't paying enough to cover your expenses or provide properly for you and your family, then it's smart to take action. That could include negotiating for an increase in salary or other compensation, taking on extra work for extra pay, or starting a side hustle. But there's a difference between hating your salary and hating your job. If you hate your salary, any of these solutions might possibly work. If it's your job that you hate, they won't.

Career experts say that the reason people hate their jobs is most often the boss. This isn't surprising when you consider that most bosses receive no management training before taking on supervisory responsibilities. It may take some thought to figure out whether you'd hate your job less if you had a different boss — or you may already be very sure about the answer. If the problem is your boss, your first step might be to explore whether there's another position in your company you could move to where you could work for someone else.

Another common reason people hate their jobs is because they feel undervalued, which may or may not have anything to do with their actual pay. If you feel unrecognized or undervalued at work, some communication may help. Begin by making sure your immediate manager is aware of the hard work you do and particularly any big successes you have had. (You don't want to be heavy-handed about this, but you do want to make sure they're aware.) Your communication strategy should also include finding out from your boss how they see your work. There may be areas where you need to work harder, or things that matter to the boss that you weren't aware of. Ask a question like, "Is there anything I should be doing to be a more valuable employee?" You may get crucial information about how to do things differently. And if your boss is smart, they will recognize that you're feeling undervalued as well.

A final reason that you might hate your job is if you feel stuck — there's no opportunity for advancement, at least not in a direction you want to go, and you're not content with staying where you are. If that's the case, then it's very likely time for a move, whether into a different part of your organization or out of the organization altogether.

What about the job market? Is now the right time to go looking for a new job? In the last few years, the United States has seen the tightest labor market in decades. In fact, the 3.6 percent unemployment rate in 2019 and early 2020 was the lowest it had been in fifty years. We all know what happened next. The pandemic hit and put an abrupt end to good economic times. In April 2020, unemployment hit a staggering 14.7 percent. After April, things improved, thanks to a series of stimulus packages and eventually the arrival of Covid vaccines. By November 2021, unemployment was down to 4.2 percent.

These statistics are only part of the picture. In the spring of 2021, people began quitting their jobs in record numbers. This phenomenon, which came to be called the Great Resignation, was a source of frustration and worry to employers struggling to fill empty jobs. Experts have debated exactly what caused the Great Resignation and what it means. But it's interesting to note that in many cases, it's paired with the acronym *YOLO*, which stands for "you only live once."

For many Americans, including me, the pandemic pierced our sense of safety and of limitless possibility. It forced many of us to consider our own mortality in ways that we hadn't before. But the truth has always been there, with or without a pandemic: none of us knows how long we have on this planet, and there's a good chance that our time will be shorter than we would wish. If your job is making you miserable, no matter what the job market looks like, now is the time to at least try to do something about that.

It's like Jim Carrey said: our decisions are always based on either love or fear, and that's especially true of our career decisions. Don't let fear keep you trapped in a job or profession that fails to make you happy, and don't let it stop you from taking a chance on a career that could bring you joy. You only have one life, and if you're like most people, you'll spend a huge portion of it at work. If you don't follow what you love, you'll never know where you might have gone.

EXERCISES TO TRY

1. Broaden Your Perspective

If you could have any job at all, what would it be? Don't worry, for the moment, about whether it's actually possible for you to get the job. (I'd argue that none of us really knows what is and isn't possible for us anyhow. We only think we do.) For this exercise, let your imagination run wild. Movie star is just fine. So is owner of the New York Yankees or captain of the starship *Enterprise*. Make a list of at least three jobs that you would absolutely love to have. (Once again, I'm considering self-employed work as a job.)

Here's where it gets trickier. For each of those jobs, write down at least three reasons why you would like to have that job. For example, for starship captain, you might list: exploring space and discovering new species of aliens, having people obey your commands, and getting any food you want any time you want from the replicator.

Now for each of these reasons you want the job, come up with at least three other jobs that have that same element. Again, use your imagination. I'll admit that there aren't too many real-life jobs where you could get to meet alien species, but you might want to work at the SETI Institute, which is actively looking for them. Or you might want to work in science fiction, where new alien species are being imagined and created. Or you could work with octopuses. Octopuses are highly intelligent, and they evolved on a completely separate path from the primates who are our ancestors. So, experts say, getting to know an octopus is as close as you can come on Earth to getting to know an alien. You get the idea.

Once you're done, you should have a list of quite a few jobs. For each job, ask yourself two questions: (1) *Would I like to have this job?* and (2) *Am I willing to do what I'd have to do to get it?*

Use your answers as a starting place to consider different jobs and different careers you may never have thought about. You may conclude that the job you already have or the career path you're already on is the perfect one for you. In that case, hooray!

If your answer to any of these questions is "I don't know," get ready for the next exercise.

2. Go Find Out

When I was a child, my parents gave me Rudyard Kipling stories to read. My favorite character was the mongoose Rikki-Tikki-Tavi, whose family motto was "Run and find out." I think that's a pretty good motto for all of us when it comes to our careers.

Most journalists know this secret: you can ask almost anyone to talk about their work, and they'll do it. People love to talk about themselves, and almost any excuse will do. This means that once you've identified someone in a job that you think you might want to have, if you get in touch and ask if they'll answer a few questions, there's a high likelihood that they'll say yes. If you have your own blog or can offer to contribute an article to someone else's blog or website, you can use that as an excuse to interview the person about their work. Or you can be straightforward and say that you're thinking of pursuing a similar career yourself.

You want to find out what the job is actually like day to day, what someone in that profession might expect to earn (many jobs are surprisingly low paying or high paying), and what education and work history would best prepare someone to get such a job. You should also ask them about their own background and how they came to be where they are.

You're *not* there to ask them to find you a job or to ask what your prospects are for landing a job in that industry or company or even whether it's a good industry or profession for you to join. They may volunteer their opinion about this, but in most cases that will have more to do with their own personality and circumstances, and maybe even their mood that day, than anything else. On the day I left my full-time job to strike out as a freelance writer – as I was walking toward the door with my personal belongings – a woman I barely knew pulled me aside to inform me that she had also been a freelance writer and that I would certainly fail because sooner or later I would "run out of work," which is what happened to her. More than thirty years later, her prediction still hasn't come true.

If someone makes a similar forecast for you, thank them politely. Consider the reasons for their prediction. If they've identified a macro industry trend that could pose challenges to your career plans, you should probably do some additional research to find out if they're right. But don't let it stop you from at least trying to get the work you want. After all, regardless of what's happening on the macro level, you are operating on the micro level – you only need one job. Only you can decide whether to try for it.

3. Imagine Your Last Job

If the job you have now were the last one you could ever have, would that be all right with you? If not, is there a clear path from the job you have now to one you would want as your final-and-forever job? If the answer to both questions is no, is there some other work out there in the world that would make you happier? Is there a different direction you could be heading in?

Do some research (see the preceding exercise) to answer these questions and to find out what doing your forever job would really be like. Identify the steps between where you are now and that forever job. Are you willing to take them?

Chapter 11

How to Reach Your Biggest Goals

In the late 1980s, in the small town of Saugerties, New York, my husband Bill had a thirteen-year-old guitar student named Jimmy who loved comedy. Before each lesson, Jimmy would insist that he had to tell Bill a joke and Bill had to tell him one. Jimmy already knew what he wanted to do when he grew up — he wanted to be on *Saturday Night Live*. And he was absolutely certain he'd get there someday.

You've probably guessed the rest of the story. Jimmy's last name was Fallon, and he did indeed grow up to be an *SNL* cast member. He stayed there for six years before moving on to host *Late Night* and then *The Tonight Show*.

Fallon is a poster child for setting an impossible goal and then single-mindedly sticking with it until you get there. With one semester to go, he dropped out of college to move to LA and start a comedy and acting career. That put him three thousand miles away from New York's Rockefeller Plaza, where *SNL* was shot every week, but it gave him the chance to perform at the

Improv and take comedy classes with a comedy troupe called the Groundlings. He got an audition for *SNL* but wasn't cast. Still, he was so focused on his goal that when he landed a role in a network television pilot, he insisted on a clause that would release him from his contract if *SNL* ever hired him. The producers only agreed, reports say, because it seemed so improbable.

By the time Fallon got a second *SNL* audition two years after his first, he was truly ready. He'd been warned that the show's creator, Lorne Michaels never laughed, but Michaels did laugh at Fallon's imitation of Adam Sandler, a recent *SNL* alumnus. Tina Fey was on hand for Fallon's audition and said he was one of only two candidates she'd ever seen who was so in tune with the show he could have appeared on it that same night. "He was shaped by it and devoted to it," she told *Rolling Stone*. "In his look, even, he has, weirdly, a little kind of Mike Myers in him and a little Dana Carvey, like he was built in a lab to succeed on *SNL*."

Will It Happen If You Want It Badly Enough?

Right here is where some people might tell you that if you just dream big enough, if you're determined enough, if you're willing to work hard enough, your wildest dreams will definitely come true. I'm not going to say that because it isn't necessarily so. Yes, there are times when a singular fixation on a seemingly out-of-reach goal will get you exactly where you want to go, as it did for thirteen-year-old Jimmy Fallon. But there are other times when it won't.

My old friend and former Inc.com colleague Kevin Daum really wanted to write a *New York Times* bestseller. As every author knows, there are hundreds of bestseller lists out there, but the *Times* list is the one that counts. Daum is a marketing consultant and expert, and he figured there'd be no better way to prove just how good he was than to publish a book about marketing and have it land on the venerated *Times* bestseller list.

He was really, really determined to get there. He was so determined, in fact, that he had the phrase "New York Times Best Seller" — in a font that resembled the *Times'* gothic font — tattooed on his chest, in reverse, so he could read it every morning in the mirror. Daum did sell his book *ROAR! Get Heard in the Sales and Marketing Jungle* to a big publisher, and it became an Amazon bestseller in its category, but it was competing with books that had much bigger marketing budgets. Despite his best efforts, it never cracked the *Times* bestseller list.

James Clear, who wrote the bestseller *Atomic Habits*, was a high school baseball star who should have had a bright future as a pro. Then one day, as a teammate was swinging a bat, it slipped out of his hands at exactly the wrong moment. The bat connected with Clear's head, fracturing his skull, crushing his eye socket, and causing brain injuries that nearly killed him. Doctors kept Clear in an induced coma to stop a series of seizures, and when he finally woke up his motor skills were badly reduced. It took many months of work before he could step onto a baseball diamond again — something I doubt I'd have had the courage to do, considering what had happened the last time.

In college, while his friends were partying, he spent his time on his studies and on his health. He went to bed early every night. The hard work paid off when he made his college team and eventually the ESPN Academic All-America Team. But no matter how big he dreamed and how hard he worked, Clear never became a pro baseball player. He's OK with that. He wrote, "Looking back on those years, I believe I accomplished something just as rare: I fulfilled my potential." He's not bitter that his potential might have been different if not for that accident. He went on to be phenomenally successful in a completely different way — as an author and speaker.

Clear gave it his best shot and failed to achieve his goal. And when that happened, he didn't let that failure define him or cripple him. The same goes for Daum. After his book failed to make the *Times* bestseller list, his reaction was more or less a shrug. He went on to focus his attention on new projects. He's now written a total of eight books, six of which were Amazon bestsellers in their categories. And as a successful serial entrepreneur, he offers consulting for other entrepreneurs. He may still have the tattoo, but he's put the failure to make it come true behind him.

Will Failure Crush You?

For me, and I suspect for many other people, the fear of failure keeps me from going after my dreams. *What if I put my all into reaching that great big goal and fail to get there? What will people think of me? What will I think of me? Will I ever be able to get over it?*

I think those are the wrong questions. I know too many people like Clear and like Daum who dreamed big, tried their best, failed, and went on with their lives. And I know too many others who've been haunted for years, not by their failures but by the things they never tried. The real risk is what will happen if we let fear, ambivalence, procrastination, or just the busyness of life stop us from going after what we really want.

Ask yourself these questions instead: *If I try for this big goal and things don't go well, what's the worst that can happen? Will I be able to recover and move on? And what if I don't try for this goal? Will I be setting myself up for years of regret?*

If you're lucky, both your life and your career will go on for many years. If you throw your whole self into something that doesn't work, you'll likely have plenty of time to regroup and try something else. If you don't, you'll have just as many years to wonder what might have happened if you had. In a weird way, going after your biggest dreams may be your safest bet.

Answer this question (no one is watching and you don't have to share this with anyone, so keep that in mind): *If I could have any job I wanted, and any life I wanted — if I could accomplish anything I wanted — what would I do?* Think about this for a moment. Have you got an answer? Good. Now imagine that no matter what you did and how you lived your life, your loved ones would be happy and proud and would approve of you completely. I realize that may be hard to imagine, but do your best. Does that change your answer at all?

Now imagine that you never again have to go to a high school reunion and answer anyone's questions about what you do. And that, for the rest of your life, no one will ever again look at your LinkedIn profile. How about now? Does that change your answer?

Now imagine that it doesn't matter at all whether you have any idea how to attain this goal or whether it's even possible for you to reach it. You really don't have to use your imagination for this one because it really *doesn't* matter whether you have any idea how to reach your biggest goals. Part of the process of going after a really big goal is doing the research to find answers to those questions. And most of us really don't know what's possible for us and what isn't. So don't worry about how you're going to get there. Just imagine where you want to go. Does that change your answer?

Here's the thing about goals. It doesn't matter that much whether a career goal is attainable or even whether you have a clue how to accomplish it. What does matter is whether your goal will take you toward something that is right for you and will make you happy. A good goal doesn't have to be reachable or reasonable. It doesn't have to be something you absolutely commit to. But it does have to be *directionally accurate.*

I first learned that term a few years ago when someone used it to describe software for measuring web traffic. The tool really was very inaccurate — it could be off by a factor of 25 percent or more. But it was "directionally accurate," meaning that it could tell you how things were trending. It showed which items were getting relatively more clicks and which were being pretty much ignored. So even though it wasn't at all precise, it did tell you what you needed to know.

That's what you should look for when you're choosing your goals — something that will point you in the right direction, regardless of whether you actually get there. The goals we set rarely wind up being our final destination. Even for *SNL*-obsessed Jimmy Fallon, *Saturday Night Live* turned out to be just a stop on the way to something else.

When you set out to reach a seemingly impossible goal, one of three things will happen. As you learn more about it, you may find there's a different goal that you like better, and you'll change your aspiration to something else. Or you may fail, but along the way you'll learn a lot about the goal you were trying to reach, and about yourself too, so you will wind up with a lot more knowledge than before you started. Or you may surprise yourself and reach your impossible goal. Every one of these outcomes is worthwhile, so long as you choose a goal that takes you in a direction you want to go.

How to Get There from Here

No matter what your goal is, whether it's a huge goal or a small one, whether it's a personal goal like getting more exercise or a professional goal like starting your own company, there's a simple, proven method for getting there. BJ Fogg, PhD, head of the Behavior Design Lab at Stanford, learned from working with thousands of people who wanted to reach their own goals that taking small steps is the best way to complete a long journey.

While researching this book, I read Fogg's book *Tiny Habits*, and it changed my relationship to big, imposing projects forever. His simple formula takes advantage of your brain's natural inclinations and helps you tackle the most difficult tasks. First, find the tiniest, easiest step you could take to get started. For example, if you want to write a book, sit down at your desk and write one word. That's it! Do that first little step as a daily habit, and then — and this is important for your brain — the moment after you do it, reward yourself with a tiny celebration, such as giving yourself a high-five or a pat on the back. This small moment of happiness creates a positive association in your mind that makes you want to come back and do the habit some more.

It doesn't necessarily sound like this approach would be effective, but I can tell you that this stuff works. In my own life, I've spent years being frustrated by clutter. Some of it was in the form of boxes of nonessential items that we brought with us from Woodstock seven years earlier and never unpacked. This was always a source of shame and self-loathing for me. But after reading *Tiny Habits* and looking at the boxes of (inexpensive) jewelry that have been sitting in packing material on my dresser all this time, I decided to unpack one pair of earrings per day and then celebrate right after by giving myself a thumbs-up. This turned my still-packed boxes into a source of pleasure rather than pain, and the habit stuck. Within a few weeks, I'd completely unpacked all my jewelry, a job I hadn't managed to tackle in seven years.

I've used the baby-step method for bigger things too, from writing pitches for important projects to straightening out our family finances, a mammoth job that had me terrified, yet turned out to be quite doable once I started baby-stepping my way into it. If you try it, I guarantee it will work for you too. Here's how to get started.

Choose Your First Baby Step

If you're a couch potato and you want to run a marathon, a lot of running experts will tell you to start by walking for five minutes and then running for one minute every day, or some such program. Fogg would say to start by putting on your running shoes and tying the laces every day. Once you've done that, you can also go walk for five minutes and run for one minute if you want to, but that's purely extra credit. This is what I mean by a baby step. It doesn't matter how huge, ambitious, or even apparently out of reach your ultimate goal is. Start with a teeny, tiny, little step.

Make It Something You Control

Your first baby step, and every subsequent step, *must be* something that is within your control. If you're job hunting, your baby step cannot be to go on one job interview, unless it's a practice interview that you set up with a friend or a coach. You're not in control of when or whether a potential employer will invite you to an interview. You may think that if you apply for a large enough number of jobs, you'll inevitably get an interview, and you're probably right about that. But your baby step or steps should be, for example, to apply for one job every day for ten days. Once you've fulfilled that step — good for you! — you can decide to apply for ten more if you want, and then another ten after that. By the time you've applied for thirty or forty jobs, one of two things will have happened. You'll have had one or, more likely, many job interviews (and very probably some job offers), or else you'll have found out that you need to change something about the approach you're taking. At a minimum, you'll have learned something valuable that you didn't know before.

Write It Down and Commit

Once you've chosen your baby step, write it down. If you're using a power journal (see chapter 4) that's a great place to write down your baby step. It's where I always write mine. But you could also write it on a piece of paper that you post someplace where you'll see it every day. Or you could write it in your calendar. That's what my coach, Wendy Capland, recommends because every baby step you take should also have a deadline. Make sure to pick a date that is realistic for you, keeping in mind how busy you are and how unexpected tasks tend to crowd into your schedule.

You can help yourself make progress toward your goal, and perhaps make it more fun, if you find yourself an accountability partner or partners and tell them about your baby steps and when you plan to complete them. Your accountability partner can be someone with similar goals so that you can keep each other honest about working toward them. Your partner can check in with you once a week, or however often is appropriate, to make sure you complete your baby steps, and you can do the same for them. Or you can set up a regular meeting or phone call in which you update each other on the progress each of you has made toward your overall goals.

Troubleshoot as Necessary

What if your deadline or check-in has gone by and you haven't completed your baby step? First of all, go easy on yourself. If you're like most people, your schedule is constantly overloaded, and items are always dropping off your to-do list. If you've missed the deadline once or twice, that's only natural.

If you're missing it over and over, though, it's time to ask yourself some questions about your baby step, because something is preventing you from completing it. Maybe you're feeling overwhelmed or intimidated. If so, it could be that your tiny baby step isn't quite tiny enough. Channel your inner BJ Fogg and break it down to something even tinier. Maybe filling out a whole job application is too much. Maybe your step should be simply to open the web page with the application on it.

Another possibility is that your baby step is frightening because it's a step toward your goal. Reaching a goal or even moving a small distance toward a goal means change, and change can be scary, even if it's change you want. Again, don't beat yourself up. You're just taking one tiny step here, and you can always stop after that. If you have an accountability partner, consider talking to them about what you're feeling. Go slow.

Acknowledge Your Baby Step

Once you've taken your baby step, your instinct may be to hurry on to the next step. I can just see you, with your running shoes laced up, raring to head out the door for your first run. That's fine, but before you take — or even consider — the next step, there's something very important you must do first: celebrate and acknowledge the step you've already taken.

It's important because every time you give yourself a reward, large or small, for taking a step of any size, you're sending a message to your unconscious mind that will make it easier the next time. Your brain appreciates rewards!

Your self-reward can be something really simple, like giving yourself a pat on the back. I do this literally. If I've taken a baby step and I need to acknowledge myself, I will reach behind me and give myself a pat. You could give yourself a small treat — eat that piece of chocolate you've been saving or let yourself take an hour or two to watch your favorite show. Or your reward can take some other form. The important thing is that you do something concrete to tell yourself you've done a good job.

One other thing I always do, and that I highly recommend, is to write down your day's accomplishments at the end of the day. Writing down your achievements, even if it was just tying your shoes, is a great way to make them concrete in your mind. The ideal time to do this is right before you go to sleep, so that you end the day on a positive note and fall asleep with a reminder of what you did right that day uppermost in your mind.

Don't write down what you're frustrated or disappointed about (you can do that in your daytime journal writing). And don't do the stupid thing I've sometimes done and write something like, "Today I went out and walked a mile and a half, but it wasn't the three miles I'd been planning." Acknowledge what you've done for the accomplishment that it is. Maybe you'll do more tomorrow.

Tonight, right before bed, I'm going to write this: "Today, I finished writing chapter 11." And I'll probably pat myself on the back.

EXERCISES TO TRY

1. Imagine Your Best Possible Future

I've done this popular exercise with members of *Inc.* magazine's solo-preneur (one-person company) community. If possible, I recommend giving yourself at least ten minutes of uninterrupted time to do this.

Imagine yourself five years from now. During those five years, everything in your life and work has gone as well as you could have hoped. You've reached your goals or are on schedule to meet them. Most of what you wanted has come true.

Decorate and furnish this future fantasy. Where do you live, and with whom (if anyone)? Where do you work, and what is your job? How do you spend your free time? What's your biggest priority? What's your greatest source of pride?

Write a description of your future life and future self, as detailed as you can make it. What would have to change, and what would you have to do for that future to become reality?

Now roll back the future to two years from now. What will have to happen and what will you need to do to be on track for that future you just imagined?

Roll back some more, and think about this time next year. What will you need to do between now and then to be on your way to that five-year destination? What about this month? This week?

Now pick one thing – a tiny baby step – that you can do right away to get just a little closer to that future. Whatever it is, write it down and commit, including a date by which you'll get it done. Once it's done, you can pick your next tiny baby step.

2. Ask Yourself Why

Have you ever gotten into one of those endless conversations with a small child where you say something and the child asks why? So you explain, and the child asks why again. So then you explain your explanation, and so on until you give up and say something like, "Because that's the way it is!"

For this exercise, access your inner four-year-old. For every important goal that you have, ask yourself why. Write down your answer, and whatever your answer is, keep asking why. Continue deconstructing this way until you've boiled your most important desires down to their very essence. Now look at what you've written. See if there are lessons you can learn from it. You may discover some alternate goals, or you may decide to rethink the approach you've been taking.

Here's an example. I've been using an app recently to try to eat healthier and lose some weight. It never occurred to me to wonder *why* I might want to lose weight – doesn't everyone? But the app asked that question, so I had to come up with an answer. If I'm honest with myself, one big reason is that my husband has lost a lot of weight recently, so I'm feeling some peer pressure. But I didn't write that down. What I did write was that I wanted to take longer and more difficult hikes.

There's a problem with that answer, which is that I haven't been doing much hiking and it has nothing to do with my weight. I haven't found a really well-matched hiking companion, and hiking on my own can seem a little lonely. Losing weight is fine, but that by itself is not going to upgrade my hiking capabilities. If I want to do longer, more challenging hikes, I need to work at finding a good hiking partner, commit to some solo hikes, or both. I'm not sure what the answer is to this, but I do know that without asking why, I wouldn't have known to look for one.

Chapter 12

The Power of Yes and the Power of No

I stared out at blue sky through the open door of an airplane about fourteen thousand feet up. I was supposed to go through that door, and I was terrified. Few things are as deeply contrary to normal human instincts as stepping through the open door of an airplane into midair. I had not fully considered that fact until this moment.

"I'm scared now," I said to my instructor, whose name — Mad Dog — was not reassuring to a first-time skydiver. Mad Dog didn't answer. He simply launched himself forward. I was attached to him by straps — it was a tandem jump, as first jumps usually are — so I went too. We somersaulted out of the plane, and there I was, falling through the sky.

How had I come to be there? It started out simply enough. My mother and stepfather lived in DeLand, Florida, and I often traveled there to visit them. They had recently discovered a fun weekend pastime: heading over to the nearby skydiving center and watching the action. Skydive DeLand was a famous and long-established skydiving school, and people came from all over the country to jump there, enjoying the beautiful North Florida weather and the views of the coastline.

We spent a morning sitting at a picnic table outside the sky-diving center, watching as one person after another floated down from the sky and landed gently, their parachutes deflating and falling behind them. Over time it came to look like the simplest, most natural thing in the world. Eventually, I asked a woman who was packing a parachute what it was like to skydive. She told me I should give it a try, that taking a tandem jump would be easy and that it was a great thrill, the most fun thing in the world.

I had never heard of tandem skydiving. Being securely at-tached to a professional who knew exactly how to steer and when to open the parachute sounded much safer and easier than tak-ing that terrifying first jump alone and relying on my own addled brain to remember those things as I hurtled toward the ground. Skydive DeLand had been around for more than twenty years. Mad Dog, despite his name and an intimidating mustache, was an expert and seasoned skydive instructor and tandem master. I'm not a daredevil sort of person, but this seemed like something I could actually do.

And so, a few days later, there I was in mid-air. I had fol-lowed my curiosity, my sense of adventure, my desire for new ex-periences, and my taste for doing things that stretched my limits. Something intriguing and exciting had come along, and although it was scary, I had said yes.

It turned out to be a picture-perfect dive on a picture-perfect day. After a few minutes of falling fast through the air, the whip-ping wind making all conversation impossible, Mad Dog opened the parachute. We floated gently over Florida, and he pointed out the river and the ocean below. A few minutes later — way too soon — he was giving me tips for how to land before guiding us in to gently touch down right outside the skydive center.

That was my only skydive; it was a huge amount of fun, but I had no intention of turning it into a hobby. Still, it was an experience I'll never forget, something I can always look back at with pride. *Yes, I've jumped out of an airplane.* Saying yes to things can take you on all kinds of adventures.

Consider Sir Richard Branson, the founder of the Virgin Group. His employees call him Dr. Yes, something he's clearly proud of. When I asked him by email how that nickname came about, he explained, "The team started calling me 'Dr. Yes' during our early days at Virgin Records, and the nickname has stuck ever since. I've always been an optimist, which makes it a lot easier to say yes and take risks! I think life is a lot more fun when you live this way and it can really help a business grow and evolve, so it's something I've always held onto."

Branson, who lives on his own Caribbean island, has started more than four hundred companies, including Virgin Megastore, Virgin Records, Virgin Atlantic Airways, Virgin Mobile, Virgin Voyages, and the commercial space company Virgin Galactic. All this wouldn't have happened without his tendency to say yes, he explained.

"The Virgin story is built on the word 'yes.' We couldn't have grown from publishing a student magazine to building spaceships if we hadn't said 'screw it, let's do it!' so often. I can't imagine what my life would be like without Virgin, so to say the word 'yes' has affected my life would be a great understatement."

Starting an airline is not an obvious next step for someone who's achieved success in the music industry, he noted. "But unlike other entrepreneurs who stick with one business, I couldn't resist saying yes to new adventures. That's how Virgin became as vast as it is now — I've said yes to so many things! And have loved learning from them all."

This includes a few things Branson has said yes to that didn't turn out so well, such as Virgin Cola, which attempted to compete with Coke but wound up shutting down. Or the time he tried to fly a hot air balloon across the Atlantic to Los Angeles and wound up in Antarctica instead, a trip he only survived by luck. Unlike me, he *is* a daredevil sort of person. He's also one of the very few billionaires who looks like he's always having fun.

The Power of Yes

There's a community of Inc.com readers who get a text from me every day. When I sent out a text about Branson and the word *yes*, some of them thought I was suggesting that they say yes to anything anyone ever asks them to do. That is most emphatically not the power of the word *yes*. There are certain things you need to do for your own benefit or to benefit those you love, such as going to the dentist or buying insurance or filing your taxes. Other than that, the things you say yes to should be things you want to do. No one else can determine what's yes-worthy to you.

Say Yes to Things That Frighten You

I'm not suggesting you should try skydiving, even though I'm glad I did. I am saying, though, that most of us let fear hold us back from doing things we want to do, and sometimes we shouldn't give in to that fear. Fear of jumping out of an airplane and smashing to the ground, or getting arrested if you do something illegal, or getting robbed or hurt in a bad neighborhood, or losing all your money if you invest it in something dubious — those are all logical fears of actual harm that you might reasonably wish to avoid. But what about the fear of looking foolish? What about the fear of being criticized? Should those things really stop you from doing something you want?

When my husband and I moved from New York to Washington State, we were partly inspired by our good friend Drew, who had moved here first and encouraged us to follow him. A few days after we arrived, Drew appeared at a local community theater in a show about the British Invasion music of the 1960s, where he played Donovan to hilarious perfection. I can still see him lovingly sniffing a flower and then tossing it to a pretty girl in the audience before being hoisted onto a chair in Donovan's signature cross-legged pose. Drew, like my husband, was a working musician and an experienced performer. Even so, between guffaws I found myself wondering how he'd found the nerve to be so funny and so completely... out there.

A week later, I learned the answer, and it was horrible. Even though he was never a smoker, Drew had been diagnosed with fourth-stage lung cancer. He had less than two years to live. Something like that will put the fear of looking foolish into perspective very quickly.

As I write this, I'm in good health so far as I know, but I am also sixty-one. Growing older is its own form of terminal diagnosis, and so the fear of looking foolish stops me from doing things a whole lot less than it used to. "'Look at me!' is where you live," someone said to me admiringly at a weekend singing workshop I attended a couple of years ago. It was quite a compliment, considering we were in a group of people who had signed up to sing and be coached in front of about sixty strangers, which is to say we were a fairly extroverted group.

I wish I hadn't wasted so many years getting here. I wish I hadn't let fear stop me from singing in front of people for all the years that it did. I still wish I didn't let fear of criticism or rejection or fear of failure stop me from doing things as often as I do. Most of all, I wish that it didn't take the fear of dying to knock silly fears like the fear of embarrassment out of us all. We waste so much time this way, and we have so little to begin with.

Say Yes to Things You Don't Know How to Do

In chapter 8, I wrote about research from HP that shows women tend to wait till they're completely qualified for a job before applying, whereas men tend to apply if they have just 60 percent of the qualifications. This finding is sometimes cited as evidence that the long-lasting disparity between men's earnings and women's results from women holding themselves back. I personally believe, as other research suggests, that women in the workplace correctly foresee that they'll be held to higher standards than their male counterparts.

There's a much fuller discussion of this issue in chapter 8, but the point here is that if you do get the opportunity to take on a task that you don't know how to do but you would like to learn, you should definitely say yes to that opportunity. In the same way, if you want to do something but don't know how, that shouldn't stop you from setting it as a goal.

My coach, Wendy Capland, took this approach, and it worked out spectacularly well. "Years ago, I found myself declaring during a workshop that I wanted to have my own television show. As soon as I said it, I thought, 'I have no idea how to do that. That was a stupid goal.'" But after the workshop was over, a woman went up to Capland and told her she was being interviewed on cable TV the following week. She invited Capland to go along and observe. This turned out to be the introduction Capland needed, and soon she had her own local cable show, which ran for three years and had 2.5 million viewers. (See chapter 11 for more on baby steps.)

A lot of people, including my husband, would take this story as a sign that the universe provides what we ask for. How else, he would say, do you explain the coincidence that within that small group of women there happened to be one who was appearing on TV the following week? I personally don't buy that, not only because it's too woo-woo for my taste but also because the evidence doesn't really support it. We all know too many instances of people in desperate need for whom the universe has provided nothing at all.

I do think there's something simpler and less mystical at work, a variant of the cognitive bias called *frequency illusion* — that is, having something on our minds causes us to notice it around us when otherwise we might not have. With or without that workshop participant being there to invite Capland to the studio, I believe — assuming she was serious about her desire to have a television show and didn't just forget about it — she would have come across another opportunity to learn about being on TV because she would have been on the lookout for it, consciously or not.

In general, for just about anything you don't know how to do, from fixing a leaky faucet to piloting a nuclear submarine, there's someone out there who does know how and would be willing to teach you. Then there's the fact that human beings are problem solvers by nature. I think if we state something we want out loud, or even to ourselves, our human brains automatically start working on solving the problem of how to make it come true. I believe this is why setting an intention or saying a goal out loud is such a powerful thing to do. In any case, the lesson is clear. Don't hold yourself back from taking a job or setting a goal just because you don't know how to get there. You can find out, I promise.

Say Yes to Things That Aren't Part of Your Original Plan

You may have a distinct idea of where you want to be in a year or in five years. You may also have a very clear idea of the steps that will get you from here to there. In fact, you may already be on that path. Yet you may be drawn to something that comes along and doesn't fit those plans at all. Perhaps it has awakened your curiosity, your sense of adventure, or your desire for a new challenge. Or maybe it just seems like fun.

These can be perfectly good reasons to say yes to something even though it may not fit your original plan. We all tend to think of our careers as heading down a straight and specific road, but in fact it can look a lot more like meandering through a forest with side trips to admire a hidden pond and backtracking to go around unexpected obstacles.

Many years ago, I was a perfectly happy freelance writer living in Woodstock, New York. Most of my clients were many miles away in New York City or even farther, and I thought it would be nice to work for more local publications. So, on a whim, I called up the business editor at the *Poughkeepsie Journal*, one of the larger daily newspapers in our area, to ask if they needed any freelance work.

Instead, the editor told me she had a job opening for a full-time business reporter and asked if I wanted to apply. Being a reporter on a daily newspaper had never been part of my career plan. I wanted to write for magazines and then graduate to books one day. Even back then, newspapers were a mostly dying breed, and I knew they didn't pay all that well. Also, I had never particularly wanted to be a reporter. The "inverted pyramid" style of writing you're supposed to use for newspaper reporting — where you put the most important fact first, then the next most important, and so on — struck me as stultifying and formulaic.

On the other hand, I'd grown up reading a thousand *Brenda Starr* comics. I'd seen *Absence of Malice* and *All the President's Men*. The idea of writing for a newspaper seemed exotic and romantic, and all of a sudden I wanted to give it a try. I applied and got the job.

Working at the *Journal* was, for me, a strange combination of charming and disastrous. We've all seen newspaper newsrooms on TV: the big open room with desks side by side, way before open-plan offices were a thing. Reporters rushing around, an editor in a glass-walled office in one corner of the room, a patrician publisher who floated through from time to time. Well, that's exactly what it was like. Founded in 1785, the *Poughkeepsie Journal* is the second oldest newspaper in the United States. I loved arriving at work in the morning at the beautiful fieldstone building, which seemed to dominate the oldest part of town, and seeing newspapers sailing on long tracks above my head as I walked through the building to the parking lot. I loved attending city council meetings and going places with my reporter's notebook in hand. But I hated the thirty-eight-mile commute from Woodstock through one of the snowiest winters on record. When spring came and that long commute meant I'd never see my garden in daylight until the weekend, I hated it even more. Working on the *Journal*'s old-style keyboard was giving me tendinitis, which I knew could quickly progress into carpal tunnel syndrome, a condition several of my newsroom colleagues already had.

It didn't take long for me to start hating the job and longing to go back to freelancing. But I told myself I needed to hang on for a year, that there was a lot to learn there, and that I shouldn't leave until I'd learned it.

Unfortunately for that plan, I wasn't very good at the job. I could write quickly, which you need to do on a daily paper, but I had no training or education in that kind of daily journalism, and my shortcomings soon became apparent. Whether because of the tendinitis, which my doctor insisted on reporting as a work-related condition, or my increasing grumpiness as I dragged myself through a job I longed to quit, or the fact that I didn't entirely know what I was doing, at the end of a three-month trial period when the paper could either hire me permanently or let me go, they chose to let me go. I had never been fired before, and it was an eye-opening experience — but not an entirely terrible one. Driving north, away from dusty Poughkeepsie and toward my Woodstock home in the mountains through the beautiful springtime landscape, I was at least as much relieved as I was upset.

A few months later, I had restored my freelance business and the *Journal* seemed like a distant memory. It was certainly a failed experiment. But I'll never be sorry that I said yes to that job because I learned so much, both about newspapers and about myself, in those three months.

Say Yes to Two-Way Doors

The *Journal's* decision to hire me and my decision to take the job were "two-way doors" — that is, decisions that can be undone if they turn out to be wrong. Amazon founder Jeff Bezos says that two-way-door decisions should be made quickly and that conflating them with the few true one-way-door decisions leads to agonizing too long and also to people failing to take risks and experiment when they should.

Selling a house, quitting a job, having a child — these are all one-way doors. But the vast majority of decisions you make are two-way doors. We may be unhappy about the embarrassment, inconvenience, or expense of changing our minds, but we can still do it. Even getting married and getting a tattoo are two-way doors, though reversing those decisions is usually painful and expensive.

In 2011, Netflix announced it was spinning off its DVD-by-mail service into a new company called Qwikster. This meant that Netflix subscribers, accustomed to getting DVDs and streaming video in one place, would now have to subscribe to two different companies if they wanted to continue getting both. Customers hated it, and there was a swift negative reaction to everything about the announcement, including the new company's weird name. Spinning off a company might seem like a one-way-door decision to you and me, but it wasn't. Less than a month after saying that Qwikster was coming, and before the service had even launched, Netflix cofounder Reed Hastings declared that the company had changed its mind. There would be no Qwikster, and Netflix would continue to provide DVDs by mail to those who wanted them. It still does that today.

The Qwikster announcement, followed so quickly by a great big "Never mind," led some to question whether Hastings knew what he was doing and even to call for his removal as CEO. In fact, he knew exactly what he was doing — he was taking full advantage of a two-way-door decision. Spinning off Qwikster had been a clumsy attempt to deal with the relative costliness of delivering DVDs by mail in a world where streaming was becoming the norm. When it became clear that this solution would create more problems than it solved, instead of sticking to his guns or worrying about embarrassment, Hastings simply reversed himself. He knew that taking his lumps for changing his mind so quickly in the short term would be better than sticking with a bad decision in the long term. Netflix's value has increased more than tenfold since 2011, and Hastings hasn't gone anywhere.

If you're deciding whether to say yes to something that appeals to you, ask yourself whether it's truly a one-way door or a two-way door. If it's a two-way door, consider giving whatever it is a try and keeping your options open in case you change your mind.

The Power of No

Yes is an incredibly powerful word, but like anything powerful, it should not be overused. I've told you some of the times when I believe you should consider saying yes to things. There are many other times when no is almost certainly the right answer.

Say No When No Is What You Really Want to Say

What do you really want? This is a question I ask myself surprisingly often. We live in a world so filled up with things we should do — grow our own vegetables, get more exercise, keep up with the news and social media, read the classics, get some fresh air every day, keep in touch with our family members and friends, rotate our tires — that I find it's sometimes difficult to distinguish between the things I really want to do and the things I know I'm supposed to do.

Think about it. If whatever you're considering falls in the category of things you don't want to do but believe you should, ask yourself what the real consequences would be of not doing it. When you really consider it, it may be that those consequences aren't so bad after all.

Say No When Saying Yes Feels Like Too Big a Risk

How much of a risk is too much? That question has a different answer for everyone. For me, taking a tandem skydive attached to a seasoned instructor constituted an acceptable risk. You may think I was nuts to do it, or maybe you think I was a coward for not doing a solo jump. Risk means something different to everyone.

As human beings, our view of risk can be inconsistent and even illogical. As a friend of mine once pointed out, some people refuse to eat nonorganic fruit for fear of carcinogens but drive down the highway without a seat belt on. We also accept different levels of risk in different spheres. For example, you may be fearless on the ski slopes but conservative about your investments. What is and isn't a worthwhile risk is something only you can decide, and there's almost never a right or wrong answer.

Say No When You'd Be Saying Yes to Please Someone Else

I have a good friend who says it's almost impossible to get her to do something she doesn't want to do. I admire that about her enormously. Just as I sometimes struggle with knowing what I really want, I struggle quite a lot with my desire to please others, or at least to avoid disappointing them. This tendency has gotten me to any number of parties that I didn't want to attend. It's also led me to take on assignments I knew weren't really right for me. My problem is that I'm a people pleaser, which is no way to live. Maybe you have a problem with this too.

I have a friend who turned seventy a few years ago. He told

me that he found that age very liberating because he no longer did things just to please others; life was now too short for that. Like fear of embarrassment, the need to please others is part of being human, but not always a part that serves us well. Don't wait until you're seventy to let go of it, because you could run out of time for the things you really want.

Say No When Saying Yes Would Take Your Focus Away from Something More Important

There's a story out there that coaches and productivity gurus love to tell about Warren Buffett and his pilot. According to the story, Buffett asked his pilot to write down twenty-five career goals. Then Buffett told him to circle the five most important. When that was done, he asked the pilot what he intended to do. The pilot said he would get to work on the top five right away, and on the other twenty as time permitted. Buffett said he had it all wrong. The twenty goals that weren't among the top five were to be avoided at all costs until the top five goals were met, otherwise they might dilute the pilot's focus and stop him from reaching the important goals.

The problem with this story is that Buffett never said anything of the kind. Or at least, he said he didn't when asked about it during an annual meeting. But there's a reason the story has been repeated and republished so many times: the underlying concept is brilliant.

Modern life can seem like an endless menu of good ideas, opportunities, and things we know we should do to improve our health or further our careers. The problem is that you can wind up like me on a Sunday afternoon trying to pick out a movie to watch. I'll look through Netflix, Amazon Prime, Hulu, and other streaming services; read descriptions and reviews of a dozen movies or more; watch half a dozen trailers — and wind up without enough time to watch any movie. We have to pare things down to what really deserves our focus, and that can be a difficult task. Making a list of lesser priorities that we should be careful *not* to focus on is a pretty good place to start.

A very successful executive once told me that what mattered in her career were the things she said no to, not the things she said yes to. I've thought about that comment a lot over the years, particularly when I've struggled myself with what seems like an endless list of priorities. When you're in that situation, the ability to say no to the things you might like to do but that aren't a top priority is a superpower. If you say no to enough stuff that's unimportant, you'll be able to truly shine when it counts.

Even Dr. Yes says no to things that don't align with his top priorities. When I asked Branson how he decides to say no to things, as every business leader must do sometimes, he answered that he gets advice from people he trusts and that he tries to learn from every setback and says no to things that would mean repeating past mistakes. Then he added, "I've also learnt to say no to opportunities that don't align with Virgin's purpose and the things I'm passionate about in life." I think that's a pretty smart approach.

Here's my very favorite story about the word *yes*. It's about how John Lennon and Yoko Ono first met. The famous Beatle was invited to preview Ono's conceptual art at a London gallery the night before her exhibit was to open. He liked the humor in the art right away. But he first became interested in the artist when he saw a small canvas hanging from the ceiling. Something too tiny to read was written on it, and there was a ladder and a spyglass nearby. Lennon climbed the ladder, looked through the spyglass, and saw that the canvas had just one word on it — the word *yes*. If it had said *no*, he wouldn't have been so intrigued, he said later.

"Even if I have no idea where I'm going or how to get there, I prefer to say yes instead of no," Branson wrote in the blog post that started me thinking about the word *yes* in the first place. "Life is a lot more fun when you say yes! It's amazing how that one little word can lead you on an incredible adventure."

What kind of adventure will saying yes bring to you?

EXERCISES TO TRY

1. Practice Asking for Time to Think

To say yes to the things you want most, you need to be good at saying no to the things that will take up more of your time and energy than they deserve. You know that sometime soon someone will ask you to take on a task that falls in this category. So – especially if you're afflicted with people-pleasing disease, as I am – practice this sentence in advance: "Can I have some time to think about it?"

Now if you know perfectly well that your answer is no, then by all means go ahead and say no. But if you aren't sure, or if you can't bring yourself to disappoint someone, then asking for time to think can be just the lifeline you need. For one thing, it will give you time to talk it over with a spouse, partner, friend, or family member, which might be enough to solidify your sense that this is something you should not take up. It also gives you the opportunity to answer the request at a time and in a manner of your choosing. For instance, if it pains you to say no in person, you could send a text or an email instead.

If you ask for time to think and the other person says no, that might make your decision a little bit easier. You can now say something like, "Well, I'm not sure, so if you really need an answer right now, I'd better say no."

2. Ask Why Not

On the other hand, you may be automatically saying no to opportunities or adventures out of instinct or habit. If someone invites you to try something new or you get the opportunity to do something that frightens you a little, but it's also something you feel drawn to, before you say no, ask yourself why not. It could be there's a good reason why no is the right answer: Saying yes would take up time or money or other resources you need for something else. Or it would mean taking an unacceptable risk. Or it wouldn't align with your goals or passions.

Either way, the important thing is that before you say no to something, you give it your full consideration. If you're saying no because you think you're not the kind of person who would do something like that or you don't feel qualified or it would take you outside your comfort zone, it could be that yes is the right answer. Or maybe not. Only you can really know.

3. Do Something Embarrassing

For too many of us, the fear of looking foolish, of doing something we're bad at, or of someone making fun of us can be nearly paralyzing. That's a sad thing, because fear of embarrassment often keeps us from doing things that might make us feel happier and freer.

Experts say that our comfort zones tend to shrink over time unless we consciously work to expand them. That's what I'm asking you to do. Find something that you'd like to do – except you fear that it would open you up to criticism or, worse, derision. What that something is, is up to you. It could be walking on the beach in your swimsuit if you're uncomfortable about your body. It could be giving a speech – most of us are uncomfortable with that. It could be singing a song or getting up and dancing at the next party you attend.

Whatever you pick, just do it. You can do it for only five minutes or only one minute. The point is to see how you feel afterward. If you feel awful, there's no need to ever do that particular thing again. But if you're like me, there's a good chance you'll feel exhilarated and relieved because it really wasn't so bad after all.

For best results, repeat this process often. The more often you step outside your comfort zone, the less confining it will be.

Chapter 13

Your Day Job and Your Dream Job

The very first full-time job I had after I graduated from college was for a small company that published a variety of fairly incomprehensible medical journals. I didn't know anything about medicine or medical journals, but I could type about eighty words a minute. Most of my time on this job was spent doing exactly that, with occasional tasks that were a bit more related to publishing. That was my day job. I spent my evenings doing what I thought of as my own writing.

For musicians, writers, actors, and other creative people, the "day job" is a familiar concept. It's the work you do to make ends meet while pursuing your true avocation in your off hours. Your day job is something you're doing just for now, until you can make a living at the work you really love — your dream job.

For decades, I lived with this day job / dream job distinction in my head. There was my "real" work — the writing that counted. And then there were my day jobs. I quickly moved on from that first, mostly administrative position to an entry-level job at a trade magazine company. It wasn't what anyone would call a dream job, and yet I loved it. My work involved lots and lots of travel to all sorts of places. Some were glamorous, such as Acapulco. Others were less glamorous, such as Tulsa or Cleveland. The truth is, I was happy either way. I love to travel, even to prosaic places, and I love hotel rooms, even drab ones. But there were very few drab hotel rooms on that job because I was writing for a readership of meeting planners, the very people these destinations most wanted to woo and impress, so they did their best to woo and impress them through me, putting me in suites, even though I was traveling alone, and treating me to lavish dinners and tours to show me the best of what their town or resort had to offer.

I was writing for a living, which in itself felt like a privilege even though the salary was pretty meager. And the job was teaching me a lot of new skills. This company's philosophy was to have the same employees write, edit, and lay out stories, often taking their own pictures as well. I learned about white space and leading, and the difference between a two-point rule and a hairline rule (which most people would call a line). I attempted to proofread, although I'm hopelessly bad at it. I pored over negatives of the film that would be shipped to the printer from which copies of the magazine would be printed in those pre-digital days.

I enjoyed the work, but I was also working late into the evening most weeknights and often traveling on weekends, when many industry conferences took place. It was the sort of job where if I called in sick, my boss would ask what I'd be working on while I stayed home. I had little time and energy left for what I thought of as my own work, the work that, I fantasized, might someday take me away from my day job and land me in a dream job.

The Uncrossable Line between Dream Job and Day Job

It seems to me that many people have a similar mental divide between the work they're doing now and the work they'd like to be doing someday. There's the job you'll have after you finally get that promotion you want or get hired by that company you've been wanting to work at or finally start a company of your own. And then there's the work you're doing today that may seem gray and mundane by comparison.

The problem isn't that thinking about your dream job will keep you from doing your day job well. The fact that you're reading this book tells me that you're probably quite committed to your career, and I'm going to guess you put your best effort into everything that you do.

But there are two big problems with this day-job-versus-dream-job way of thinking. First, it can affect how you feel about the things you've already accomplished. Let's say you get a promotion to a non-dream job, or you get a raise or land a big customer, or you complete a project that turns out to be a resounding success. It's time to bask in the glow of your own achievement! But when you do, is that a perfectly complete pleasure? Or do you qualify it in the back of your mind with *yes, but*? Yes, but this isn't the job I really want. Yes, but that new deal I just landed is making a lot of money for my employer when I really should be landing deals for myself at a company that I own. Yes, but this isn't my real career; I'm still waiting for that career to get started.

Psychologists talk about *goal ambivalence*, "conceptualized as an approach-avoidance conflict...in which a person simultaneously hopes for and fears the attainment of a personal striving." Some studies suggest that people with goal ambivalence get more ambivalent about their goals the closer they come to attaining them. I've experienced this myself. For example, the trade publishing company where I worked launched a new magazine devoted to business travel. I wanted in from the moment I heard about it, and I lobbied for a job there. Once I got the job, I also asked for a fancier title — senior associate editor, a step down from the managing editor and editor in chief, but clearly higher up the food chain than anyone else who worked there. I got that title too. After less than three years at the company, it was quite an acknowledgment of the work I'd done and the skills I'd acquired, and it should have made me happy. But it didn't. My head was still full of *yes, but.*

Robbing you of the joy of your own achievements is one drawback to dream-job-versus-day-job thinking. The second is even worse. It can hold you back from your dreams.

That's the bad rep that less-than-dream jobs get. You get a fine arts degree with the goal of becoming a fashion designer. Instead, you land a job doing illustrations for a sports equipment catalog. You promise yourself you'll apply for entry-level fashion jobs, such as patternmaker, or maybe even for a fashion internship, but you never do. Some would say your illustrating job is too cushy and has made you too soft to face the challenges of the highly competitive fashion industry. But I don't think that's true. I believe it's something else.

The more you work away at your day job with the catalogs and the more you fantasize about your dream job in fashion, the harder it gets to actually go after that dream job. You start wondering whether you really have enough talent for fashion design or if you're only good enough for catalog illustration. Once you start thinking that way, you're in trouble because applying for a fashion job is no longer just about filling out a job application and sending a portfolio. It's suddenly about finding out whether you have what it takes for the career you've spent years wishing for. That's a lot of significance for what should just be a simple little job application! Once you give a simple action like applying for a job the power to change the way you think about yourself, it becomes really difficult to do.

Meantime, you're very good at your catalog job. They've given you a raise and an assistant and even invited you to help design their new product line. All this keeps you so busy you barely have time to stay up on fashion trends, let alone apply for a fashion job. Eventually, you decide it's better this way. You're doing well, you enjoy your job, you just got another raise, and you obviously aren't cut out to be a fashion designer or you would have been one by now.

The problem isn't that your catalog job has made you soft. Believe it or not, it also isn't that you don't have the time to keep up with fashion or fill out fashion job applications. You could make the time if you truly wanted to. And it's not that you aren't talented enough for fashion design. The truth is, you don't know whether you're talented enough because you never really tried to find out. Finding out would have been too frightening. It's been too easy for too many years to fantasize about working in fashion while leaving the actual task of applying for a fashion job for another day. I know because a version of the same thing happened to me.

Don't get me wrong. I definitely have a dream job. Not only do I get to write for a living, which is pretty good all by itself, but millions of people read what I write every month. Some of them pay to get a text from me every day, which still feels amazing to me a year after I started doing it. Besides *Inc.*, I get to write for CNBC.com and Insider. As one writer friend of mine put it, that's a pretty nice trifecta. And now I'm writing this book, which is something I dreamed of doing for years.

But there's another kind of writing I love — personal essays. I have stacks of them: pieces I've written and revised over and over, shared with my writer friends for critique, and not submitted anywhere for publication. Why not? Because I'm shy. Because these essays are about my life, my mother's Alzheimer's, my disastrous first marriage, my miscarriage. If someone rejected them, I'm not sure that I could bear it. I did publish one in a literary journal started by a friend of mine because I felt reasonably confident that if I sent it to him, he wouldn't reject it. And that's pretty much it. As to the rest, I've revised and revised and revised. Sometimes I find myself undoing the changes I'd made earlier.

Somewhere along the way, I convinced myself that I wasn't that good at essays, that this was the reason I had virtually never published any. I never considered that the reason might be that I had only sent out two of those essays, one time each, in all the years I'd been writing them. The writing I do for *Inc.* and others, fun and meaningful as it was, somehow was still a day job inside my head. The essays were a dream job, and part of me was too afraid that sending them out could be the death of all my dreams. This is where building a mental wall between my day job and my dream job has gotten me.

Crossing the Uncrossable Line

It doesn't have to be this way. The truth is, just about every job is part day job and part dream job, and the sooner you and I stop thinking of a job as either/or, the better off we'll be. The trick is to figure out which parts of your job are dreamy to you, and how to do more of them, and which parts feel like day-to-day drudgery, and how to do less of them.

To accomplish this, start by unlearning everything you know about what your ideal job "should" be. If something is your dream job because you think it will impress someone else — your parents, your siblings, your former schoolmates, your spouse, or your potential dates — I'd highly recommend doing something else. According to one analysis, we spend, on average, thirteen years and two months of our lives working. Other than sleeping, which we do for twenty-six years, it's the thing we'll spend the largest portion of our lives doing. By contrast, we spend only one year and one month on romance, and one year and three days socializing with those friends we might be trying to impress with our great jobs. If you think about it this way, it seems pretty silly, at least to me, to spend those thirteen-plus years on something you don't love.

I also think you should consider not spending too much of that time on things that you think are good for your career, if they're things you don't enjoy. Yes, you have to pay your dues, and that probably means doing work that's not as fun or important as you might like. But I also know from experience that people will tell you something would be good for your career when what they really mean is it would make their own lives easier. If you're doing something you don't love because it's good for your career, ask yourself if you see a clear path from what you're doing to where you want to go. Also ask yourself whether getting that promotion you're looking for will mean doing more of or less of whatever it is you don't love.

Back at that trade publishing job, I was asked early on what my aspirations were. I said I wanted to "manage people." This was an outright lie. I had no particular desire to manage people. I was a writer; I wanted to write. Why did I say it? It hadn't taken me long to see what the career path was in this place. The more successful you were, the higher up the hierarchy you climbed, and the more people you had reporting to you, the less writing you did. For me to say I wanted to write would have meant I had no desire for promotion. To say I wanted to manage was telling them I was on board with the career they were offering me, that I could have a future there and would not necessarily be looking to move on soon. I did want to be promoted, and I saw no reason to sabotage my own chances with too much honesty.

But then a funny thing happened. I started getting promoted and being given more responsibility. I began getting rudimentary management responsibilities. I started learning to edit and supervise less-experienced writers, a completely new skill for me. All of this made me feel successful. It wasn't what I'd always wanted. It wasn't that much fun. But I was climbing the ladder, and I wanted to do more of it.

When I moved to the business travel magazine, I got more responsibility, plus I got a rare chance to be in at the creation of a brand-new magazine. I might have stayed a lot longer. I might be there still, or in some job very like it. But fortunately for me, the job stopped being fun. The new travel magazine was getting a lot of attention inside and outside the company, and its editor wanted to make a mark. This was a company where late evenings and working weekends were the norm to begin with, and working on the business travel magazine meant working extra hard. As I started feeling more and more spent and exhausted, I began asking myself what I was doing it for. When I quit to freelance, to my eternal satisfaction, they hired two people to replace me.

It is very, very easy to let other people's definition of success take up space in your head, which is why you must constantly guard against it. So strip away everything you know about what you should want to do or how anyone other than you defines success. Look at every part of your job, and ask yourself: *Does this make me happy? Does it seem meaningful?*

If the answer is 100 percent no, and it's not obvious to you that this job will soon lead to one you really want, consider making a change. (More about that in chapter 10.) But I'm guessing the answer is partly yes and partly no. Some parts of your job feel meaningful and might even make the world a slightly better place. Some parts make you feel happy and valued. Some of the things you do are what you always wanted to do. Other parts of your job are drudgery — boring, bureaucratic, and serving no real purpose that you can see. Some of the people you deal with are obnoxious and disrespectful. Some of the tasks are things you dread.

I got a lot of insight about day jobs and dream jobs from Patrick Meehan, who passed away in 2018. Meehan was a high-level executive at Christie's and Phillips/LVMH before becoming a vice president at business and technology research firm Gartner. When I interviewed him, he explained to me how every job in existence is some combination of the meaningful and the tedious-but-necessary. "Managing costs and maintaining things is every executive's day job," he said. "Everyone wishes they could spend 100 percent of their time on things that add value. But even the CEO spends a lot of time poring over mundane things like the budget. We all have day jobs, and we have to pay for innovation and inspiration."

I thought about that comment for a very long time because, of course, he was right. Any great job you can think of is some combination of delight and tedium. Movie stars have to get up at four in the morning so they can sit in a chair for hours while makeup is applied. Even the president of the United States has to spend some of his time making phone calls to campaign donors and recalcitrant members of Congress or sitting through boring state dinners. No job, no matter how dreamy it seems, is 100 percent dream job. There are, on the other hand, plenty of jobs that are 100 percent day job. But you can and should expect better.

Don't make the mistake of thinking either/or or *yes, but* the way I did for so many years. Instead, see your job for what it likely is, a mix of day job and dream job. Only you can decide whether that mix is right for you. But whatever it is, you can make it better by finding ways to cut down the day job and add dream elements wherever you can. If you do this right, it might make you more valuable to your employer. It might also make you happier. That's the best reason to do just about anything.

EXERCISES TO TRY

1. Redesign Your Job

What's the first thing you do when you start working for the day? And then? And after that? Make a list of everything you do, right up to when you quit for the evening. If necessary, go through a whole day writing down what you do or making a voice note on your phone every time you switch to a new task. Your job isn't the same every day, so list any tasks you would do on different days of the week or at different times in the month, quarter, or year. When you're done, you should have a pretty long list of what you do in your job. Check it over to make sure that it's a complete list of everything you do on the job.

Now draw a line down the middle of a piece of paper (or your screen, if you're doing this digitally). On one side, write the heading "Dream Job," and on the other, "Day Job." You can change those headings to something else if you'd rather, such as "Love" and "Hate" or "Fun" and "Boring."

Now put every task on your list under one of your two headings. If you feel like you're learning valuable skills that you want and can use, it goes under "Dream Job." The same goes for anything that feels meaningful to you or aligns with your highest aspirations. Parts of your job that you enjoy should also go under "Dream Job," even if they don't fit in with your larger career aspirations. Everything else belongs under "Day Job."

Now, for every item under "Day Job," ask yourself: (1) *Can I get someone else to do this instead of me?* (2) *Can I just skip doing this at all, or will there be consequences?* (3) *Can I make this task more fun, quicker, or both?*

In many cases, the answers to all three questions will be no, and that's OK. But I'm hoping you'll be able to come up with some things you can try that will make your job a little bit less of a day job.

For every item under "Dream Job," ask yourself: (1) *Can I find ways to do more of this kind of work, perhaps by volunteering for more of these tasks with the free time I gained by cutting down my day job tasks?* (2) *Are there similar tasks I'm not doing now that I might enjoy, and can I add these similar tasks to my job?* (3) *Are there skills I need to learn in order to take on these new tasks or to do my existing dream job tasks better?*

Again, the answers won't always be yes. But taking these two lists together and working on spending more time on dream job tasks and less on day job tasks should give you some ideas about changes that will make your current job more dreamy.

2. Don't Abandon Your Dreams

If you have dreams you've failed to pursue, find ways to revive and go after them. Pick a first baby step, write it down, and commit to having it done by a specific date. (For more details on this approach, see chapter 11.) Remind yourself this is just a baby step, and it carries no deep significance about your abilities or your future or anything else. Make it more effective by adding an accountability partner, someone who will check in with you to make sure you did your baby step and congratulate you for doing it, no matter what the final outcome is. You'll do the same for them when it's their turn.

Chapter 14

The Dirty Little Secret about Success

In 2017, Amazon announced that it was planning to open a second headquarters, far from its original headquarters in Seattle, a city that was growing ever more expensive, in large part because of Amazon's presence there. The new headquarters, called HQ2, would bring fifty thousand jobs to the lucky location where it landed, and Amazon invited local governments to compete for the privilege with bids explaining what their location had to offer and what sorts of financial incentives they could provide the company.

Two hundred and thirty-eight cities and counties in the United States and Canada sprang into action, putting together bids that they hoped would lure HQ2. Many observers derisively called the whole process a beauty contest. In true beauty-contest style, Amazon named twenty semifinalist locations in an apparent bid to get them to improve their offers. The company spent months reviewing its options while local leaders waited and hoped.

Amazon picked two lucky winners, announcing that it would

split its new headquarters between them, bringing twenty-five thousand jobs to each. One was Crystal City in Northern Virginia, and the other was Long Island City in Queens, New York, where the state and city had put together $3 billion in incentives and former Governor Andrew Cuomo had joked he would change his name to Amazon Cuomo if it helped.

But then things went wrong. There was resistance from Queens, where local legislators balked at the deal, in some cases claiming they hadn't understood the size of the tax breaks being offered. Protests sprang up over Amazon's imminent arrival and its anti-union stance. It's not clear whether any of this would have been enough to stop the deal from going through, but the company didn't wait to find out. It pulled out, citing opposition to its presence, and affirmed it would go forward in Virginia, where it had been planning to expand in any case. In the end, the high-profile search for HQ2 looked like a waste of everyone's time and a misstep from a company that doesn't make them often.

But that wasn't the whole story. Almost exactly two years after Amazon pulled out of Queens, a Bloomberg report revealed what had really been going on at the company during the hunt for HQ2. Amazon founder Jeff Bezos had become envious of Elon Musk, the founder of Tesla. Tesla had received a $1.3 billion incentive from Nevada to build its giant battery factory there in 2014. A frustrated Bezos demanded to know why Amazon wasn't being offered similar incentives, insiders told Bloomberg. When an Amazon executive sent out a celebratory email after getting a $40 million incentive for building a new facility near Cincinnati, Bezos complained that the sum was too small. He told his lieutenants to play hardball — he wanted billions, not millions.

Think about that for a minute. Bezos was the world's richest person. Amazon, with more than a million employees, is among the largest employers in the United States. By any reasonable measure, you'd have to consider that Bezos, who started the whole thing from a garage in Bellevue, Washington, might be the most successful entrepreneur of all time. You'd think all this would make him happy. Instead, he was jealous of Musk.

To me, the lesson you can learn from this incident is that, in some ways, there is just no such thing as success and certainly no such thing as contentment with one's accomplishments. Bezos is the wealthiest and arguably most powerful person on Earth — owner of one of the world's most prestigious newspapers; the most dominant person in publishing, retail, food provision, and perhaps entertainment; and an important player in space exploration. His company hosts so much of the internet that he can, if he chooses, destroy countless other companies with the flick of a switch. If the person at the helm of all this can't be satisfied and content with his own accomplishments, what hope is there for the likes of you and me?

I love this story because it's so extreme, but the truth is that something like this has probably happened to you. It's certainly happened to me. When I first started writing columns for Inc.com, I kept hearing rumors that some of the other columnists were getting hundreds of thousands of page views a month. Some were even getting a million. For many years, that was my dream too. *If I could just get to a million page views, life would be golden. A million people would be reading what I wrote. What a thrill that would be!*

Then it happened — for one month. *If only I could get back there*, I thought. *If I could get a million readers every month, I would be happy.* You can guess the rest. I did start hitting a million page views just about every month, and more. But meanwhile, I learned some of my colleagues were getting 3 and 4 million. My 1 million readers started to seem pitiful.

And there you have it. The dirty little secret about success is that, for most of us, there is no "there" there — it's an endless journey with no destination. There's a Haitian proverb, "Dèyè mòn gen mòn," that translates as "Beyond mountains, there are mountains." In Haiti, the poorest and in many ways most troubled nation in the Western Hemisphere, the saying is usually taken to mean that when you overcome one huge obstacle, you'll find yourself faced with another. It's also a pretty good description of the country's topography; the name Haiti actually means "land of high mountains" in the language of the Taino, its original inhabitants. But I think it's a pretty good description of the quest for success as well. Climb any mountain and the very first thing you'll see is the next mountain waiting for you.

A Talk with My Nineteen-Year-Old Self

At sixty-one, I've been thinking about this a lot. Depending on your own age and point of view, I may seem ancient or not-all-that-old. Most of the time, I don't feel old. I'm still full of all sorts of ambitions: career ambitions, creative ambitions, and even ambitions about things like hiking and horseback riding. And yet, reality tells me that more of my career is behind me than ahead of me, and while I have no intention of slowing down for the foreseeable future, I also know that if I want to relax and hang out with my husband without constantly shutting myself away in my office for one deadline or another, if I want to be able to read all the books I want and travel more for fun than for work... well, the time to do all of that is not infinite.

I've started thinking about my career as a whole — what it means and what I still want to accomplish. And I often find myself thinking back to myself at around nineteen, a college English major who spent her time reading for pleasure when she wasn't reading for class. I can see her so clearly in her first couple of years away from home, with her long black hair and bohemian wardrobe that made her stick out in any crowd at the Midwestern college she attended. She had big dreams, that girl, and big worries that none of those dreams would come true.

I imagine sitting down with her at the Sheepshead Café in Iowa City for a cup of steamed milk and honey, her beverage of choice in those days. "So this is you at sixty-one," I would begin, and I'd go on to tell her about all I'd done since I was her, the dreams that didn't come true and those that did, the things that went wrong and the many more that went right. When he was ninety-nine years old, my indomitable stepfather looked at a baby in a carriage and remarked, "Wouldn't it be great to do it all over again, make all the same happy mistakes again?" I'd tell my younger self about the happy mistakes she was on her way to making, and the ones, like her first marriage, that would make her awfully unhappy when they happened but would still land her exactly where she needed to be.

I wonder what she would say in response. The career I have now is nothing she hoped for or planned — her ambition was to be a novelist. Would she be disappointed that her dream didn't come true or happy that the girl who dreamed of becoming a writer really did become one — and had a million readers a month? When I ask the question that way, when I think about all the things that she — I — will do along the way, I realize that I know the answer. She would be proud of me.

And I'm willing to bet that your nineteen-year-old self would be proud of *you*. Remembering back to that younger self, before your career got started, is a great antidote to that mountains-beyond-mountains thing where you forget to feel proud of the goals you've already reached in your haste to chase after the ones you haven't reached yet.

What's Your Condition of Satisfaction?

My coach, Wendy Capland, uses a phrase that I love: *condition of satisfaction*. She might ask, for example, "What would be the condition of satisfaction that would make you happy and satisfied with a job, an offer, or a situation?" I've started asking myself a question that I invite you to ask yourself too: *What are the conditions of satisfaction that would make me feel that I am successful?*

My husband the musician says that guitarists know the perfect number of guitars to own. It's exactly one more than whatever number they already have. My friend the horse trainer says that horse people use a similar rule to determine the perfect number of horses. I think it's incredibly tempting to fall into that way of thinking when you're trying to determine the condition of satisfaction for your own success. One more promotion. One more increase in income. One more location for your business. One million more readers for my column.

Instead of falling into this trap, can you think back to what made you want this career in the first place? Was it to earn a good living? Have an adventure? Travel? Help people? Express your creativity? Learn new things? Change the world?

Will one more *whatever* bring you any closer to that original purpose? Or is the job you have now completely separate from that purpose? If so, it might mean you need to rethink your job, but it could also mean you've found a different purpose or you're already achieving that purpose right now.

Considering all this, what is your condition of satisfaction? What should it be?

For many people, including me, the condition-of-satisfaction question is answered at least partly in dollars (or whatever your currency is). Money means completely different things to different people. It could mean love, security, safety, a better future, the ability to improve the world through giving, a scorecard that shows you're winning the game of life, or a better education for your children. We all see money in different ways, depending on what part it has played in our lives so far.

If you were raised in a family where money was a constant lack, where people ignored their toothaches because they couldn't afford the dentist, where rent and utility bills were often overdue, you'll see money in a different way from someone who grew up with doormen and maids and summer homes. Earning a good living might be important in both cases, but the reasons for that will be different, and your definition of what a good living is may not be the same.

How much money does it take to be successful? At one end of the scale you have Bezos, fighting hard for $1 billion in tax incentives for Amazon when his own net worth at the time was already more than a hundred times that much. At the other end of the spectrum are *sadhus* and *sadhvis*, Hindu ascetics who give up all worldly possessions and survive by begging. Somewhere in between are adherents to the FIRE (financial independence, retire early) philosophy, many of whom cut their expenses to a minimum so they can save most of what they earn and then live as long as possible without needing to earn any more.

When it comes to money, it's pretty much impossible to say how much is enough. As with guitars and horses, the answer always seems to be just a bit more than you already have. If you've ever experienced an unexpected windfall, you probably know what I mean. You might have considered buying things that you previously couldn't afford. But did you stop worrying about money and how you would cover your financial obligations? If you're like most people, the answer is no.

You're the only one who can know how much money is really enough for you. However, there is a body of psychological research correlating income with happiness and well-being, and the findings are worth considering. In 2018, in perhaps the largest of these studies, researchers at Purdue University used data collected from 1.7 million people in Gallup surveys to determine the optimal level of income for maximum happiness. They found that an individual (not family) income of $60,000 to $75,000 was enough to create emotional well-being and that an income of $95,000 led to satisfaction with one's life. Income over that $95,000 threshold seemed to make people slightly *less* happy, they found. "Money is only a part of what really makes us happy, and we're learning more about the limits of money," lead author Andrew T. Jebb said.

You Are Already a Success

I don't know whether $60,000 or $95,000 would make you happy. I don't know how you define success for yourself or what that definition should be. I do know, though, that success is a slippery thing that often feels just barely out of reach. Too many people go through their entire lives always thinking that success is just around the next corner. That seems to me like a terrible shame.

I'm going to make a radical suggestion. Whoever you are, wherever you are, however old you are, and however much you earn, *you are already a success.* Right now, just as you are. That doesn't mean you don't have goals and ambitions — of course you do. It also doesn't mean you don't have bigger and better things ahead of you — you very well may. But it does mean it's time to stop dreaming of being successful "someday." Stop waiting for that one big break or the next promotion or a higher income to say to yourself that you're a success.

Say it to yourself right now, for two important reasons. First, when you believe you are successful, it will come across in all your interactions. You'll have more confidence to pursue what you really want, and that will bring you actual success, whatever that means to you.

The second reason is more circular and more subtle but no less important. Believing you're already successful will make you happier — and I think happiness is the truest measure of success. In other words, the more you say it and the more you think it, the more it will be true.

EXERCISES TO TRY

1. Have a Conversation with Your Younger Self

This was a fascinating experience for me, and now it's your turn. Picture yourself during your teenage years or whatever time in the past seems most appropriate to you. Look in old photo albums, yearbooks, or social media posts for pictures of your younger self if it helps.

Sit down and tell your younger self about everything you've accomplished in life so far: what you're most proud of, what makes you happiest, and what you still hope to achieve. Listen to what your younger self says in response. I'm guessing that younger you will be impressed, but if not, remember that young people sometimes have unfulfillable dreams. Your younger self should be proud of you, even if they don't know it.

2. Declare Yourself a Success Right Now

If you were successful, what would you do? What clothes would you wear? What car would you drive? What foods would you eat? Where would you go? Who would your friends be?

Well, abracadabra – as of this moment, you are successful. I don't want you to do anything you truly can't afford right now. But within financial reason, can you start doing, wearing, and eating things in accordance with your new status as a successful person? In particular, can you choose friends, acquaintances, and perhaps romantic partners that go with your successful self? The motivational speaker Jim Rohn famously said that you are the average of the five people you spend the most time with. Now that you're a success, who are the five people you'd most like to spend time with?

On a piece of paper or in your journal, list the things you might do and the people you might reach out to now that you're a success. Review your list, and then do as many of them as you can.

Chapter 15

How to Build Your Own Confidence

"Look over the top of my head and skewer him!"

It was the first day of the Natural Singer Workshop. As instructed, I'd arrived with a song to sing. Claude Stein, who's been running the workshop for close to forty years, had me singing the first two lines of the song over and over. Meanwhile, he urged me to stand straighter, sing louder, and let my feelings out.

My relationship with singing? It's complicated. When I was in high school, I sang in the 92nd Street Y Chorus, which meant performing in front of big audiences. I could be shy about a lot of things, but singing wasn't one of them. Then I went to college and left singing behind. By the time I married Bill, other than singing along with the radio, I hadn't used my singing voice in a very long time.

Bill was a real professional singer-songwriter with a four-and-a-half octave range. I found this sufficiently intimidating that I mostly didn't dare sing a note around him. But there we were in a community of musicians, and singing just kind of came up.

One day I agreed to sing harmony onstage with one of our musician friends. I practiced the song over and over. I worked out a harmony that I thought sounded pretty good. But when I stood onstage, with a microphone in my hand, my voice deserted me. It went squeaky. It went off-key. The power of my fear had overcome the power of my voice.

I decided I was sick of being afraid to sing. I'd thought about taking Stein's workshop for years but never quite had the nerve to do it. The next time he gave it in our area, I signed up.

Our first task was to say what we hoped to gain from the workshop. "I don't want to freeze onstage anymore," I said. And now here I was, with sixty people watching. "Look over my head and skewer him!" Claude said.

Skewer whom? The imaginary man in the song? My singer husband, for not encouraging me to let my voice out? The real answer was that I needed to skewer myself for being so hesitant for so long and for letting my fear of embarrassment deprive me of one of life's great joys. I had spent years muzzling myself like an idiot when there was nothing and no one to silence me. So I did it. I looked over Stein's head and sang the lines again, angry and loud, and even I could feel their power.

"Did that feel frozen to you?" he asked.

No, it didn't. Not anymore. By the end of the workshop, I was done with freezing and done with feeling too shy to sing. Am I a great singer? Absolutely not. Will I ever be? Unlikely. Do I still have a lot to learn about singing? You bet. But am I able to carry a tune and convey the emotion behind a song in a way that can make the audience happy they came out to listen? Yes, I can. But only because I believe that I can.

It turns out that for singing, as for so many things, such as walking on a tightrope or controlling a misbehaving horse, confidence by itself can make the difference between ability and inability. Don't get me wrong. If you can't carry a tune, all the confidence in the world won't help you, as the famously tone-deaf heiress Florence Foster Jenkins proved. She was so confident she once rented Carnegie Hall and gave a concert there, and all her belief in herself didn't help her singing one bit. But if you have the slightest bit of ability, confidence will often make the difference between failure and success. Believe that you can, and you can. Believe that you can't, and you can't. It's really that simple, so which would you prefer?

The other thing about confidence is that it affects what other people think of you, even when they really should know better. If someone asks you whether you can handle a task you've never done before, and you answer forthrightly that you know you can, chances are they'll trust you with it. Cast your eyes downward and mumble that you'll do your best, and they'll start looking for someone else. The someone else they give the job to probably won't know what they're doing any better than you do. I've seen confidence trump actual skill again and again over the years. I bet you have too.

Four Myths about Confidence You May Have to Unlearn

So how do you go from unconfident to confident? I believe that confidence can be learned. But first, if you're anything like me, you'll have a bunch of lessons to unlearn, lessons you may have learned as a child, especially if you were raised in a family where boasting was frowned on. If you were a girl, you may have been taught that acting confident was unladylike. So let's start by challenging some of the myths about confidence.

Confidence Is Not Arrogance

The difference between arrogance and confidence is other people. It's confident to say, "I'm good." It's arrogant to say, "I'm better than anyone else" or, worse, "I'm better than you."

There's some unfortunate quirk in human nature that makes

us unsatisfied with the notion that we're just good — we can't be happy unless we know we are better than others. I'm reminded of this every time I hear Bill or one of his guitarist friends express their admiration for another player with the odd statement that listening to that guitarist play makes them want to go home and throw away all their guitars, as if there's only room for one really great guitarist in the entire world, and everyone else should just give up and go home.

Confidence is actually the opposite of this. It's knowing you yourself have value no matter what anyone else may have to offer. I believe the urge to compare ourselves with others arises from the opposite — from insecurity and a need to know that, worthless as you may be, there's someone even more worthless out there. Resist the urge to think this way.

Confidence Is Not Boastfulness

What's the difference between expressing confidence and boasting? There are a lot of possible answers to that question. You could say that boasting is a lie or an expression of vanity, while confidence is simply telling the truth. Sometimes the difference between a boast and an expression of confidence depends on context. "I've closed more deals than anyone else in my department" sounds like one thing if you say it to your boss when requesting a plum assignment, and another thing if you say it on a first date.

But the truth is that boastfulness and confidence are really a matter of opinion, of expectations, and of custom. If, like me, you were raised by people who put a high value on modesty, then saying the slightest thing about how good or successful you are might feel like the world's biggest breach of etiquette to you, as it often does to me. If you were raised with different values or in a different culture, it might feel completely natural. My favorite example of this is the incomparable South African singing group Ladysmith Black Mambazo, best known in the West for performing on the Paul Simon album *Graceland*. On the album, the group sings the song "Homeless," whose lyrics resulted from a collaboration between Simon and Ladysmith's late leader, Joseph Shabalala.

The song ends with this passage in Zulu: "Kulumani sizwe / Singenze njani / Baya jabula abasi thanda yo / Ho." This is Ladysmith's standard way of ending a song, and it translates roughly as "We hereby proclaim that we are the best at singing in this style." The group once frequently participated in Zulu *isicathamiya* (a cappella harmony) singing competitions until they had won so many times that they were banned from the competitions. So their statement about their own ability is likely true. Is it boasting or confidence? You decide.

You get to decide for yourself as well. It's not up to anyone else how confident you feel or how much confidence you do and don't express. There's a wide spectrum, and it's up to you where you want to be on it. If someone else thinks you're boastful, that's their problem, not yours.

Confidence Is Not Bad Karma

Whether or not you've ever studied Greek drama, you're probably familiar with the concept of hubris, an excess of pride that leads to disaster. "Pride goeth before destruction, and an haughty spirit before a fall," it says in Proverbs (16:18, KJV). Most of us, perhaps instinctively, feel this is right, as though the fact that its builders called the *Titanic* unsinkable is what put an iceberg in its path. I'm sure, with hindsight, they wished they'd never said that. But it's also true that an unusually mild winter made April 1912 the worst April for icebergs in the North Atlantic in fifty years.

There's a serious problem with the notion that too much confidence equals bad karma and that modesty equals good karma. That problem was on full display in 2014 when Microsoft CEO Satya Nadella, who grew up in India, was being interviewed onstage at a high-profile conference on women in technology. He was asked his advice for women in tech who felt uncomfortable asking for a raise. "It's not really about asking for the raise, but knowing and having faith that the system will actually give you the right raises as you go along," he answered. That probably sounded pretty bad to a roomful of women who were well aware, as Nadella should have been, that women have never achieved pay equity with their male colleagues and that the gender pay gap is particularly huge in the tech industry.

Then he made things worse. He went on to say that not asking for a raise is among the "superpowers" some women have. "That's good karma. It'll come back because somebody's going to know that's the kind of person that I want to trust. That's the kind of person that I want to really give more responsibility to."

Not surprisingly, Nadella was immediately criticized by just about everyone, including many of the women in the audience, who immediately began posting about it to social media. To Nadella's credit, he quickly walked back those comments and wrote in his book *Hit Refresh*, "In some ways, I'm glad I messed up in such a public forum because it helped me confront an unconscious bias that I didn't know I had."

Ah, if only his original statement had been true. If only silence, being a team player, and remaining modest about your own abilities were a sure path to being properly appreciated and compensated, life would be a lot simpler for most of us. But of course, the world doesn't work that way. Keeping your head down while waiting for others to notice how smart and responsible and hardworking you are won't help you in most situations. In fact, Harvey Mudd College president Maria Klawe, who was interviewing Nadella that day, said then and there that it was one of the few things she disagreed with him about. She added that in her own career, failing to ask for the compensation she deserved had cost her quite a lot of money over the years and warned the women in the audience not to make the same mistake.

Confidence Won't Make People Hate You

If you're a man, I apologize. Feel free to skip to the next section because for you, displaying confidence is not a problem. It's considered manly and, if anything, is considered a likable quality that will make people want to work with you and be friends with you. Confident women, however, are not always so lucky. Think about how confident women — as opposed to shy, insecure ones — are depicted in popular culture. They are preyed on by young, cute men who take advantage of them, or they are unfavorably compared with the shy, "sweet" women our culture seems to prefer. Think Veronica versus Betty, or Jean Hagen versus Debbie Reynolds in *Singin' in the Rain*.

The zillion books and movies and television series telling women to be sweet and demure and not to let their pride in their own accomplishments shine out can easily convince women that displaying confidence is a very bad idea. But there's a big difference between popular culture and real life. And in real life, in my experience, the best things happen when people are honest with themselves and each other about their own worth.

If you believe you need to act shy and insecure to be liked or to land a job, ask yourself if you're prepared to keep acting that way forever. If you have to pretend to be weaker than you are to make people like you or hire you, are those really the friends or the employer you want? Or do you want to be around others who admire you for everything you've done and everything you are, who encourage you to feel strong and powerful, who believe in you and are glad that you believe in yourself?

How to Develop Confidence

If I've convinced you that confidence is really a good thing, how do you get it if you don't have it? Let's start with one more thing that confidence is not — it's not a reflection of objective reality. That can be a tough idea to absorb because for many of us, including me, confidence does result from a change or changes that happen in the real world. My confidence in myself as a writer appeared over time in direct proportion to real-world success — getting assignments in publications I pitched, publishing books, getting to a million page views a month on Inc.com. In other areas where I haven't been as successful, I still completely lack confidence. But the thing is, that's nonsense and I know it because the two things have little or nothing to do with each other.

Years ago, when I was working at the trade magazine company, a colleague decided to show me the ropes. He gave me all kinds of advice, most of it useful, and generally treated me like a younger sister who should look up to him and learn from him. His status as wise older brother came crashing down one day when the company had a reorganization in which he was laid off. Afterward, he sent me an email full of conjecture and purported inside information on the internal changes that had led to the shake-up. By that time, I really was an insider, and I knew that most of what he said about what had happened was wrong.

For years, I'd assumed that his great confidence resulted from the fact that he was more successful and knowledgeable than I was. By the time he was let go, I didn't think that anymore. But in the meantime, he'd had the confidence to ask for and obtain a lot of things I never got, such as a one-on-one meeting with the CEO and a plum speaking spot at a conference the company put on.

It's taken me decades since then to grow my own confidence. I now think I wasted an awful lot of time for no good reason. I wonder what would have happened if I'd gone through my entire career feeling as sure of myself as he did. Who knows where I might have gone?

It's not that confidence, or the lack of it, is independent from reality. It just depends on how you interpret that reality, because everything that happens, good or bad, becomes part of the ongoing story about the world that we tell ourselves throughout our lives. The story you tell yourself determines how you feel about the world and your own place in it.

Let's take a simple daily activity that frequently rattles my own confidence — driving. I grew up in an urban environment and only drove on very rare occasions until I was well into my thirties. After my first book came out, my publicist got me an interview on a local television station on Long Island. The prospect of answering questions on live TV didn't faze me at all, but the fact that I was going to have to drive 144 miles, some of it in heavy traffic, to get to the TV station from Woodstock had me terrified. Even at the time, I knew there was something odd about this.

After that, we moved to the West Coast, with its famously packed freeways. One day, I was driving home at rush hour, and as often happens on freeways, all the traffic sped up and then slowed down rather abruptly. I had stayed a safe distance away from the car in front of me, but the driver behind me hadn't, and he slammed into my car from behind, totaling my car and propelling it into the car in front of me.

I wound up with a check from my insurance company and a case of whiplash that got better with treatment. But the next time I found myself on the freeway, it didn't feel safe or natural anymore. Nothing had changed. The roads weren't any different, and neither was the traffic. The only thing that had changed was the story I told myself about driving on the freeway. I'm guessing the same sort of thing has happened to you, where something that once seemed frightening and dangerous came to feel easy and safe with familiarity, or where something that had seemed safe and harmless became frightening after a traumatic experience. Nothing is any different, except for what you believe about it.

With that in mind, start asking yourself what stories you're telling yourself, what limits those stories put on you, and whether those limits are helping or hurting you. How many times have you been absolutely sure you couldn't do something, until someone you trusted persuaded you to try? How many things have you convinced yourself you're just not good enough for, and let that belief stop you from finding out?

Instead, try asking yourself the question: *Why not me?* If anyone in the world could reach that stretch goal you've set for yourself, your greatest ambition, why shouldn't that someone be you? Take a good look at where you are. Chances are, you deserve to be confident. Chances are, you deserve to give that distant goal a real try.

Confidence doesn't happen overnight. Like anything else, you get there with baby steps, and those steps should take you outside your comfort zone. For one of my most popular Inc.com columns ever, I interviewed confidence expert and author Becky Blalock. She gave me this piece of advice: take a small step outside your comfort zone at least once every day. We all have a comfort zone — things we're comfortable doing and know we can do well. For you, that might be performing the tasks in your job that you've done many times before, for example. And then there are things that are definitely outside your comfort zone. For many people, this includes speaking in front of a large audience.

The thing about comfort zones is that the more you stay inside them, the smaller they get, and the more you step outside them, the bigger they get. Use this fact to your advantage. I have a sign that hangs on my office wall that I painted myself, and it says, "Did you do something scary today?" More often than I'd like, the answer to that question is no. But whenever I can answer yes, even if the scary thing was something minor that really shouldn't be scary, such as reaching out to a friend I haven't spoken to in a long time, I know I've made my comfort zone just a tiny bit bigger, and that small change will carry over into other areas, such as sending out a pitch when I know I'll most likely be rejected.

The other way you can build up your confidence is through other people. You should have people in your work life and personal life who make you feel capable, who can help you navigate some of the challenges you face, or both. When a task or a situation has you feeling truly daunted, ask yourself who you know who's been there or might have special insight or might be able to give you useful advice. Then reach out and ask for help. Being confident doesn't mean that you never need help. Being confident means that you understand asking for help can be a sign of strength rather than weakness.

Your friends, partners, loved ones, and family members should be there to help you too, with encouragement and reassurance when your confidence flags. Sometimes asking the people in your life for their support can be even scarier than asking your work contacts or colleagues to help you. But that help should be there when you need it. If the people in your life aren't helping you build your confidence, ask yourself why not. And if there are people in your life who don't believe in you, do what you have to do to keep them from getting inside your head.

Confidence is just too important to go through life without. When I think back now, it seems criminal — all the time I wasted wondering whether I was good enough to try for a job or project or role, instead of just trying for it. All the useless years I silenced myself, when I could have, and should have, been singing instead. All the opportunities and all the fun I missed, when there was no one stopping me but me. I'm begging you. Don't make the same mistake.

EXERCISES TO TRY

1. Why Not Me?

On a piece of paper or in your power journal, list five things you'd love to do but haven't attempted because you don't think you're up to the challenge or because you believe you wouldn't be given the chance.

Now, choose one of those things that you will actually set out to do. You can pick the easiest thing on the list or the most ambitious; it's up to you. Underneath that goal, write, "Why not me?"

Next, write a list of any obstacles you believe will prevent you from reaching your goal. Depending on the goal you chose, there may be many or just one. Write down the names of anyone you can think of who you can ask for help in overcoming those obstacles.

Look over the list you've made. What you have is a road map for getting to the job or opportunity that you wanted. Is it still what you want? If it isn't, go back to your original list of five aspirations and choose another one. If it is, decide when and how you will take the first step in that direction. This may be a good time to revisit the exercise "Your Best Possible Future" from chapter 11. You can use that same process to plan and execute the first step toward your goal, and then the next, and so on.

2. Expand Your Comfort Zone

Write a list of four things that you would like to do but that are outside your comfort zone. These could be job-related, such as making a pre- sentation at a conference, or they could be completely non-job-related, such as completing a challenging hike or cooking a complicated rec- ipe – or, like me, getting up and singing. Whatever your four things are, they should ideally be things that just take you outside your com- fort zone a little bit. You don't need to throw yourself in the deep end.

Now, for the next four weeks, pick one of those things. Write in your calendar on Monday that you will complete this task before the end of the week. At the end of the week, if you've completed the task, give yourself a star. (Yes, you should draw or paste a star on your cal- endar! Rewarding yourself right away when you take on a challenge will make you keep doing it.) If you didn't get it done, you can either push it to the following week or choose something else – but please don't try the same challenge for more than two weeks. If you fail twice to do it or even try it, pick something else instead.

At the end of four weeks, review your four challenges and how you did. Think about your comfort zone. If you did the challenges, I'm guessing that your comfort zone will be a little bigger than it was four weeks earlier and that you'll have gained more confidence in other areas as well.

PART FOUR

WORK + LIFE = ?

Chapter 16

Why You Have to
Stop Working So Hard

In December 2013, a badly overworked copywriter in Indonesia named Mita Diran tweeted, "30 hours of work and still going strooong!" It was the last tweet she would ever send. A few hours later she collapsed and fell into a coma. The next day she died of heart failure, having never regained consciousness. Her death was widely blamed on exhaustion and on her habit of guzzling Krating Daeng, a caffeinated Thai beverage said to be the inspiration for Red Bull.

Something about this news item hit me hard. At the time, I was halfway through my two years as ASJA president, a prestigious and challenging but unpaid job, so I was working full-time as a writer at the same time. I was also running a popular reading series at a bookstore-and-café. I was constantly running from one thing to another, working through the weekends, perennially late for wherever I was supposed to be.

On top of that, Christmas was coming. Christmas was always a big deal in our household, with stacks of presents for the family and a huge New Year's Day party we hosted every year. I loved all of this, but it was cramming too many clowns into the clown car that my schedule had become. I was constantly angry — at Bill for ever wanting any of my time, at my editors, at the work itself, at Christmas for existing, and mainly at myself for all the commitments I was missing or just barely meeting and the half-assed job I was doing. I knew I should be happy to have so much good stuff in my life, but instead I was miserable nearly all the time.

In the midst of all that, the story of Mita Diran was a jolt. I started wondering what I was doing and where it would lead. So I did what I often do when facing a dilemma — I wrote about it. The resulting Inc.com column, called "10 Reasons to Stop Working So Hard," was one of my first to go viral. Friends reported that it had been forwarded to them from people who didn't know they knew me. One got it in a blast email from her daughter's school with a note that said the piece "really resonated with us." Apparently, I wasn't the only one struggling with questions of workaholism and work-life imbalance.

Mita Diran's age when she died was never reported or released by her former employer. But from the many pictures of herself she posted on social media, she appeared to be in her early or mid-twenties. Based on her social media feed, her thirty-hour work binge was only slightly unusual. It seemed she often got home from work after midnight, and in one tweet she said she'd gotten home after 2 a.m. every night for a week. In another, she wrote: "So it's 2AM, Friday night and I'm at the office, nibbling on junk food with 9 other creatives. I'm actually okay with this." As with many of her tweets, she added the hashtag #AgencyLife, suggesting that this was the norm in her industry. At 4:45 that same morning, she tweeted that she'd finally gotten home.

I keep wondering: What if someone had been able to warn her? What if someone had taken her aside, somehow given her a look at the future, and let her know that all the devotion she poured into writing marketing copy meant that she wasn't going to get to live the rest of her life? She might not have believed the warning, of course. But if she did, do you think she would have made that trade willingly? I don't.

Are You Trading Your Health for Your Career?

Diran's case is extreme, but a lot of us do trade some amount of our physical and mental well-being for our devotion to our jobs. Every time you go to bed too late or wake up too early, every time you skip exercising because you're on a deadline or eat junk food at your desk because you lack the time and energy to provide yourself a healthy meal, every time you let the stress of work eat away at you or you go for days without spending any time outdoors, and every time you spend hours sitting in the same spot, you are chipping away at your good health. You may not suddenly fall over like Diran did, but in time, this chipping away is liable to catch up with you and cause serious harm.

That's one excellent reason we all should work less. Here are a few others.

1. Getting Enough Sleep Matters Even More Than You Think

In 2007, Huffington Post founder Arianna Huffington collapsed from exhaustion and sleep deprivation while reading emails on her phone. She woke up in a pool of blood with a broken cheekbone. Since then, she's been a self-proclaimed "sleep evangelist," writing two books about the importance of getting enough rest and founding Thrive Global, a website devoted to health and stress reduction.

Bragging about how little sleep you get has fallen out of fashion, which is a good thing. Sleep tracking, on the other hand, has taken off, with health-conscious people increasingly obsessed with the quantity and quality of their sleep. Eight hours of sleep a night became the ideal, often sought after and rarely achieved (at least by me). Then, in 2018, a Penn State sleep expert named Daniel Gartenberg upped the ante by arguing that eight hours of sleep isn't even enough, because most people spend some of their time in bed either falling asleep or slowly waking up, so that you need more time in bed to get eight hours of actual sleep.

If you're failing to get enough sleep because of devotion to your job, that's a really bad (and counterproductive) idea because being sleep-deprived will affect your work performance — a lot. According to the Division of Sleep Medicine at Harvard Medical School, being awake for twenty-four hours causes the same level of mental impairment as a blood alcohol level of 0.10 percent, which would make it illegal for you to drive in all fifty states. Sleep deprivation particularly affects your prefrontal cortex, the part of the brain responsible for logic and complex thought. One result of this is that people who are sleep-deprived often don't know that they are because their judgment is too impaired for them to realize it.

You may think none of this applies to you because you never stay up for twenty-four hours straight. But you can achieve the same effect by not quite getting enough sleep for enough nights in a row. According to the Harvard Medical School website, sleeping for just six hours a night nine nights in a row will give you that same level of impairment on the tenth day as staying up for twenty-four hours — or being drunk enough to have a 0.10 percent blood alcohol level.

Have you ever gone nine nights in a row with no more than six hours of sleep? Even if you felt perfectly fine and well rested, you weren't. Your prefrontal cortex was simply too impaired to tell you how tired you really were.

All of this might be disturbing enough to make you start taking sleep seriously, and I haven't even gotten to the *really* scary information yet. Here it is: sleep deprivation, even a small amount of it, increases your risk of Alzheimer's disease. Scientists have learned that, during deep sleep, cerebrospinal fluid washes through our brains, removing the beta-amyloids, protein fragments that are believed to cause Alzheimer's. Have you ever been close to anyone who had Alzheimer's? I have. My mother lived with it for more than fifteen years while it slowly robbed her of everything, including her ability to walk, speak, and feed herself. . Since reading about this research, I've thought a lot about how she spent weekends in the country with my retired stepfather, then rose at 4 a.m. to beat the traffic back into Manhattan, and how she stayed out late at night, then rose early for work the next day. This is not a disease you would wish on your most hated enemy. I don't care how wonderful your job is — it isn't worth it if it keeps you from getting a healthy amount of sleep.

2. You'll Be Better at Your Job

This is a lesson I learned the hard way in 2012, at my first in-person board meeting as president of ASJA. Shortly before that meeting, I had started as an Inc.com columnist, and I was determined to do well at both things, both of which were highly important to me. I traveled to New York City the evening before the board meeting and then sat in my hotel room that night, working on a column. I'd been scrambling hard for days, trying to get everything done. With less than six hours to sleep before I had to get up for the board meeting, I crawled into bed, the column just barely completed.

The next morning, I crawled out of bed again and made my bleary-eyed way to the conference room for the board meeting. There was just one problem. I was the president, therefore I was the one leading the meeting. I couldn't glance at my email or momentarily let my mind wander, as I'd done at countless meetings before. (I bet you have too.) I had to be as focused and mentally alert as I could be for every minute of the meeting, which would last from about 9 a.m. to about 4 p.m., with a break for lunch.

I got through the meeting without falling asleep in my chair and without doing anything outstandingly stupid, which was an accomplishment in itself, given how tired I was. I don't think we made any terrible decisions that day. But fifteen highly accomplished and very busy people had pulled themselves away from their work and families to join me at this meeting to plan a path forward for our organization, and I'm sure some of them left thinking it hadn't been a good use of their time. Worse than that, it was a missed opportunity to do what we were there to do: plan a strategy for the organization's future.

I was painfully aware of how badly I sucked at my job that day. It was a valuable lesson in setting appropriate expectations for my own energy level and my own brain. I'll get into brain science more in chapter 19, but for now, the important thing to remember is that the amount of time we can think clearly and perform at our best on any given day or in any given week is a lot shorter than we would like it to be, and a lot shorter than we think it is.

On the other hand, the list of things to do that we all keep in our devices, on paper, or even just in our heads is a lot longer than we would like it to be. We will never get to the end of that list, and we will never be able to do all the things that we think are important. Even if we do, new important things will come along to take their place. This is why productivity experts so often tell people to take the bottom items off their to-do lists and focus on no more than three tasks each day. In a world of multiplying opportunities, obligations, and work overload, learning to do less and to protect your own energy level is a superpower.

3. You'll Be More Creative

There's a reason for the old cliché about people getting great ideas in the shower, and a reason so many people have "aha moments" when they're hiking, fishing, or otherwise relaxing. Brain science tells us that when we take our minds off work for a time, something called the *default network* in our brain makes connections between its different functions, and those connections help spark new ideas and innovation. An exhausted, overworked brain that spends all its time trying to solve immediate problems or be productive has no opportunity to activate the default network or make those connections, and little time to think about the larger issues because it's too busy dealing with day-to-day problem-solving.

Think of the times you've had your most creative or most powerful ideas, and when you've come to clarity about a difficult decision you had to make. I'm willing to bet that many of those were times when you were away from work and away from the distractions of modern life, walking, doing yard work or house cleaning, on vacation, or — yes — in the shower. Whenever that happened, it was a demonstration of the power of your default network. You can harness that power more often, but only if you give your overworked and overstimulated brain a chance to turn off.

4. You'll Have Better Relationships at Work and at Home

When I wrote that my husband had asked me to make a little time every day to talk to him, a writer acquaintance of mine posted my column to social media and commented that she was shocked at the idea that I didn't have time to talk to my own spouse. In fairness to me, he may have been exaggerating just a teeny bit. But you don't need to get to that point to know that being overworked and exhausted, especially if it goes on for a long time, is bad news for your relationships with your family members and friends, not to mention for your social life.

In 2009, a former palliative caregiver named Bronnie Ware published a blog post that's been read more than 8 million times, titled "Regrets of the Dying." She'd gotten in the habit of asking her patients if there were any things they wished they'd done differently. Nearly every male patient expressed a wish that he hadn't worked so hard, she wrote, and another frequent regret was that patients had failed to keep in touch with their friends over the years. So those of us who work long hours (including me) are officially on notice that we may someday come to regret not having prioritized relationships over work.

It may be less obvious to you that working long hours and overloading yourself is also bad for your relationships with your colleagues, your boss, and anyone who reports to you. Why? For one thing, an exhausted and overworked person is usually a grumpy one. You can try your hardest to be the nicest version of yourself, but if you're overtired, you're probably miserable, and if you're feeling miserable, you're probably making the people who interact with you unhappy. Moods, particularly bad ones, tend to be highly contagious.

There's an even bigger problem, though — overwork doesn't happen in a vacuum. If you work all weekend to meet an unreasonable deadline, you're setting the expectation that it's fine to give you more deadlines like it — that you'll willingly sacrifice the time you're supposed to have for rest, relaxation, socializing, and spending time with your family whenever your employer or customer wants you to. You may think you're being a valuable employee, but in fact, the opposite is true because, as we've seen, working too many hours means depriving your customer or employer of your best work, your creativity, and the kinds of insights only a rested brain can produce. Worse, you're putting your coworkers in the unpleasant position of having to match your impossible work hours or risk looking like slackers by comparison. And if you have people reporting to you, overworking yourself may lead them to think you expect them to overwork themselves too.

I realize that in almost every job there are all-hands-on-deck moments, such as preparing for a big presentation or filling an unusual order, dealing with an unexpected crisis or a seasonal spike in demand, such as at holiday time. But in too many workplaces, these moments when you have to give your absolute all seem to arrive every month or even every week instead of once in a great while. Where is the dividing line between the reasonable expectation that people put in extra effort at a special crunch time and the unreasonable view that crunch time is a frequent or even ongoing state? I don't know. But I do know that an awful lot of employers are on the wrong side of it.

5. Work Matters Less Than You Think It Does

Just as tiredness clouds our judgment so that we can't tell how tired we are, overworking and hyperfocusing on our jobs distorts our judgment about how important those jobs are. Companies these days like to talk about their missions — missions and visions are very much in vogue. A few years ago, I set out to find some of the worst ones for a column, and I found one company that said its mission was "to make every brand more inspiring and the world more intelligent." Lofty goals, but in case you were wondering, what the company actually did was manufacture stick-on labels.

That's a ridiculous example. But it's much, much too easy to get pulled in by lofty claims or lofty ideas about the significance of our own work. Simple math tells us that if you work at least fifty-five hours a week, as many people do, and if you sleep eight hours a night, as everyone should, you'll spend at least half your waking hours at work during your full-time career. Chances are, you'll feel a lot better about that if you believe your work means something. This dynamic may make it easier for you to convince yourself that making just a little more money for your company's shareholders or helping someone market their product more effectively is making the world a better place. At least until you take a step back and really think about it — the kind of thinking you can only do when you're rested and have a reasonable amount of time off.

But what if you do work for an organization that truly is making the world better, by treating disease or helping people in need or preserving the natural world? In that case, the temptation to work too hard is going to be particularly acute. You have to resist that temptation, though, because as we've seen in chapter 2, working longer hours doesn't necessarily mean you'll get more done — people who work sixty hours in a week get less done than those who work forty hours. And if you're chronically tired, you simply can't do your best work.

In the hallway outside my office door, there's a picture of my mother and stepfather, both of whom have been dead for several years. I didn't plan it this way, but every day when I leave my office, the first thing I see is the two of them, her in her eighties, him in his nineties, sitting on a deck near a beach, holding hands and clearly devoted to one another. They both worked extremely hard throughout their careers and cared a great deal about their jobs, but, other than as a means of providing retirement funds, those jobs didn't seem to matter a whole lot by that point — and even less now.

When my job is making me crazy, which happens more often than I'd like to admit, seeing them right at eye level outside my office door is a healthy reminder not to take things so damned seriously. As Bronnie Ware's patients knew, a day will come when all the things we worry over — deadlines and sales trends and everything else — will seem pretty insignificant. Until that day comes, our most important job is to keep that in mind.

EXERCISES TO TRY

1. Set a Firm Quitting Time

This is something I've tried to do several times throughout my career with only middling success. But I'm going to keep trying because I know how important it is. Set a time for finishing work every day, and commit to leaving work at that time, no matter what. As always, make changes in baby steps. If you find yourself (as I sadly do) still at your desk at 9:00 every evening, don't set a quitting time of 5:00 and expect it to stick. Instead, plan to leave at 8:30 or even 8:45. Once you've done that successfully for a couple of weeks, you can inch your quitting time a little earlier if you'd like.

What if there's a drop-dead deadline or a piece of work that absolutely, positively has to get done? Well, then you might have to work past your quitting time for that particular evening. But before you do, make sure to stand up and walk away from your desk and your work for at least five or ten minutes. Do something completely non-work-related, such as taking a walk or calling a friend to say hello. When you return to your desk, ask yourself again if it's really, truly necessary for this work to get done tonight. If the answer still is yes, you can go back to work. But, at least for me, the act of breaking my brain out of work mode for just a few minutes often gives me the perspective to see that what I was obsessing about just a little while ago really isn't that urgent or that crucial.

2. Have a Conversation with Your Older Self

In chapter 14, I invited you to have a talk with the younger self from your past. Now it's time to meet with the older self from your future. The older version of you is ninety-five years old and living in a retirement facility, but older you is still as sharp and clear-minded as you are today. It's been at least twenty years since older you had a job. Instead, older you spends time enjoying visits from family members and friends, playing cards, going for slow strolls around the park, reading, and watching your favorite movies.

Sit down and tell older you about the work you're doing right now. Explain why it's important, if it is, and what difference it makes in the world and in your own life. Explain why it matters for you to do the job as well as you possibly can. Also tell your older self about anything that you missed because of that job, whether it was cooking dinner for your family more often or trips that you wanted to take but didn't or events that you wanted to attend but couldn't.

Imagine what your older self would say in response. Assume that your older self loves you and approves of you — after all, the choices you make and the life you live are your older self's choices too, and we all love ourselves, or we should. But older you may have some perspective on whether filing that report when you said you would is really all that essential. And the vantage point of a ninety-five-year-old may be a better viewpoint from which to differentiate things that are really important from those that only seem that way.

Chapter 17

Why Your Relationships outside Work Can Make Your Career

In 2017, researchers at Carnegie Mellon University did an experiment to determine how having a supportive spouse might affect your career. One of the things I love about this study is that the researchers did not content themselves with just asking people whether their spouse was supportive or not, which is a highly subjective notion. Instead, the researchers brought 163 married, heterosexual couples to their lab and offered one spouse the following choice: either they could do some simple puzzles, word searches, or mazes, similar to ones they had likely done as a child, or they could give a speech. The speeches would be video recorded and evaluated by a panel of judges, and the three best would win prizes worth around $200.

Then they withdrew and unobtrusively recorded each couple's interactions while the spouse who'd been offered the choice made a decision. Trained independent observers who did not know what result the researchers were looking for evaluated the video and determined which spouses were more supportive, and which less so.

The choice between doing puzzles and making a speech that might win you a prize was intended to mimic the kinds of decisions we all make throughout our careers. How often have you had to choose between doing something familiar and predictable, something you'd been doing for years, and taking a risk that could lead to failure and public embarrassment but might also bring greater rewards (volunteering to give a presentation, for instance)?

Not surprisingly, the researchers found that those who had a supportive husband or wife, one who encouraged them to go after the prize and told them they could do it, were more likely to choose the speech over the puzzles. (Once participants made their choice, the researchers explained that there wouldn't be a speech contest after all and instead held a random drawing for the prizes.) But it is surprising how much this business of having, or not having, a supportive spouse seems to affect pretty much everything we do. When researchers followed up six months later, those who had decided to take the challenge — and who had the most supportive husbands or wives — reported that they'd learned more and grown more in their abilities over the past six months than their unsupported peers. They also seemed to be generally happier.

In other words, they were thriving. "The thriving perspective posits that people must fully embrace life and its opportunities to achieve optimal health, happiness, and well-being (to thrive) and that close relationships are integral in this process," the researchers wrote in their analysis of the experiment. Having someone who loves and supports you will help you succeed in work and life because their support will help you find the confidence to take risks and try new things. Taking risks and trying new things can lead to either failure or success, but not doing those things just leads to stagnation, which is rarely a recipe for happiness or career growth.

One reason I love this research is that it's consistent with my own ongoing one-marriage experiment. Most everything I've set out to do has come with a lot of encouragement and support from my husband Bill, who seems to genuinely believe I can do anything I set my mind to. (Admittedly, I didn't tell him beforehand when I decided to try skydiving — he probably wouldn't have been encouraging about that.)

About eight years ago, I was feeling at something of a crossroads in my career. The economy was picking up, demand for written content was growing, and for the first time, instead of having to search for work, I was turning work away. I knew I couldn't pursue every opportunity and that the choices I made would have a lasting effect on my career. It was time for some serious strategizing. I sat in the living room with Bill one day and talked through my options. I was writing a few columns a month for Inc.com back then, and I thought that I could do more. I was also writing for the websites and publications of major technology companies, doing content marketing, in the lingo of the industry. I enjoyed this work, and the pay was much better than for work like writing for a magazine's website. If I wanted to maximize my income, if I wanted to ensure the most comfortable retirement possible for us, this was the kind of work I should pursue. It was the kind of work most of the writers I knew were focusing on.

But the more I talked it through with Bill, the clearer it was that the writing I did for Inc.com, and occasionally for *Inc.* magazine, was really the work I wanted to do. Bill understood that my making this choice might have implications for our financial future. But he encouraged me to do it anyway, just like the supportive spouses in the Carnegie Mellon experiment. By the end of the conversation, I had decided: I was going to do less content marketing and try to do more for Inc.

This was risky not only because I would earn less but also because I wasn't sure what the opportunities were for me at Inc. But

I also knew that I had one life and one career and a finite number of years in which to do whatever I wanted to do. And so, the next time I was at Inc.'s office, I made a point of telling one of the senior editors that I wanted to do more.

As it happened, Inc. was looking to run more articles on its website. It worked out very, very well, but Bill didn't know it would when he encouraged me to do it. He only knew that doing the work I loved most would make me happy.

Would I have made the same choice if I had been single? Maybe. That's why it can be so hard to put your finger on exactly why having a supportive person in your life makes a difference. And yet, having lived with Bill's support for twenty-six years, it's very clear to me that it does. The choices that move you ahead in your career nearly always carry some risk. You take a chance on moving to a new job or a new company or out on your own. You raise your hand to ask for more responsibility or for a promotion. You share your ideas and push for them, rather than keeping them to yourself. You say your opinions out loud and help make decisions instead of just going with the flow.

Every time you do any of that, there's an opportunity for horrible, humiliating failure. (For example, there was the year I pushed ASJA into having two regional conferences instead of one, which seemed like a good idea to me but proved to be a very bad one.) There's always the potential for catastrophe, but things just don't seem quite as catastrophic when you're sharing your life with someone who believes in you and who will help you get through the bad times, whatever they may be.

For a year or so, I volunteered to answer phones for an emergency hotline. The people who called me were nearly always freaked out, usually for good reason since they were in the midst of an emergency. But I'll never forget one of those calls. The woman on the phone, along with her husband and kids, was in a dire situation. It was a winter night and they had run out of fuel to heat their home. To make matters worse, one of their windows had been broken by a tree branch, leaving them defenseless against the single-digit cold. But unlike most of my callers, they were not freaking out. The husband set about covering the broken window with cardboard while the wife stayed on the phone as I worked to organize an emergency fuel delivery. I was single at the time, and I was forcefully struck by how much difference it made to tackle a problem as part of a two-person team.

Giving as Well as Getting Support

There is a flip side to having a supportive partner, and that's being a supportive partner yourself. Giving support, I find, is considerably trickier than receiving support, especially if, like me, you're both self-critical and critical of others, have big ambitions but are never satisfied with any achievement or piece of success, and can look at whatever anyone else is doing and think you see a better approach. I'm not as good at being supportive as Bill is, but I'm working on it.

When Bill and I moved from Woodstock to Snohomish, it was, as one family member noted, about as great a distance as we could go and still remain in the continental United States. Woodstock had been my home for more than twenty years, and leaving there felt like pulling myself up by the roots. It meant leaving my friends, my garden, my writing group, the asparagus plants I'd nurtured for years until they finally started producing, the tiny peeper frogs who sang to us from the marshy field near our house every spring night, and the blanket of stars on moonless nights, when the sky was so dark you could see the milkiness of the Milky Way. I loved it there, but I had known for a while that it wasn't the right place for Bill.

We arrived in Washington in early November, and at a Thanksgiving gathering that year, one of our new friends looked at me and asked, "Why did you move?" The meaning of his question was clear. It was obvious what Bill had gained from relocating, but what had I gained?

I thought for a moment about how best to express it. "I have a selfish desire to be married to a happy person," I finally said, and as I said it, I realized that it was exactly true. Things can be great for you, but if your partner is unhappy, it will be hard for you to be happy. Your career can be going strong, but if your spouse feels at a dead end, it will be hard for you to feel successful. Sharing your life with someone means sharing how they feel, good and bad, so that supporting them is really the same thing as supporting yourself.

What If You're Single?

But what if you don't have a partner? Does that mean you're out of luck when it comes to the kind of support that can help you take risks and build your career? Not at all, because support can come in all shapes and sizes. In Bill's world of musicians, I've seen friends support each other over and over in so many ways, looking for gigs together, playing on each other's albums, sharing the stage, sharing contacts, even sharing instruments and each other's homes. In chapter 5 I wrote about moais, groups formed for mutual benefit, an Okinawan concept that I think can apply to many of the groups we join and form. If you don't have a partner or spouse, a group of friends or peers such as this can give your confidence the same sort of boost and help you regroup if you fail.

While this certainly isn't true for everyone, for some people, family members can provide the same sort of encouragement and support. When we moved, I had to leave most of my many house plants behind. I was especially sad to part with a sprawling pothos plant in a very large clay pot. Thinking about it even now, I remember the day it arrived in my cubicle, a small plant back then, in the days when I worked at the trade magazine. I'd recently been promoted from trainee to associate editor and was about to go on my first reporting trip. To celebrate, out of the blue, my mother sent me a flower arrangement, and the pothos plant was part of it. For decades, I kept it in my office wherever I worked, a living reminder of her love and support that lasted for years, even after she herself was gone. By the time we moved to Washington, it was well over thirty years old. While the original plant was too huge to come along, I had several smaller descendants grown from its cuttings. One of them is in my office, a few feet away, as I'm writing this now.

I can still remember the lunch my mom put together for me and an acquaintance of hers who worked for Time Inc., when I had just graduated from college and was looking for my first job. "My daughter won't blow her own horn, so I am going to do it for her," she said, and she proceeded to tell her acquaintance about everything I'd achieved so far. At the time, my mother was an office manager in a large and powerful advertising agency conglomerate; before that she'd been a movie actress and then helped create Broadway theater productions. Having this smart, accomplished woman willing to go to bat for me made a big difference.

None of us is born confident, and we are not meant to find our way through this thicket of life on our own. We may climb mountains and slay dragons, but most of us do it at least partly because we know there's someone in our life who firmly believes that we can. We all deserve that kind of support. If we look hard enough, we can find it.

EXERCISES TO TRY

1. Name Your Support System and Make the Most of It

Who are the most supportive people in your life, the ones who you know will always be there with encouragement and maybe even practical help when you need it most? Make a list of three to five names.

You might include your spouse, partner, or significant other, but list other people too – a longtime friend, a family member, or someone else entirely.

These people are a tremendous resource for you. Are you making the most of this resource? I am not suggesting that you lean on people harder or demand more from them than they are willing to give. Instead, I'm suggesting that you think strategically about who can best help you with the particular challenges and decisions you're facing and how to get the specific support you need. For example, Bill is a deep thinker when it comes to managing interpersonal relationships, so when I'm struggling in my dealings with someone else, I know he can offer insights that might really help.

Often the most effective way to get support from someone in your life is to figure out exactly what support you need and then ask for it. For example, you might say, "I'm feeling nervous about this presentation I have to give. Will you talk through it with me?" or "Will you help me figure out which direction to take my career?" That's pretty much what I asked Bill and what led to my deciding to prioritize writing for Inc.com.

2. Learn to Be a Better Support System Yourself

When it comes to getting emotional or practical support, as with so many things in relationships, it's important to give in order to get. Ask yourself if you're the support system to your partner, friend, or family member that you would like that person to be to you. That can be very challenging (believe me, I know!) because if you've known that person long enough, you've probably watched them make the same mistakes over and over, which can be even more frustrating for the person watching than the person doing it. Sometimes it can be hard to figure out what you can say or do that would actually be helpful, and if you do figure it out, it may be hard to get yourself to say or do it.

But one thing you can always do in almost any circumstance is ask a simple question: "How can I help?" And then listen to the answer.

3. Grow a Support System from Scratch

What if you feel like you have no support system because you're single or your partner isn't the right person to help build your confidence or talk through career questions? What if you don't have a friend or relative to be that person in your corner?

If so, now is the time to change that. Start by considering all the people in your life and asking yourself who seems like they might have potential to be part of your support system. Then ask that person to help you think through a problem or difficult decision, and see how it goes. Remember that you won't ever get everything you need from any one person, even if it's your spouse. Ask people to help you where they can, and find others to help where they can't. Like the stand under a table, the wider your support system, the better.

If you don't have anyone in your life who seems like a good support for you, it may be time to meet some new people. Consider trade groups, online get-togethers, clubs, employee groups, local people in your profession, workshops, college courses, and any other way you can think of to meet people who might have similar interests, similar jobs, or similar outlooks to yours. Don't expect to make friends with someone on Monday and then have that person help you through a difficult situation on Tuesday. Friendships, like all relationships, take time and patience to develop. But if you find someone who really seems to be on your wavelength, that time and patience will be a very worthwhile investment.

Chapter 18

Making Work Work for Parents

I recently read a *Harvard Business Review* piece by Stanford professor Nicholas Bloom titled "Don't Let Employees Pick Their WFH [work from home] Days." It was an odd opinion coming from Bloom, who is known as a work-from-home advocate. He famously conducted an experiment with one thousand employees of Trip.com, a ginormous Chinese travel agency, and proved that those who worked remotely were more productive than their on-site colleagues. He even gave a TEDx Talk about it. Now here he was arguing that — unless your company is fully virtual and no one ever comes to the office — no employee should have the option to work from home five days a week.

What changed his mind? A few things, but here's the biggest: motherhood. Bloom explained that his team at Stanford had surveyed thirty thousand working-age Americans since May 2020, asking them whether they would rather work in an office or at home. Most said they wanted to work in the office at least one day a week, but 32 percent said they wanted to work from home full-time, and a disproportionately high number of the people who said that were mothers with children at home.

If mothers want to work remotely, why not just let them? This is a bad idea, according to Bloom, because his earlier research with the travel agency had shown what most of us intuitively know: if you're doing your job at home and you have colleagues doing the same job in the office, they're more likely to get promoted than you are. This is true even if you're working harder. The travel agents he studied were more productive than their peers, yet they were 50 percent less likely to get a promotion over the twenty-one months he tracked them.

Put these two findings together, and you've got an obvious problem, Bloom wrote. "Single young men could all choose to come into the office five days a week and rocket up the firm, while employees with young children, particularly women, who choose to [work from home] for several days each week are held back. This would be both a diversity loss and a legal time bomb for companies."

According to Bloom, this obvious problem had an equally obvious solution. He advised the company leaders who read *Harvard Business Review* to set the same work-from-home rules for everyone, without taking their preferences into account, and simply tell employees which days to be in the office and which days to work from home. Don't give additional work-from-home privileges to mothers with children at home or anyone else.

Reading Bloom's article got me really angry. It seemed such an obvious instance of punishing the victim when in fact it was the system that needed fixing. Instead of making life harder for working mothers than it already is, why not change our workplaces so that people who work from home are on a level playing field for promotions with their on-site peers? Or better yet, change the rules and format of the workplace to make it easier, or at least less ridiculously difficult, for mothers to work in the office and care for their children too.

I got on the phone with Bloom to ask him these questions. It turned out he knew a lot more about the trade-offs of work and parenthood than I did, not only because he'd done the research but also because, unlike me, he actually is a working parent. When I made my case that companies should change to make life easier for working parents, he challenged me to come up with what those changes should be. He said that working from home really is not the equivalent of working in the office for most jobs, and especially not managerial jobs, where things like going out for coffee with colleagues and learning what goes on behind the scenes are really essential and difficult to do by Zoom.

What about on-site childcare? It certainly helps, Bloom said. He and his wife used it for their toddler daughter because it was the best option they could find. But she hated being dropped off at 9 and was ecstatic to be picked up at 5. "It made me nervous about putting children in for longer," he recalled. So parents who use on-site childcare may need to limit their workdays to 9 a.m. to 5 p.m., he said. "For many well-paid jobs, that is not enough hours."

What I learned from that conversation is what most working parents already know — much of the time, there really is no good solution. Instead, there's an infinite variety of individual work-arounds involving trade-offs and sacrifices, help from grandparents and nannies, after-school programs, part-time work, and sometimes parents, usually mothers, leaving their jobs altogether. None of it is perfect, and all of it seems unfair to at least one of the people involved.

But if we don't have good answers, we can at least try to ask some good questions that might point us in the right direction.

Where Does the Myth End and Reality Begin?

We've all seen countless mothers who have enviable careers, smart and well-behaved children who get good grades, spotless homes, and a home-cooked meal every night. These women also have perfect figures (they obviously put in lots of time at the gym), flawless hair and makeup, and designer clothes. The problem is, none of them are real. They're on TV. You know at least some of these mothers — Alicia Florrick from *The Good Wife*, Lorelai Gilmore from *Gilmore Girls*, Miranda Hobbes from *Sex and the City*, and Clair Huxtable from *The Cosby Show* among many, many others. It isn't always easy, but they always manage to pull it off with style.

I love TV shows as much as anyone, but they often seem designed to make us feel bad about ourselves. Whatever you do doesn't look anything like what your favorite characters do — and you yourself don't look anything like they do either. This might lead you to think you just aren't trying hard enough. Believe me, you are trying hard enough.

Of course, it isn't just television. We all know real people who just seem to have this stuff all sewn up. I'll never forget a visit to a couple who were friends of my husband's before we got married. She had four children who were all thriving, and she was slender and beautiful, with a perfect haircut. She had a job as an executive. We stayed the night, and when we woke up the next morning, she greeted us with freshly baked scones that she must have started making around five o'clock that morning.

I very much enjoyed our visit, but I did a certain amount of muttering under my breath as I compared myself to her. And that, of course, was the whole problem in one sentence — I was comparing myself to someone else. Comparing ourselves to anyone, in fiction or in real life, is always a recipe for trouble.

We berate ourselves because we don't have as fancy a job, as beautiful a home, as accomplished children, or as fun a marriage as the people down the street. Or we congratulate ourselves because we don't feed our children fast food or let our lawn go to weeds like our other neighbors. All of it is nonsense. The more we compare ourselves to others, whether that makes us feel good or bad about ourselves, the less we're living our own lives — and the harder it is for us to see what really matters.

What Will You Choose to Give Up?

My role model through most of my life was the Parisian author Dominique Desanti. She and my father had been childhood friends, and even though they lived in different countries, they saw each other whenever the opportunity arose. I was starry-eyed around her, the only successful author that I personally knew. She and her husband had an open marriage and kept two apartments, so her home life was complicated, to say the least. It wasn't something I wanted to try myself, but it did seem to be exactly what she wanted. Everything in her life appeared to be precisely on her own terms.

I would have tea with her every now and then. On one of those last visits, I filled her in on my life since the last time we saw each other. My career was going well. I was happily married. But I didn't have everything I wanted. I was disappointed that our attempts to have a child hadn't worked out. She looked at me sternly. "You never get everything," she said. It was a striking admonition coming from the one person in my life to whom I'd thought it didn't apply.

I don't know what Desanti wished had been different in her own life. But I do know she was right. We never get everything we want, and everything we do get means giving up something else. That applies to those of us who aren't raising children and even more to those who are. It even applies to Nicholas Bloom. When I asked him whether it was inevitable that parenthood negatively affects people's careers, his answer was surprisingly personal. "I quit McKinsey," he said. "I was there for a year and a half [as a management consultant]. After my first kid was born, it was clear it was not a career I could do plus spend time with my kids. It would be impossible. You're on the road. I'd never be around."

Bloom says he's lucky. Educated at Cambridge and Oxford, and with a PhD from University College, London, he was well positioned to enter academia. He acknowledged that his professorship at Stanford is a pretty nice fallback position.

"Kids may make people happy," he said. "They improve mental health. I wouldn't want to try and claim that for anyone, having kids or not having kids is a good or a bad decision for their career. It's just, from a personal perspective, it influenced my career. Probably I'm earning less. And I'm happy. I'll never have any regrets."

Can You Lose the Guilt?

As I was thinking about this chapter, I sent out a call asking working parents to tell me what was most difficult about combining parenting with their careers. I was astonished at how many wrote back to say that what made it most difficult was feeling guilty all the time: guilty about their kids when they were working, guilty about their work when they were spending time with their kids, guilty about neglecting their marriage or romantic relationship, and guiltiest of all if they ever took any time to do anything just for themselves, even if it was something they needed for their physical well-being, such as a workout or a yoga class.

April Crichlow is chief marketing officer at Centrical, an employee engagement and performance platform for large companies. She was formerly global head of marketing at SAP SuccessFactors, the human resources software division of the giant tech company SAP. She's also the mother of two children under ten. She said she often feels guilty around other parents in her community, usually mothers, who don't have jobs outside the home and can turn up for PTA events, help with fundraisers, and get thoroughly involved in their children's schools. That guilt is intensified if a work trip keeps her away from a special event, such as a school performance. "People tell you all the time that those years are short," she said.

Then again, sometimes she compares herself to mothers at work who have full-time nannies or other help and can spend more hours on the job than she can. "When you're not working, you're thinking, 'Oh my gosh, I should be working.'"

Is there a fix for all of this guilt? Crichlow said it comes down to setting the right expectations, for others and for yourself. "I think that the guilt comes from the expectation that we have to be there for everything because, again, we're comparing ourselves to the parents who can be there for everything." Added to that, she said, is "the old-school way of thinking that you should be available for your kids all the time."

A better approach, Crichlow told me, is to let others know what you can do and where you'll need help. "I think a lot of moms put undue pressure on themselves to try to be fully Mom all the time." If you're working outside the home, she added, "I don't think it's humanly possible to do it all. I think you have to be okay with the things that you prioritize, and no one can do that but you."

The chance for that kind of prioritization came up recently when Crichlow got an exciting invitation from one of the other mothers she knew in her New York City neighborhood. This other mother was an executive at the Museum of Modern Art. She invited Crichlow and some other moms she knew from the neighborhood to an evening event at the museum.

Unfortunately, the event conflicted with a picnic for prekindergarten students and their parents at her daughter's school. Her husband was surprised that she would consider missing the picnic — he assumed her daughter's event would take precedence. "Normally, I'd think, 'I can't go to the museum,'" she said. "And then I thought to myself, 'Wait a minute. I have the right to reset the expectations and the narrative. It would be good for Mom to go to the museum because I would come back relaxed, and

I'd have the opportunity to do something cultural and be among other moms.'"

It meant asking her husband to do something that she normally wouldn't have. "I had to think that this is the joy of parenting together — we can carry the load together." So Crichlow asked her husband to take her daughter to the picnic, and she went off to the museum. And, it turned out, everyone had a good time. "We have to set boundaries," she said. "And we have to give ourselves space to take care of ourselves. I don't know how we do that except by just doing it, and breaking through the guilt and doing it, and having fun, and saying, 'I'll do that again.'"

Psychotherapist Angela Ficken should have the answer to the guilt conundrum if anyone does. Not only does she specialize in stress reduction but she also has a three-year-old. When I asked about guilt, she said, "Is there a solution or a magic wand? If there were, I would be a billionaire. I would market that, believe me."

Despite being a stress-reduction expert, Ficken sometimes feels guilty if she chooses to do something for herself, such as spend time with a friend or get a mani-pedi when she could be spending time with her daughter. "I love spending time with my daughter, and I also want to do this thing for me," she said. "One way to manage the guilt is thinking about *should* versus *prefer*. Should exists for a reason. I *should* do laundry so I have clean underwear. I *should* go grocery shopping so I have food. But…I *should* spend time with my daughter? What would I *prefer* to do? Would I prefer to spend time with my girlfriend whom I haven't seen in a few weeks, or would I prefer to play with my daughter? Well, I can play with my daughter tonight when I get home, so I actually would prefer to see my girlfriend."

Thinking about it this way can soften the whole issue a little, Ficken said. "It doesn't have to be so bloated and saturated with guilt."

What Are You Teaching by Example?

There are many different aspects of parenting, and one we don't always think about is modeling, or teaching by example. Most children grow up using their parents as a template for how to live in the world, so that the behaviors you display as a parent, working person, and human being may be repeated by your children later on.

When we say no to things that are too much for us to handle and when we take time for ourselves, Ficken said, "We are modeling for our children that we can take care of ourselves and it's okay to be selfish. That doesn't have to have a negative connotation. When we donate time to ourselves, we actually increase our overall well-being so that we have more energy to be present, whether for our families, our partners, our girlfriends, or ourselves."

My own parents were good role models in some ways and bad ones in others. But one thing I learned from them, because they both modeled it strongly and consistently, was that they took their work very seriously and always did their absolute best at everything they undertook to do. This led to each of them being quite successful at their very different jobs, although it also meant that both of them, my father in particular, were sometimes unavailable when I was growing up.

I'm not the only one. I've changed some identifying details in the following story, but it's all true. There was a prominent journalist who was a friend of a friend of mine. This journalist traveled the world on assignment, and her stories appeared, often on the front page, in one of the nation's most widely read newspapers. She won many awards and accolades. However, the journalist also had a son and, my friend said, struggled with guilt over leaving him behind when she was off on assignment. She agonized over the priorities she had chosen and how they were affecting him.

The years passed, and the son grew up to be a musician. He put the same work ethic into writing, performing, and recording his songs that his mother put into her front-page stories. On the night of the Grammy Awards, she accompanied him to the ceremony, and when his name was announced as a winner — one of the youngest ever in his category — the camera panned over to her and the whole world could see her gigantic smile.

Parenting is a marathon, not a sprint. Being a working parent can mean an ongoing struggle among priorities, and a constant search for least-bad solutions. Our society doesn't always accommodate working parents, and our workplaces were designed for a time when one spouse was always home. Even so, you may one day look back and discover that you got it right after all.

EXERCISES TO TRY

1. What If You Just Stopped Feeling Guilty?

I realize that feeling guilty is part of being a parent and that it's not easy to turn the guilt off. But, just for a moment, try to imagine what it would be like if you did. Don't imagine that you finally do everything right, but merely that you do everything the same as you did yesterday and the day before – only all of it is fine with you. If you could reach this desirable state, what would be different? What would stay the same?

Try going just one day with no guilt – one twenty-four-hour period when, every time you think a guilty thought, you stop and say to yourself, "Today is No-Guilt Day. I can feel guilty about this tomorrow." At the end of No-Guilt Day, ask yourself how you feel and whether you'd like to have another No-Guilt Day sometime soon.

2. Choose What You Will Fail At

When I interviewed Oliver Burkeman, author of the book *Four Thousand Weeks: Time Management for Mortals*, he made a suggestion that I immediately fell in love with: choose what you will fail at because it's impossible to succeed at everything. (Cooking is one of the things he says he's willing to fail at.)

If you're trying to balance work with parenting or with caring for a family member who needs it, there's no question — you *will* fail at some things. So decide in advance which things you'll fail at, and then try to revel in your own failure.

PART FIVE

YOUR WHOLE SELF

Chapter 19

You Have a Brain —
Here's How to Make the Most of It

M any years ago, a neuroscientist named Josh Davis was scheduled to give a presentation at a large conference. The conference was in a destination city, so his wife cleared her schedule
and arranged for vacation time so she could accompany him. The
presentation was scheduled for a Monday, and on Saturday, just as
Davis and his wife were planning a day of sightseeing, he learned
that a more senior colleague of his was going to give almost the
same presentation that Davis had planned.

"As the more junior person, I had to change my presentation,"
Davis, now the chief scientist at the Mentora Institute, said in an
episode of the podcast *Intersections*. This meant he had less than
two days to create a new presentation to give to a huge audience,
even though his wife had gone to a lot of trouble to be there with
him so they could enjoy the city together.

If it had been me, I would have been overcome with frustration, anxiety, and flat-out fear. I'd have apologized — grumpily —
to my spouse and sent him off to explore the city on his own.

I'd have been furious at my colleague for stealing my thunder, at myself for not having come up with something more original, and at my husband for getting to have a good time while I had to slave away in our hotel room. I'd have ordered a gallon of coffee and maybe some pastry from room service, popped open my laptop, and struggled to contain my roiling emotions long enough to get a new presentation written.

Fortunately for Davis, as a brain expert he knew better than to do any of that. He spent the next couple of hours strolling around the city with his wife and then had a nice leisurely lunch. "The stress levels started to reduce," he said. "Yeah, it was still on my mind. I knew I had to do it. But there were breakthroughs occurring in my mind as I started to realize what was important for me to do here with this audience, and what messages I had that really were unique. I was able to stay so focused on my purpose because of that."

Not wanting to abandon his wife any longer than necessary, he rewrote his presentation in two-hour and one-hour work sessions over the next day and a half. Working in that limited time had surprising benefits because it forced Davis to zero in on what was most essential to include in the presentation. "My mind automatically started going to this place of, 'What is important here?'" he recalled. "The work I did was so on point, and I managed to reuse a lot of existing content from other things."

How did the presentation go? "People loved it. It was a big hit," he said. "I've been able to use it again and again. And I got to spend time with my wife — she was happy that she'd come."

I'm not sure many of us would have the nerve to go for a leisurely stroll while facing the pressure of having to rewrite a major presentation. The knowledge that helped Davis make that choice is the basis of his book, *Two Awesome Hours: Science-Based Strategies to Harness Your Best Time and Get Your Most Important Work*

Done, which is a quick read and full of information Davis has collected over the years about how to get your brain working at its best. The title comes from his conviction that the majority of us spend most of our time on the job working with less than our best brain power, and that some of this is inevitable. But, he argues, if we pay attention to what helps and what hinders our brain function, most of us can achieve two hours of awesome productivity and creativity, which is enough to get our most important tasks done. Most people don't have two daily hours when their brains are working at their best, he says. Many have none at all.

Davis understands what few of us do — that people are not machines. I know how obvious that might sound. Yes, we all know we're not machines — in theory. In practice, though, we expect ourselves to work with the same consistency and dependability as a machine, even if we've already been working for many hours. Even if we haven't had the proper amount of sleep, leisure, exercise, or nutrition. Even if we are distracted, worried, frightened, or emotionally drained. We may know that we're not machines, but we expect ourselves to act as though we were.

I used to expect machinelike consistency and stamina from myself, but researching Inc.com columns over the years about how to operate at your best eventually cured me of that expectation. Over time, I've adjusted my approach to work to take my own humanity into account and to make room for my personal habits and preferences, such as relaxing and reading for a while in the morning and working into the evening. It was painful, but I slowly let go of the belief that through sheer self-discipline and force of will, I could *make* myself do whatever needed to get done. If you're still clinging to that belief, I hope this chapter will help you let it go as well.

If you must think of your brain as a machine, think of it as a very expensive, high-performance sports car. Yes, you can fill it up with low-octane fuel, skip its needed maintenance, drive it for thousands of miles without stopping to let the engine cool down, and slam on the brakes and push the accelerator to the floor over and over again. But if you do that, your sports car won't perform the way you want it to. And the more you do those things, the less well it will work.

So how do you treat your brain like the high-performance vehicle that it is? Begin with the simplest fact about your brain, which is that it is an organ inside your body. I realize that I'm once again stating the obvious, but it's astonishing how many people act like their brains and their bodies have nothing to do with each other. They stay up late, arrive at their desks hung over, eat pastry for breakfast and French fries for lunch, and then blame their colleagues for being too boring when they can't stay awake through the team meeting that afternoon.

Many of the things Davis and other experts recommend as ways to make your brain work better will sound very familiar because they're also the things countless physicians and health experts and probably your mother have said you must do to stay healthy. This may sound like I'm nagging you to be healthier, and of course I do want you to be healthier in the long term. But for the purposes of this chapter, let's forget about the long term. These are all things that will help you be more alert, more quick-thinking, and smarter in the here and now. Use these tactics as short-term solutions when you want your brain to be working at its best. You can return to your usual habits, healthy or not, the rest of the time.

Sleep

In chapter 16, I dived into the topic of how lack of sufficient sleep can affect your long-term health and even put you at risk for Alzheimer's disease. Research has shown that getting only six hours of sleep a night for nine nights produced the same effect as a 0.10

percent blood-alcohol level. You probably wouldn't show up to work with that much alcohol in your bloodstream and expect to be as smart, efficient, and alert as if you were completely sober. Expecting yourself to perform at your best when you're even moderately sleep-deprived is just as unrealistic. Don't do it.

Nutrition

People talk about "brain food," but what is that, exactly? It's not entirely clear since the short-term effect of various types of food on mental function hasn't been studied as widely as it could be. According to Davis, here's what we do know:

1. Carbs aren't brain food. Eating carbs might give you a very brief (fifteen-minute) boost in mental function, but after that they will drag you down, which may lead you to eat more of them, and then more after that, and…it's a losing battle. If you want to do your best work, avoid carbs, especially those that can spike your glycemic index, such as sweets, white bread, and pasta.

2. Fats, on the other hand, may be a better brain food. In one experiment that Davis cites, subjects experienced a three-hour boost in brain function after consuming fats. You've probably heard by now that there are "bad fats," such as animal fats and saturated fats, and "good fats," which come from things like nuts and fish and contain omega-3 fatty acids. Davis notes that in the long term, those omega-3 fatty acids seem to help brain function, while saturated fats seem to harm it.

3. Caffeine may be good for you. A growing body of evidence seems to show that up to about four cups of coffee a day is fine (unless you're pregnant, in which case you should avoid it). According to Davis, an estimated 80 percent of the world's population consumes caffeine

daily in some form, which is to say that most of us have a caffeine addiction (I know I do).

While drinking coffee or another caffeinated beverage is definitely beneficial, Davis warns against a very common error: increasing your caffeine intake when you're feeling particularly tired or when you're short on sleep. "Have whatever your normal dose of caffeine is," he advises. "Having more than that will just make you jittery and anxious."

Hydration

Most of us don't realize how much of an effect water has on our mental function and our moods. I learned this lesson myself the hard way on a trip through southern Utah with an old friend. We set out on a multiday backpacking trip through the desert carrying plenty of water — or so we thought. Then we saw a sign at the trailhead that said we needed one gallon per person per day on the trail, and we had about half that much. We asked a passing park ranger for advice, and he said we'd be OK because the weather wasn't all that hot. So off we went, figuring we'd ration our water just to make sure.

We were thirsty over the next two days, which was to be expected since we were rationing water. What was more surprising was the dramatic effect it had on our moods and our relationship. It turns out that dehydration can make you very grumpy, and we found ourselves squabbling over just about everything. Eventually, we came upon a stream. We immediately cut our planned hiking route short and instead camped next to it for two nights. We had a water-treatment kit with us, and we drank and drank and drank.

Davis has some simple advice that we should all follow. If it's been two hours or more since your last drink of water, have some. (Soda, beer, juice, and especially coffee don't count.) This alone can noticeably improve your mood and energy level.

Learning about the importance of hydration has turned me into one of those annoying people who carry a water bottle everywhere. I'm also inordinately fond of those old-fashioned water carafe-and-glass combinations where the glass fits over the top of the bottle and doubles as a lid, something you're likely to see on the set of a period drama. They turn up in antique stores and flea markets, and my husband bought me one a few years ago that sits on its own special coaster on my desk. I find that if I fill it before starting work in the morning, it's empty by the end of the day without my having thought about it. Sometimes just having a container that you like within easy reach is enough to get you drinking more water without any extra effort.

Movement

You know by now that regular exercise is important for your overall health and will lengthen your life. That's the long-term benefit of exercise. In the short term, exercise is a great idea because it's proven to improve your mood. In fact, a Harvard study found that people who spent an hour more a day moving than their sedentary counterparts had a 26 percent lower risk of depression, and that benefit held even if they were doing everyday activities such as climbing stairs or folding laundry instead of "official" workouts. There's no doubt at all that regular exercise will make you both healthier and happier.

I'm not here to tell you about the health benefits of regular exercise. I am here to tell you that brief bits of movement — too brief to have any real health effect — can nevertheless change your mood and improve your brain function within moments. Years ago I interviewed an executive coach and stress expert named Jenny Evans who suggested something so simple and quick that anyone can do it in any circumstance, and it's absolutely brilliant. When you're feeling stressed — your boss has just chewed you out, you realize you're going to miss an important deadline, you just lost a deal or a promotion you were counting on — do some vigorous exercise, but only for thirty to sixty seconds.

This could amount to running up one flight of stairs, doing a handful of lunges or jumping jacks, running in place, or putting in your earbuds, turning on some dance music, and dancing around your office or the parking lot for one minute or less. That's not enough time to work up a sweat, so you won't need to fuss with your clothes or change your shoes. Set a timer, and when your thirty or sixty seconds are up, you're done, she said.

How can such a short bit of exercise make any difference at all? It's because of evolution, Evans explained. When you're under stress, hormones such as cortisol flood your system to produce the fight-or-flight response that helped keep your ancient ancestors safe from an attacking enemy or other threat. Those hormones caused them to spring into a short burst of action, either to run away or to fight back. So thirty to sixty seconds of movement is enough to satisfy that urge and put some endorphins into your system instead. Years ago, I was on a flight that had just arrived, and I saw a tall man stand up to leave his seat and bang his head painfully on the low ceiling above him. He turned around and punched that ceiling hard, even though it was a silly thing to do and there were about a hundred people watching him. You've probably seen, or even had, such reactions yourself. That's how powerful stress hormones can be and why a short burst of exercise is such a good way of dealing with them.

Beyond that, Josh Davis says, you can use exercise to maximize your productivity and effectiveness during your workday and especially before giving a presentation or participating in an important meeting. "In the next thirty minutes to five hours, how do I want to be thinking and feeling?" he says. "If you engage in some moderate exercise — a forty-minute brisk walk, a twenty-minute light jog on a treadmill, ten minutes going up and down stairs — that is an extremely reliable way to reduce anxiety that will get you in a more positive mood and able to collaborate more effectively. Use it when you really need to hit the reset button."

Davis uses this tactic himself. "Now that I know this, I build it into my preparations. If I'm traveling and I'm going to present, I'll jog in place for fifteen minutes in my hotel room if I need to." This sort of thing is common among the most seasoned presenters. Tony Robbins, for example, famously bounces on a minitrampoline before heading onstage.

Knowing What to Do When

I used to start my workday by reading my email and answering anything that required a response before digging into my real work. It seemed like such a logical approach. I could get any urgent matters or questions that needed answering out of the way, giving good service to my clients by providing a rapid response. I even wrote a column about how all the efficiency experts were wrong about the need to confine email to an hour or two in the late afternoon. At the time, I was ASJA president, and I argued that if I didn't answer my email promptly, I would prevent others from getting on with their jobs because they'd have to wait for me to respond to their questions or requests.

Besides, reading email is so enticing. It doesn't seem to take much brainwork or energy. Every time you answer someone's question or solve someone's problem and hit "send," you're filled with a small sense of accomplishment. It seemed like the perfect way to ease myself into the workday.

But then I interviewed Davis. He made me see that starting the day with email was a terrible idea because of decision fatigue. Although we're mostly unaware of it, every decision we make, even if it seems inconsequential, costs us mental energy. "We make a lot of decisions without noticing," he said. "Email involves a lot of decisions: Should I send this right now? Am I including the right people? Did I say it the right way? A lot of people try to pack that in right before they're going to give a presentation or do something creative, and they're affecting their ability to do that effectively." Conversely, later in the day, when you're worn out from more important tasks, is a great time to tackle email and a terrible time to try to get yourself to do something creative or make an important decision.

Tackling your most challenging creative work first thing (which I try to do, though I don't always succeed) and leaving email and other mundane tasks for later is one way that timing things properly can help you be much more effective. Another is to pay attention to your emotional state. Your mood also has a big effect on your ability to work productively, even though you might not want to admit it.

I know I don't want to admit it. I figure I should be able to do my best work whether I'm feeling happy, confident, and fresh or miserable, worn-out, and full of self-doubt. But I'm slowly learning to stop expecting machinelike consistency from myself and to recognize the massive effect my emotions have on my ability to function. I'm a very moody person, and when I'm feeling happy, it's easy to get into the flow of work. It's a great time to write pitches or meet with potential clients — people feel my bright mood, and it makes them want to work with me. When I'm down, the opposite is true, and everything drags. At those times, the best thing I can do for my productivity is to get up from my desk and find some way of getting out of my bad mood, such as going for a walk, watching something really absorbing on TV, or talking with a friend.

Dealing with Distractedness

Most of us strive (or at least wish) for a workspace with few distractions and a relatively quiet setting in which to do our most thoughtful work. We're right to want that, Davis says, since a calm, quiet environment is best for optimum brain function. But most of us also think that, once we're in our workspace, we can concentrate fully on our work, and with nothing to pull us away from it, we can knock out hours and hours of focused productivity.

That is pure fantasy. The human brain isn't wired to focus on one thing for hours on end. Instead, its natural state is to constantly scan whatever is in our environment, paying particular attention to anything new or unexpected. Once again, blame evolution. "Detecting approaching people, animals, flying objects, and so on is a straightforward survival strategy, whereas staying focused on one thing without keeping an eye on potential dangers would leave us fairly exposed," Davis writes in *Two Awesome Hours*.

What should you do about it? Begin by eliminating your most compelling distractions. If you want to focus on an important task, you should — of course — have email and social media notifications turned off. Davis also suggests putting your smartphone somewhere you can't easily reach it, such as on the other side of the room. If you start looking at Instagram or checking the latest news, you can lose half an hour or more before you realize it.

Once you've removed the most compelling distractions, don't be afraid to let your mind wander. In fact, you should expect it to, Davis says, because that's the nature of the human brain. He recommends looking out the window or, if you don't have a window with a good view in your workspace, gazing at a poster from time to time during your workday. Whatever you do, don't get angry at yourself when your mind wanders away, because that's what it was designed to do. Looking out the window, or at your poster, is a sufficiently boring activity that your attention should naturally snap back to whatever you were working on within a few minutes. In chapter 16, I talked about your brain's default network, which helps you solve problems while your attention is elsewhere. You just may find that, once your mind is done wandering, the solution to whatever you were working on will have magically appeared.

EXERCISES TO TRY

1. Break the Email Habit

How much time every day do you spend on email? More importantly, what time of day do you read and respond to email? If you're in the habit of reading email at the beginning of the day, try putting it off till late afternoon. The same goes for Slack messages, chat, texts, phone calls, and social media. And if you're accustomed to starting the day with some other mundane task, such as filling out paperwork, set that aside for later as well. Instead, when you first arrive at your desk in the morning, tackle your biggest, most important task, the one that requires all your creativity and problem-solving skills.

Try this for a week or, if you can't manage a week, for three days. At the end of that period, ask yourself whether doing your most important work at the start of the day helped you make more progress on the tasks that are most important and meaningful. Also ask yourself whether dealing with your email (or Slack, etc.) a bit later in the day created any major problems for you or for anyone you work with. If the answer to the first question is yes and the second one is no, consider making this a permanent change.

2. Commit to Sleep

Most adults require between seven and eight hours of sleep a night, and, as I mentioned in chapter 16, some researchers believe that means you need at least eight-and-a-half hours in bed (since you don't spend 100 percent of your time in bed sleeping). Just for a week, try to get those eight hours. Temporarily set aside other priorities you might have to make sure you have plenty of time for sleeping – ideally enough to wake up without an alarm. While you're at it, up your "sleep hygiene" by shutting down all electronic devices at least half an hour before bed. That includes the television. You can improve sleep hygiene even more by taking a bath and/or having a cup of herbal tea before bed, having some light exercise, such as a walk, during the evening, and eliminating all light from your bedroom.

You don't have to do all these things, and you don't have to do any of them forever. But just try for one week to prioritize sleep over other things, even if you don't feel particularly sleep-deprived. Remember that humans are very bad at knowing when they haven't had enough sleep. At the end of the week, check in with yourself and see how you feel. Ask yourself if your work is going well or badly. You may find that improved sleep really does make you feel better.

3. Create a Schedule That Takes Your Brain into Account

You might start the typical workday with a set of tasks you want to either accomplish or make progress on. Executive coaches and other career experts often recommend putting the most important of these into your calendar, in effect making an appointment with yourself.

This is a good idea, but try taking it a step further by making sure to block out a time when you know you're at your most creative and energetic to work on your most important and meaningful task for the day. For many people, this might be first thing in the morning, although for me it's late afternoon to early evening, which just tells you that everyone is different.

Chapter 20

How Mindfulness Can Help You in Work and Life

Years ago, Bill and I were driving somewhere. I was sitting in the passenger seat, and for some reason, I got to thinking about how much of my life I'd spent with my mind fixed firmly on the future, anticipating, planning, and worrying. Especially worrying. So much time spent worrying, and it had done me so little good.

I sighed. "Someday, I'll learn to live in the present moment," I said. "But I don't know when that will be."

Yes, I know how ridiculous that is. I knew it as soon as I said it. But there it is: this business of mindfulness and being in the present moment has always been challenging for me. I'm excellent at planning, organizing, and anticipating. I pride myself on finding solutions to future problems before others even realize they're problems. But when it comes to staying in the present moment, noticing what's around me and what I'm feeling — really experiencing my life? That's always been much, much more difficult. If you're like me, good at planning and organizing, bad at just letting go, maybe it's difficult for you too.

Even the idea of mindfulness has been tough for me to get my head around. A few years ago, I took a weekend meditation course with the authors and Tibetan Buddhists Joel and Michelle Levey, and on the first day they gave us an exercise that's turned into a daily habit for me. When you first wake up in the morning, they said, before you get out of bed and before you reach for your smartphone or other device, do three things. First, be awake to the fact that you're awake. Second, find three things to be grateful for, even if they're just the sunlight streaming through the window or the fact that your body is alive and functioning for one more day. Then, set an intention for the day.

The second and third of those practices seemed straightforward enough, but I spent a lot of time wondering how to do the first one. How do you wake up to the fact that you're awake? What does that mean, exactly? I know when I'm awake, but how can I really be awake to that knowledge?

Eventually, I came to a solution that may or may not have anything to do with what the Leveys intended. All I can say is, it works for me: I pet one of our cats. When I wake up in the morning, one or both of them are invariably next to me, within easy reach and happy to be petted. (My husband is there too, but he sleeps later than I do, and I don't want to wake him up.) The feel of the soft fur under my hand is a tactile reminder that I'm there, awake and alive in that moment, surrounded by warmth and love.

And, really, mindfulness can be as simple as that. At least, I believe it can. It can be a profound, mystical, spiritual experience, achieved after hours of practice and meditation and study, but it can also be as simple as petting a cat. I like to think of mindfulness as one of those maps in a shopping mall with a big red dot that says, "You are here." That's it. You are here, not anywhere else, not anyone else, and not any time else. That big red dot can be a reminder that you are here now, that we are all here now, and that's really all that any of us have.

Choppy Surface, Calm Below

So how do you use mindfulness? How can it help you at work and in your daily life? A few years ago, for my column, I posed that question to Chade-Meng Tan. Meng, as he likes to be known, is a former Google engineer; in fact, he was the company's 107th employee. He studied meditation and mindfulness and began giving a highly popular course at Google called Search Inside Yourself. When we talked, right after the publication of his bestselling book based on the course, his official title at Google was "jolly good fellow (which nobody can deny)." Since then, he's retired from Google, continued as an author and movie producer, and become cochair of One Billion Acts of Peace, a nonprofit that encourages ordinary people to help solve the world's biggest problems through small actions.

"Mindfulness is about the training of attention in a way that allows your mind to stabilize," he explained when we talked. He compared it to the ocean. "The surface is choppy, but the bottom is very calm. If you're able to go deep inside, you can access that calmness and exist in a world where you can be calm and in action at the same time."

How do you achieve this admirable state? Meng spends a lot of time in meditation, but it's not the only way to achieve mindfulness, he said. "Gaining this skill turns out to be very easy." A great place to start is to focus your attention on your breath from time to time throughout the day, whenever you think of it or — especially helpful — when you feel yourself getting tense. Focus on your breath for three breaths. Or just one breath. "You don't have to train very deep," he said.

The stress and upset of failure are physical sensations, Meng explained. Calming your mind by focusing on your breath will not only settle your emotions but it will settle your body as well. He talked to me about the vagus nerve, which I had never heard of. I learned later that it's the longest nerve in your body, connecting your brain to your digestive system. According to information on the National Institutes of Health website, the vagus nerve is "the main component of the parasympathetic nervous system, which oversees a vast array of crucial bodily functions, including control of mood, immune response, digestion, and heart rate."

You can use this powerful nerve to increase your own calm with an absurdly simple technique. When you inhale, your heart naturally speeds up, but when you exhale, the vagus nerve releases a neurotransmitter that slows your heart rate. You can both increase your sense of calm and increase the variability of your heart rate — which has all kinds of health benefits — by slowing your breathing and making your exhalations longer than your inhalations. The simplest way to do this is by counting. For example, count to four while inhaling and count to five or six while exhaling. As you become calmer, you can increase those counts if you want to slow your breathing further, which will help you relax more.

But mindfulness isn't only about achieving inner calm. It's also about being awake and aware and fully in the present. It's about understanding two seemingly contradictory truths. First, the present moment is all we have and all we truly know. Second, many of the things that make us desperately anxious or frustrated or angry don't really warrant that much emotional energy, which becomes clear when we consider them in the grand scheme of things. This is why the question "How much will this matter five years from now?" can be so powerful.

That brings me back to Josh Davis, the neuroscientist from chapter 19. Some of his most intriguing advice is about how to best use the few moments in every day when you are fully awake and aware.

What does that mean? Davis writes in *Two Awesome Hours*, "In one regard we are very much like computers: almost everything we do — from flossing our teeth to answering a day's worth of emails — we do by following neural routines, the human version of computer programs, which guide our thoughts, feelings, and behaviors."

In other words, we spend much of our time more or less on autopilot. It's not our fault. Our brains evolved this way, and for good reason. As Davis explains, one influential theory says that humans are "cognitive misers," conserving mental energy whenever we can so we can use it for advanced problem-solving when we need it.

You're probably aware that you do some things by rote, like brushing your teeth. For me, the process goes like this: I put toothpaste on my electric toothbrush and turn it on. I start my brushing routine, as always, in the upper right corner of my mouth. Three minutes later, the toothbrush turns itself off and my teeth are clean, but I have no memory of actually brushing them. That happened automatically while my mind wandered away to the day's plans or the movie I watched the night before. Driving or walking to a familiar destination is another time when autopilot kicks in for many people. If you've ever missed a turn you were supposed to take because it required you to deviate from your usual route, you know what I mean.

According to Davis, this business of operating by rote doesn't just apply to things like tooth brushing and commuting, but to nearly everything. You may believe you go through your day thoughtfully, constantly making fresh decisions about what you do, but that mostly isn't true. The vast majority of the time, you're gliding along well-worn neural pathways, completing tasks the same way you've done them before, and using as little mental energy as you can.

To be clear, this does not mean you don't care about these tasks or that you're not putting your best effort into them. You're probably doing them very well because they're things you've done many times before and you've learned how to do them right. If you're not on autopilot, it usually means you're a complete beginner at whatever you're trying to do and so the task requires your absolute attention.

Understand all that, and you'll see why the few times we come out of autopilot during the course of an average day are so very valuable. Davis calls these moments "decision points," and they generally happen at one of two times. Either you've just completed a task and are ready to move on to something else, or you were in the middle of a task but have just been interrupted.

That second instance seems ironic, at least to me. So many of us who do thought-intensive work such as writing try our best to arrange our work lives to cut interruptions to a minimum. This is why so many successful people get up at five or even four in the morning — they love having a couple of hours to work without fear of interruption while everyone else is asleep. Then there are those of us who like working late at night for the same reason. It's not that we prefer to miss out on sleep or time with our loved ones; it's that working without interruption lets us really disappear into whatever it is we're doing.

We're not entirely wrong to dislike interruptions. Researchers at the University of California, Irvine found that it takes the average worker twenty-three minutes to get back on track after an interruption. But according to Davis, an interruption can make you more productive instead of less because it gives you a rare opportunity to really ask yourself whether what you were doing beforehand was truly the most effective use of your time. When you get interrupted, he says, "a gift has just occurred."

It's a gift most of us try to reject. When we're interrupted, we try our best to get back to what we were doing quickly, picking up exactly where we left off. When we complete a task or finish a phone call or leave a meeting, we immediately look around for the next thing to do or check the next item on our to-do list, and we jump right in.

That's a shame, Davis says, because a decision point is an opportunity that you should value. It's a rare moment in your day when no autopilot routine is running, and therefore your brain is completely awake and engaged. It is, therefore, a perfect moment to make a smart decision, and since Davis is focused on greater productivity and effectiveness, he suggests using that moment to decide how best to spend your time. Instead of jumping into the next task right away, he says, take five minutes or so to really think about the best way to use your next chunk of time.

Perhaps you have a large, important project you need to get started on. You may be tempted to jump on in, but should you? Maybe you have an important meeting in half an hour, and your time would be best spent preparing for that meeting so you'll be able to answer any questions that arise. Or maybe it's the end of a long and arduous day, and your mood and energy level are low. In that case, starting on the big project may lead to frustration and perhaps exhaustion. Answering your email, which is relatively easy and can give you the satisfying feeling of accomplishing something, might be the right choice. Or maybe you're feeling upbeat and energetic, and you have nothing on your schedule for the next two hours, making this the perfect time to start on a more challenging task.

If you think about it, Davis says, you almost certainly know the best way to use your time right now. The important thing is to take those few minutes or so to think about it and make a deliberate choice. It might feel like you're wasting time, but spending five minutes deciding how you'll spend your time is way better than immediately starting a task that isn't the best use of that time. Decision points don't come up often, he notes. If you had ten of them in a day — which would be quite a lot — and took five minutes for each, you'd still lose less than an hour.

Why do we tend to jump so quickly into the next task or back into the task that was interrupted? Because sitting with a decision point is mentally uncomfortable, Davis explains. Not knowing what to do, even briefly, is an unpleasant feeling for most of us. We may find ourselves thinking about everything we have to do, and it may all crowd into our brains at once. At least, that's what happens to me, something my husband calls my "litany." And so we grasp at something — anything — to start working on. The moment we do, we activate one of our neural routines, although we probably aren't aware of it. Being in the routine is much more comfortable for our overtaxed brains, and we breathe a sigh of relief, happy to feel productive again and to lose the awful sensation of not knowing what to do with ourselves.

Davis doesn't often use the term *mindfulness*, but that's what he's talking about. That unpleasant sensation of being outside all your neural routines and completely aware is all about being mindful. And his suggestion to use those decision points to your advantage is just one example of how mindfulness can help you be more successful and more present when you're at work.

Mindfulness is also what many people are after when they meditate. I realize meditation can seem like an uninviting activity to some people, and if you feel that way, you can certainly find mindfulness without it. But meditation has many scientifically proven benefits: It can change the brain to literally make you smarter and can reduce the effects of aging on the brain. It can lower your blood pressure, reduce pain, and help with a variety of illnesses, as well as anxiety and insomnia.

Not only that, but research shows that meditation can make you happier. Richard Davidson, a neuroscientist at the University of Wisconsin, led a twelve-year study on the brain and found that twenty minutes of daily meditation made people measurably happier. The person with the happiest brain activity Davidson ever measured was a Tibetan monk named Matthieu Ricard, originally from France, who sometimes meditates for an entire day at a time.

And meditation may be both easier and more pleasant than you think. I'm a complete amateur when it comes to meditation. But years ago, I took a meditation class where the teacher impressed upon us that five minutes of meditation every day carries much more benefit than hours of meditation once in a while. I took that to heart and started meditating for five minutes a day, not every day, but whenever I had time and remembered to. Those five minutes, when I did them, made a big difference to my mood and my sense of calm. Over the years, I've tried to increase my meditation practice, and I'm now up to nine minutes a day, still not every day, though I'm more consistent. Nine minutes may be as far as I ever get, and if so, I think that's fine. If you're a more serious meditator, good for you. You're helping yourself in countless ways. But if you've been reluctant to try it, consider just a couple of minutes a day.

Also, consider guided meditation, which I think is a lot easier and more enjoyable for many people. There are any number of recorded guided meditations out there to try. Many people love the guided meditation series that Oprah Winfrey and Deepak Chopra have uploaded to YouTube. If you have Netflix, the *Headspace Guide to Meditation* series is a fun (and animated!) way to start practicing meditation with meditation master and former circus arts student Andy Puddicombe.

But even without meditation, there are many ways to be mindful because mindfulness is at least as much an attitude as it is a specific practice. One of the best ways I know to understand this is to consider the difference between a regular walk outdoors and an "awe walk." In early 2020, before the pandemic spread in the United States, researchers at the University of California, San Francisco, conducted an experiment where they told people to take a fifteen-minute walk in nature once a week. Some randomly selected members of the group were given one additional instruction, to seek to experience awe during their walk, defined as "a positive emotion elicited when in the presence of vast things not immediately understood." Both groups were also asked to take a selfie at the beginning and end of each walk.

Researchers followed these subjects for eight weeks, during which time they filled out daily surveys about their emotions. The awe group had a marked increase in emotions like gratitude and compassion, and a marked decrease in feelings of distress. But what was really interesting was those selfies. Over the eight weeks, the awe group took up less and less room in their own selfies, devoting more and more space to the nature around them. And when experts in reading facial expressions reviewed the selfies without knowing which group was which, they identified the awe group as having noticeably happier smiles. Mindfulness can be as simple as that. Noticing the beauty that's around you, and around us all. Trying to look beyond ourselves. Finding wonder, because it's there to be found.

For me, it's about crows. I'm a bird lover, and I've always been fascinated by crows and ravens because they are highly intelligent, among the very few types of creatures other than humans that use tools. For example, they will tear a stem off a bush, bend one end into a hook shape, and then poke that hook into a rotted log, "fishing" for grubs, which are a tasty snack from a crow's point of view. After I took the Leveys' workshop and was driving home, I saw crows in the trees and decided to make them into my own personal mindfulness cues. Now, every time I notice crows around me, usually once or twice a day while walking or driving, they remind me to let go, for a moment, of my constant thinking, planning, and worrying about the future and instead to be here in the present moment, which is always enough and is all we have.

Mindfulness can be an incredibly powerful tool for a calmer, happier, more thoughtful life. And it can be as simple as a big black bird sitting on a telephone line.

EXERCISES TO TRY

1. Use Breathing to Hack Your Nervous System

In yoga, there's a controlled breathing practice called pranayama that can calm your nervous system. In its simplest form, you breathe in for a count of, say, four beats, and then breathe out for a count of six beats. The numbers can vary, but the important thing is for your exhalation to be longer than your inhalation. This simple act will activate your vagus nerve to slow your heartbeat and communicate to your body on a physiological level that all is well.

There are various ways to use mindful breathing to increase mindfulness and calm. Here's one easy technique that Bhava Ram (formerly Brad Willis) from chapter 1 recommends. Focus on your breath and mentally say "I" on the inhalation and "am" on the exhalation. That should increase your level of calm in almost any circumstance. Some other inhalation/exhalation words that work well are *let/go* and my own favorite, *just/this*.

2. Take a Walk in Nature

You don't need to go for a long hike in the woods, although that's a lovely thing to do. A walk in a park or along a river or lake, if there's one nearby, can also be effective. If you like, try mindful walking. Simply focus your attention on what's around you and on the sensation of your feet rising and falling as you go along. You can do this for just a few minutes – believe it or not, it's a form of meditation – and then go back to walking as you normally would.

Or make it an awe walk. Look around you and just let yourself marvel at the vastness and wonder of our world.

3. Find Your Own Crows

Using crows as a reminder to be mindful has worked so well for me that I've turned it into a permanent mental practice. If, like me, you spend too much of your time reviewing the past or planning the future, I invite you to find a mindfulness cue of your own. It should be something you see perhaps once a day or a few times a week, or it could be something you encounter more frequently. It might work best if it's something in nature – the top of a nearby mountain might work, or a grand tree that you pass on your way to and from work. Whatever it is, it's there for you. Make it your own mindfulness companion.

Chapter 21

What Do You Really Want?

It's a simple question, and yet for most of us, it can also be a co-nundrum. That very much includes me. For example, if you had to choose, would you rather be successful or happy? The logical answer would seem to be to choose happiness. After all, if you think about it, our quests for wealth, renown, creative fulfillment, and even love and family really boil down to a search for happi-ness. We pursue these things because we believe they'll make us happy, and we feel disappointed and cheated if they don't.

For readers of Inc.com and other aspiring entrepreneurs, few figures are as compelling as Apple cofounder Steve Jobs. More than a decade after his death in 2011, Inc.com columnists keep writing about him because he continues to fascinate our audi-ence. Jobs was enormously proud of what he accomplished at Apple and of his own role and influence in the world. He was certainly driven, clearly loved the company he'd built, and loved working there every day. But was he actually happy? It didn't seem that way. His former colleagues at Apple describe him as some-one who was tough to work for, often acted like a bully, and was famous for berating employees whose work didn't live up to his exacting standards. One entrepreneur I interviewed remembered that before his first encounter with Jobs, his boss took him aside and said: "I just want you to understand that, whatever Steve says, you shouldn't take it personally." And Walter Isaacson's biography of Jobs describes a man who frequently threw tantrums and cried, someone who was "driven by demons."

I have no inside knowledge of what Jobs was really like or how he felt, but from the available information, it seems to me that he was not happy at all. But I also suspect that he didn't think of his own happiness as a particularly relevant goal. He almost said as much in a 1994 interview with the Santa Clara Valley Historical Association. "When you grow up, you tend to get told that the world is the way it is," he said. "Live your life inside the world. Try not to bash into the walls too much. Try to have a nice family life, have fun, save a little money."

But that's not good enough, or at least it wasn't for him. "Life can be much broader once you discover one simple fact," he said. "And that is, everything around you that you call life was made up by people that were no smarter than you, and you can change it. You can influence it. You can build your own things that other people can use." Once you learn that lesson, Jobs said, "you'll never be the same again."

For Jobs, his love of the company he'd built and the work he was doing and the influence he could have on the world was the point, and happiness was definitely not. Some people described him as monk-like, which is ironic when you consider the research (discussed in chapter 20) that suggests that Tibetan monks may be the happiest people in the world. But the descriptor fits. Jobs had a happy marriage and a family, but his devotion to Apple and his work there was so complete that even when he knew he was dying of pancreatic cancer, even after he'd had a liver transplant, he remained CEO.

When he finally stepped down, he said it was because he could "no longer meet my duties and expectations as Apple's CEO," but he remained on the board of directors. At the time, he had only six weeks left to live. On the last full day of his life, he called Apple CEO Tim Cook to discuss one of the company's upcoming products, according to a SoftBank executive who was there at the time and said Cook interrupted their meeting to take the call. Jobs died the next day.

For Jobs, the choice between happiness and achievement was a simple one — achievement trumped everything else, including family, friendship, and most of life's pleasures. It was so important to him that it filled his mind during the final hours of his life. Our culture in the United States reveres that kind of total devotion, especially in entrepreneurs, athletes, and creative artists. I think many of us believe that this kind of single-minded focus is necessary to achieve great success — and also that it guarantees great success. But neither of those things is true.

Is unwavering devotion to your work truly necessary if you want to reach the heights of achievement? Consider Facebook founder Mark Zuckerberg, another highly successful billionaire entrepreneur with a world-changing company. In 2015, and again in 2017, he took the full four months of paternity leave that all fathers of newborns at the company are entitled to. At the time of his second paternity leave, Facebook was in the midst of controversy. It was clear that Russian operatives had used the service in their efforts to manipulate the US presidential election. Many CEOs would have concluded that their continued presence in the office was needed at such a difficult time. Instead, shortly after his daughter August was born in 2017, Zuckerberg posted this: "At Facebook, we offer four months of maternity and paternity leave because studies show that when working parents take time to be with their newborns, it's good for the entire family. And I'm pretty sure the office will still be standing when I get back."

As for the notion that total devotion somehow guarantees

success — I'm guessing you know plenty of people who've thrown every ounce of effort and devotion they could into an endeavor and still saw it fail. And while Jobs was unquestionably a product design and marketing genius, he also was very, very lucky. He grew up in the region that would later be known as Silicon Valley, and there were many technology companies in the area already. At age twelve, he phoned HP cofounder Bill Hewlett, who lived in nearby Palo Alto, and requested spare parts for a technology project. Hewlett agreed to give Jobs the parts and later also gave him a summer job. Perhaps his biggest piece of good luck was that in high school he became friends with Steve Wozniak, who was as brilliant at engineering as Jobs was at product design. Woz designed a digital "blue box" that produced tones to outsmart the phone system, allowing for free long-distance calls (long-distance calling was quite costly at the time). Jobs suggested selling the devices, and it became their first entrepreneurial venture. In 1976, Woz created what would become the Apple I computer, and the pair founded Apple in the Jobs family garage.

My purpose here is not to diminish Jobs's undeniable role in starting Apple or reshaping the entire tech industry. My point is that luck and timing are part of every single success. You can bring total devotion and even genius to something and still fail at it.

You Can Follow Your Heart

Which brings me back to my original question: What do you really want? If total devotion isn't necessary for success, and it doesn't guarantee success, it seems to me that this knowledge leaves you free to follow your heart. You just need to figure out where it wants to go.

Oliver Burkeman, author of *Four Thousand Weeks: Time Management for Mortals*, observes that a typical human life expectancy works out, very roughly, to four thousand weeks. That's the amount of lifetime each of us can reasonably expect to have.

Meantime, we live in a world of what he calls "infinite inputs." In other words, "Emails or work or demands from the boss. Small businesses you want to launch. Things you want to initiate. Family obligations. Bucket list destinations. There's no end to any of those. We have the capacity to imagine infinite possibilities. And yet here we are with — if we're lucky — roughly four thousand weeks of time. So there's a lack of fit between the goal and the reality right from the start."

Contemplating this reality could be very depressing, especially if, like me, you've already used up a substantial portion of your allotted four thousand weeks. But, Burkeman said, it can also be very liberating and even empowering: "When you stop fighting that impossible battle, you can drop back down to reality and get going on a few things that really do matter."

What Matters to You?

What are those few things for you? I have no idea, and neither does anyone else except you, because the answer to that question is different for each of us. The problem, or at least part of the problem, is that the world is filled with people who will tell you with great confidence what the most important things in your life should be. There is so much competing advice out there about what really matters that it's impossible to follow it all. In chapter 16, I mentioned Bronnie Ware, a nurse who worked with dying patients in their last few weeks and often asked them if they had any regrets about their lives. She distilled their answers into a blog post about the top regrets of the dying, and the second item on her list is "I wish I hadn't worked so hard." She said that she heard this regret from every single one of her male patients. Follow that logic and you might conclude that throwing too much of yourself into your career could be a mistake.

But on the other hand, women only a few years older than me chafed under the expectation that the moment they had a husband, or perhaps a husband and a child, they would set their careers aside for the more important job of housekeeping and child-rearing. It was an expectation that caused misery for many generations of capable women who wanted meaningful careers but weren't allowed to pursue them. The idea that career is ultimately unimportant and family is the only thing that matters didn't work for them, and it definitely doesn't work for me.

Then, some people will tell you that your health should be your top priority, since you won't be able to do anything else well if you lose it, and that makes a lot of sense. A healthy body is definitely among the things just about everyone should want. But how you achieve that and how much you set aside other goals in order to make time for things like exercise and cooking healthy meals and getting enough sleep is a conundrum that few people I know have solved.

Once, I was at a writers' event where I heard a speaker, the author of a book about making dinner, argue that it truly is important to eat a home-cooked meal every night, and what she said made a lot of sense. Listening to her, I started thinking about how to rearrange my life so as to cook dinner at home more often.

And that's how they get you. She was right, of course — there is a lot of value to preparing a home-cooked meal for your family. But there's also great value in taking a walk with your partner or spouse, reading a book (which has proven brain benefits), playing a game with your kids, or even just relaxing in front of the television at the end of a working day, because we all need some time to turn off all our concerns and just relax. Every worthwhile thing you decide you want means giving up another worthwhile thing you also want. Believing otherwise is a mental trap I fall into all the time, and I bet you do too.

But all this overload might be a good thing in a way because no matter what you do, you will fail when measured against at least one of these frameworks. You won't do everything right because, as Burkeman would say, it's mathematically impossible.

Which brings me back to Bronnie Ware and "Regrets of the Dying." The number one regret on her list is this: "I wish I'd had the courage to live a life true to myself, not the life others expected of me." She wrote that this was the regret she heard most often from dying people.

This seems like vital information. It tells us that we all have a job to do, and it's an urgent one: find a way to silence all the voices about what we're supposed to care about most and figure out what we actually do care about most.

The fictional detective Nero Wolfe is highly sought after for his uncanny ability to solve crimes, but what he cares about most is his orchid collection. In the mystery *The Red Box*, he's persuaded to take on a case after being given a letter signed by six of the nation's top seven orchid growers asking him to do so. Wolfe has such disdain for the seventh grower that if he'd also signed the letter, the detective would have refused. ("He splits bulbs!" Wolfe says.)

This kind of thing is entertaining only because it's all too real. Most of us know people whose desires and priorities seem very far removed from our own ideas about what matters most. If you've never met anyone like that, spend an afternoon at a Star Trek convention or a coin collectors' event, and I promise you will.

The challenge for all of us is to find the thing that's as important to us as Wolfe's orchids are to him and then fill our lives with it, whatever it is and whatever anyone else may think. That, I suspect, is why we're all so fascinated with Steve Jobs. Not just because he created what would become the most valuable company in the world. Not just because nearly all of us have products in our homes and our pockets that either were made by his company or copy its designs and ideas. But because he did exactly what Ware's patients wished they had done — he lived a life true to himself and not at all what others expected of him. After his parents scrimped to send him to college, he dropped out, then sat in on a calligraphy class. He took LSD and traveled to India on a spiritual quest, returning with a shaved head and wearing traditional Indian clothing. He ate mostly fruit. At Apple, he was famous for parking in handicapped spots, for no apparent reason other than his own convenience.

And, yes, he absolutely found the thing that he loved. In 2005, he gave a now-famous commencement speech at Stanford where he talked about being ousted from Apple after a power struggle with then CEO John Sculley. "At 30 I was out. And very publicly out. What had been the focus of my entire adult life was gone, and it was devastating," he said. Eventually, though, he decided to return to the world of high tech. "Something slowly began to dawn on me — I still loved what I did. The turn of events at Apple had not changed that one bit. I had been rejected, but I was still in love." He went on to found the computer company NeXT and then returned to lead Apple in 1997.

When he made the speech, Jobs believed himself cured of the pancreatic cancer that would kill him six years later. It's safe to say he died with few regrets about anything, and certainly none about working too hard. He told the Stanford graduating class that he had lived his entire adult life with the goal of avoiding exactly those sorts of regrets.

"When I was 17, I read a quote that went something like: 'If you live each day as if it was your last, someday you'll most certainly be right.'" That quote made a big impression on him, he said, and since then he looked in the mirror every morning and asked himself, "If today were the last day of my life, would I want to do what I am about to do today?" Whenever the answer was no for too many days in a row, he knew it was time to change something.

Remembering that you're going to die one day is the best tool there is for helping you make important choices, he added. "All external expectations, all pride, all fear of embarrassment or failure — these things just fall away in the face of death, leaving only what is truly important.... You are already naked. There is no reason not to follow your heart."

If you follow your heart, where will it take you? And how can you know if that's the right direction to go? Asking yourself Jobs's daily question is a pretty good place to start.

EXERCISES TO TRY

1. Describe Yourself to a Stranger

Imagine you're sitting next to a stranger on a long train ride. The stranger asks, "Who are you?" They aren't looking for your name, but for you to say who you are, the things that you consider most important. Your answer can be as long as you want and can include whatever information you like.

Write down your answer. For each piece of information you include, ask yourself: *Am I happy with that?* If you aren't, ask yourself if there's anything you can do to change it.

2. Do a Should versus Want Review

Pick a workday from the past week. Grab your calendar and review the day. Remember as much of the day as you can, and ask yourself why you did each activity. There are three possible answers: because you wanted to, because it was expected of you, or because even though you may not have wanted to do it at that moment, you chose to do it in pursuit of something you wanted. Did you eat oatmeal for breakfast because you enjoy it or because it was expected of you? Or did you eat oatmeal instead of the donut you wanted because your goal is to feel and be healthy?

Do this exercise over a few days, and compare the activities you did because they were expected of you to the ones you wanted to do and to those you did in pursuit of a goal. Try to be as accurate as you can. This may give you some information about what you really want to do, as opposed to what you think you're supposed to do.

Chapter 22

It's Your Job to Make Yourself Happy

Years ago, I interviewed the late writer Daylle Deanna Schwartz about her new ebook, *How Do I Love Me? Let Me Count the Ways*, which she was giving away for free. Schwartz was one of those writers I admired quite a bit and was also slightly envious of. She'd written more than a dozen books, some of them with fun titles such as *All Men Are Jerks — Until Proven Otherwise*. She'd made a mark for herself in the music industry because she'd been a teacher and when some of her grade school students insisted a white woman like her couldn't be a rapper, she decided to prove them wrong. She was a successful speaker, something I was trying to be, and she was absolutely fearless.

Schwartz talked about ways that we all could and should work to make ourselves happy, from eliminating toxic people from our lives to taking a pledge to do something nice for ourselves every day for a month. She told me that she didn't normally eat sugar but had recently taken great delight in eating a package of Twinkies. She talked about accepting yourself just as you are and about choosing the same upscale brands of things like coffee or soap for yourself that you would if you were buying them as gifts for a friend. "Every time you use it, it's a reminder that you're worth more," she said.

The column I wrote from our interview is titled "11 Simple Ways to Make Yourself Happy Every Day," and I think it has been viewed more than any other column I've written. It's been seven years since it was published, but month after month, thousands of people read it. Most of them seem to have found the piece through Google, and I love this. It suggests that lots of people out there are searching phrases like "how to make myself happy" or "how to be happy." Those people are on the right track. So long as you don't harm anyone else, it's your job to make yourself as happy as you can possibly be.

I realize this is very predictable advice in a book that has "self-care" in its title. But whether your chief concern is your own happiness, the happiness of those around you, or even making the world a better place, it's still great advice to follow.

"Robert Louis Stevenson wrote, 'There is no duty we so much underrate as the duty of being happy,'" said Gretchen Rubin, author of *The Happiness Project* and *Happier at Home*, among other books. I interviewed her because she has studied happiness and its value perhaps more than anyone else in the world. "I thought about this a lot," she said. "What does it mean to have a duty to be happier?"

In a world full of suffering and injustice, some people might think trying to make yourself happy is inexcusably selfish and possibly amoral. But that's the wrong way to look at it, she explained. People who are unhappy may be defensive and isolated. "In fact, research shows that happier people are more interested in the problems of other people and the problems of the world. They're more likely to vote, they're more likely to volunteer, and they may give away more money. They have healthier habits. They make better team members and better leaders. They're more patient, they have a better sense of perspective, and a better sense of humor." Seeking happiness truly is a win-win proposition.

So how do you become happy? Hunting down happiness is more difficult than it might seem, partly because, research has shown, most of us are really bad at knowing beforehand what will and won't make us happy. In fact, Oliver Burkeman argues, the best way to find happiness is not to aim for it at all, because if you do, you likely won't get there. "You do have a responsibility, but it's to meaning," he said. "If you get that right, something like happiness, more often than not, might come along for the ride."

I think Burkeman is onto something here. Not that it's pointless to seek happiness — I think it's certainly worthwhile to try — but that the key to happiness may lie in living a meaningful life, whatever that is to you. In the search for happiness, pay attention to what brings meaning to your life, whether it's taking care of your family, doing what you consider to be important work, or even growing rare orchids like Nero Wolfe.

Beyond looking for meaning, there are some other powerful things you can do that can lead to a happier life.

1. Be Generous

A fascinating experiment, conducted by researchers from Simon Fraser University in British Columbia, showed that it truly is better to give than to receive and that money actually can buy happiness — if you spend it on someone else. In the experiment, participants were given an envelope containing either $5 or $20 and a note instructing them either to spend the money on themselves that day, or else spend it on either a gift for someone else or a charitable contribution. When researchers followed up with those subjects later that evening, those who'd spent the money on gifts or charity were measurably happier than those who'd spent it on themselves, even though there had been no such difference before the experiment began.

Humans are profoundly social creatures, deeply connected to one another whether we realize it or not. Most of us instinctively know that being kind or generous to others makes us feel good, but we may not realize how powerful that effect is.

2. Step Outside Your Comfort Zone

One way to make yourself happy that Rubin said surprised her is to try new things and "stretch" yourself, rather than stick with what you do well. "I'm somebody who thought familiarity and mastery would make me happier," she said. You would think, especially at work, that doing something you know how to do well and knowing you're doing a really good job would lead to the most happiness. But that's not how it is, she said. "The research is very compelling. It shows that people are made happier with novelty and challenge, even though a lot of times, when we have novelty and challenge, we might feel insecure. We might feel frustrated or stupid or inefficient. We might feel scared. But when we get through these things, we feel this feeling of growth that's so important to happiness."

This is why Rubin, who writes rules and mottos for herself in different situations, uses this rule, especially when making important decisions: "Choose the bigger life."

Choosing the bigger life can mean different things to different people in different situations. But it usually entails trying something new, taking some sort of risk, and possibly making a fool of yourself. All of this was in play when I went to the singing workshop described in chapter 15. I was somewhat uncertain before I did it, but beyond all doubt, it made me happier.

3. Don't Let Happiness Be Conditional

"People have kind of this tomorrow policy where they think, 'I'll be happy *once*,' or 'I'll be happy *if*,'" Rubin said. You know the kind of thing: I'll be happy once I lose twenty pounds. I'll be happy if my spouse gets a new job. I'll be happy once I get married.

That kind of thinking rarely works, Rubin said. "What the research shows is that typically when those things happen, they don't really give us the happiness boost that we anticipated ahead of time." For one thing, as we get nearer to meeting one of these goals, our thinking adjusts to take it as a given, she explained. By the time we get there, we're already hanging our happiness on another conditional event, such as when our spouse gets a promotion or when we have a baby. Thus, happiness becomes a destination at which we never actually arrive.

But even if that doesn't happen, even if finishing school or getting that promotion or finally finding the right partner really will make you happier, putting happiness off is making very poor use of your limited time on this planet. As you're pursuing goals that will eventually give you a better life, ask yourself: *What can I do to make myself happier today? Like right this minute?* It could be taking a nap or talking with a friend or going out dancing or something as simple as soaking in a hot bath. Whatever it is, go get it if you can. Happiness is a habit. And the more you get in that habit, the more you exercise your happiness muscle, the happier you'll be later on, whether or not the thing you've been waiting for comes true.

4. Don't Be Afraid of Happiness

Why would anyone be afraid of happiness? A lot of people are, including me at one time. I was frightened that happiness equals complacency, that if I let myself be happy or took any pleasure in my own accomplishments, I would stop trying so hard. I would lose my edge. Wendy Capland patiently talked me through this during an entire coaching session, explaining that I could simultaneously be both completely satisfied with the career and the life I already had and completely driven to achieve more.

I know I'm not the only one to fear happiness in this way, so I asked Rubin about it. "An old boss of mine once said that ambitious people can never be happy because part of ambition was never being satisfied," she said. "I think that's a false choice. You can be ambitious and looking forward, and work on your happiness as well." False choices like these can be very comforting, she said, because they allow you to disregard whole areas of your life.

If you believe happiness is bad for you, as I once did, it can be an excuse to go ahead and be miserable. You don't have to make the effort — and it does take effort — to deal with the things that might be dragging you down. But pitting happiness against ambition isn't just a false choice — it's the opposite of true. When you're happier, you're more energetic and more confident. You're more likely to put yourself out there and take the kinds of risks that can advance your career. Being happier makes you a better boss and a better employee. Other people are drawn to happiness, so it can help you when you're trying to land a sale or make a pitch or go after a promotion. If you make yourself happier, you might be surprised to find you've made yourself more successful as well.

And that's the whole point of this book. The notion that a successful career and a happy life are somehow at odds with each other is one of the most destructive myths plaguing us today. You may not be able to "have it all," whatever that means. But you can have this: a satisfying work life, career success, ambition and growth, and a life outside work where you care for yourself and your loved ones. All those things really matter, and you are entitled to all of them.

EXERCISES TO TRY

1. Make a Happiness List

Five years ago, when my career was going well but I wasn't feeling much joy in my life, Capland challenged me to do this exercise, and I'm glad I did. Make a list of all the things that bring you happiness, which could be anything from horseback riding (which was on my list) to talking to your kids to baking a cake to reading mystery novels. Now see how many of these things you can fit into your daily or weekly life. It's like the most fun to-do list ever.

2. Try a Random Act of Kindness

The classic random act of kindness is to pay for the car behind you at a toll booth or drive-through restaurant. In one spectacular such occurrence in December 2020, nine hundred drivers in Brainerd, Minnesota, each paid for the meal of the car behind them at a Dairy Queen, creating a chain of random acts that lasted until the store closed for the evening, when the final driver donated $10 to restart the process the following day. It continued for two and a half days.

Random acts can be anything from picking up litter to putting a candy bar in your mailbox for the letter carrier to find. Do whatever makes you happy, because after all, that's the whole point.

3. Wish Others Well

This exercise is something Chade-Meng Tan recommends for everyone, and one that he says will ultimately add to your own success. Begin by silently wishing success and happiness to the people you know and like whenever you see them. Once you have that down, expand it to acquaintances, like the person serving you behind the deli counter. Over time, expand this to include people you don't know at all, like the drivers of other cars on the highway, and eventually even to people you don't like.

The idea is to create a mental habit so that whenever you see anyone, your first instinct is to wish them well. "The people you meet will pick this up unconsciously," he explained. That will help you do better at your job. But the real benefit is to your own state of mind, because wishing happiness to others automatically makes you happier as well. Try it and you'll see.

Epilogue

One Small Thing

So here we are, at the end of the book. I feel as if I've flooded you with ideas and approaches and exercises. Are you wondering where to begin putting any of it into practice? Start anywhere you like. But do me a favor: start small.

I'm a real believer in the idea that the smaller your first step, the greater your odds of success. I think this because I've seen it work that way many, many times, both for myself and others. So please don't do a lot all at once. Just pick one small thing that appeals to you, that feels natural to you, and try it out tomorrow. Today, if you can.

If it's helpful and it becomes a habit — great! You can stop there, or you can try adding something else. If it doesn't work for you or doesn't make you happy — fine! Drop it and try something else.

All I ask is that you keep trying new things, keep experimenting, and stay curious. Don't let fear or inertia stop you. In this fun, crazy, scary, dazzling world we live in, you have to keep trying new things because what worked yesterday probably won't work next week. It might not even work five minutes from now. So try something — anything. Then, if you like, come find me at www.mindazetlin.com, email me at minda@mindazetlin.com, or message me on LinkedIn or Twitter (@MindaZetlin). And let me know how it goes.

Acknowledgments

This book began with a title, *Career Self-Care*, that managed to perfectly capture the concepts I've dived into in a decade of writing my Inc.com column. That title, and all the inspiration that came with it, was a gift from my agent Janet Rosen of Sheree Bykofsky Associates. Without Sheree and Janet, I might never have published any books at all.

Thanks to everyone at New World Library, especially Georgia Hughes and Kristen Cashman, and to Judith Riotto. It makes a huge difference to a writer when her editors really get what she's trying to say and have good ideas about how to say it better.

Huge thanks to Laura Lorber, Graham Winfrey, Scott Omelianuk, and everyone at Inc.com and *Inc.* magazine, as well as my columnist colleagues, especially Bill Murphy Jr. You all are the smartest people I know.

Thanks to the American Society of Journalists and Authors (ASJA), my tribe for more than twenty-five years. So much of the work I've done has resulted from connections made through

ASJA that I can't imagine what my career would have been like without it.

Thanks to the early readers of this book, especially Cindy Ferraro and Vanna Le, who made me feel like I was on the right track. Thanks also to the hundreds of early subscribers to my daily texts, the first audience for many of the themes and ideas that turned into this book.

And finally, thanks always to my husband Bill Pfleging, who always provides wild ideas, dinners, endless cups of coffee, and even more endless love and support.

Notes

Chapter 1: Taking Care of Yourself Is a Radical Act

p. 3   *"I'm going to work harder"*: Interview with Brad Willis (aka Bhava Ram) for Minda Zetlin, "This 5-Minute Exercise Will Make You a Better Leader," Inc.com, June 5, 2014, https://www.inc.com/minda-zetlin /this-five-minute-exercise-will-make-you-a-better-leader.html.

p. 5   *"for fear the station will stop sending me"*: Brad Willis (aka Bhava Ram), *Warrior Pose: How Yoga (Literally) Saved My Life* (Dallas: Benbella Books, 2013), 46.

p. 6   *"They taught me more about the world"*: Willis, Warrior Pose, xviii.

p. 6   *"I have to push forward"*: Willis, Warrior Pose, 44.

p. 10   *Show Your Worth*: Shelmina Babai Abji, *Show Your Worth: 8 Intentional Strategies for Women to Emerge as Leaders at Work* (New York: McGraw-Hill, 2022).

Chapter 2: The Disappearing Line between Life and Work

p. 20   *the mere expectation that employees check their email*: William J. Becker et al., *Killing Me Softly: Organizational E-mail Monitoring Expectations' Impact on Employee and Significant Other Well-Being*, Virginia Tech, December 12, 2019, vtechworks.lib.vt.edu/handle/10919/96394.

p. 22   *"With every passing year"*: Caroline McHugh, "The Art of Being Yourself," TEDxMiltonKeynesWomen, Milton Keynes, United Kingdom, December 2, 2012, https://www.youtube.com/watch?v=veEQQ-N9xWU.

p. 22   *more than 15 million self-employed people*: Rakesh Kochhar, "The Self-Employed Are Back at Work in Pre-COVID-19 Numbers, but Their Businesses Have Smaller Payrolls," Pew Research Center, November 3, 2021, https://www.pewresearch.org/fact-tank/2021/11/03/the-self-employed-are-back-at-work-in-pre-covid-19-numbers-but-their-businesses-have-smaller-payrolls.

p. 23   *"Leaders are owners"*: "Leadership Principles," Amazon Jobs, https://www.amazon.jobs/en/principles.

p. 24   *people who work sixty hours a week*: John Pencavel and the Institute for the Study of Labor (Bonn, Germany), *The Productivity of Working Hours*, discussion paper no. 8129, April 2014, https://ftp.iza.org/dp8129.pdf.

p. 24   *multiple other studies have had similar results*: Ron Friedman, "Working Too Hard Makes Leading More Difficult," *Harvard Business Review*, December 30, 2014, https://hbr.org/2014/12/working-too-hard-makes-leading-more-difficult.

p. 26   *"Everybody struggles with work-life balance"*: Interview with Wendy Capland for Minda Zetlin, "7 Secrets to Solving the Work-Life Balance Conundrum," Inc.com, June 29, 2015, https://www.inc.com/minda-zetlin/7-secrets-to-solving-the-work-life-balance-conundrum.html.

Chapter 3: What If You Showed Up at Work as Yourself?

p. 31   *a scathing exposé*: Jodi Kantor and David Streitfeld, "Inside Amazon: Wrestling Big Ideas in a Bruising Workplace," *New York Times*, August 15, 2015, https://www.nytimes.com/2015/08/16/technology/inside-amazon-wrestling-big-ideas-in-a-bruising-workplace.html.

p. 31   *"Strive to Be Earth's Best Employer"*: "Leadership Principles," Amazon Jobs, https://www.amazon.jobs/en/principles.

p. 36   *she had a calf who died shortly after birth*: Lynda V. Mapes, "Tahlequah, the Orca Who Carried Her Dead Calf for 17 Days, Is Pregnant Again," *Seattle Times*, July 27, 2020, https://www.seattletimes.com/seattle-news/environment/tahlequah-the-orca-who-carried-her-dead-calf-for-17-days-is-pregnant-again.

p. 37   *"I was coming out as a gay Black man"*: All David McKnight quotes in this chapter are from an interview for Minda Zetlin, "Why You Need to

Be Your Real Self at Work," Inc.com, March 18, 2014, https://www.inc
.com/minda-zetlin/why-you-need-to-put-your-real-self-in-your
-professional-image.html.

p. 39   *"Consider emotions as simply physiological sensations"*: Interview with
Chade-Meng Tan for Minda Zetlin, "How to Be Happier at Work: 3
Tips," Inc.com, May 22, 2012, https://www.inc.com/minda-zetlin
/how-to-be-happier-more-calm-googles-happiness-guru.html.

Chapter 4: The Power of Journaling

p. 42   *his invention: the bullet journal*: Ryder Carroll, Bullet Journal free video
tutorial, https://bulletjournal.com/pages/learn.

p. 49   *for better retention and comprehension*: Cindi May, "A Learning Secret:
Don't Take Notes with a Laptop," *Scientific American*, June 3, 2014,
https://www.scientificamerican.com/article/a-learning-secret-don-t
-take-notes-with-a-laptop.

p. 51   *one-sentence journaling*: Gretchen Rubin, "Why I Started Keeping
a Daily 'One-Sentence Journal' (Ok, a Not-Quite Daily Journal),"
Gretchen Rubin (blog), August 6, 2007, https://gretchenrubin.com
/2007/08/why-i-started-k.

Chapter 5: Who's Your Tribe?

p. 55   *Blue Zones*: Dan Buettner, "The Secrets of Long Life," *National Geographic*, November 2005, www.bluezones.com/wp-content/uploads
/2015/01/Nat_Geo_LongevityF.pdf.

p. 56   *social isolation and loneliness*: "Social Isolation, Loneliness in Older
People Pose Health Risks," National Institute on Aging, April 23, 2019,
https://www.nia.nih.gov/news/social-isolation-loneliness-older-people
-pose-health-risks.

p. 56   *early humans who lived in groups*: Jennifer Evans, "Groups Are the
Driving Force of Human Evolution, Wilson Says," Rice University,
News and Media Relations, Office of Public Affairs, April 6, 2012,
news2.rice.edu/2012/04/06/groups-are-the-driving-force-of-human
-evolution-wilson-says.

p. 58   *Wendy Capland*: All Wendy Capland quotes in this chapter are from
an interview for Minda Zetlin, "The Career-Boosting Technique Even
Smart People Don't Know," Inc.com, July 8, 2020, https://www.inc.com
/minda-zetlin/career-success-advice-networking-mentorship.html.

Chapter 6: How to Have a Conversation
with Anyone, Anywhere, Anytime

p. 69   *"He that has once done you a kindness"*: All Benjamin Franklin quotes
in this chapter are from "Poor Richard's Almanac and Other Activities,"
chap. 10 in *Autobiography of Benjamin Franklin* (New York: Henry
Holt, 1916), Project Gutenberg edition, https://www.gutenberg.org
/files/20203/20203-h/20203-h.htm.

p. 70   *the Ben Franklin effect is a result of cognitive dissonance*: Shana
Lebowitz and Weng Cheong, "Harness the Power of the 'Ben Franklin
Effect' to Get Someone to Like You," Insider, updated July 3, 2020,
https://www.businessinsider.com/ben-franklin-effect-2016-12.

p. 70   *a very clever car salesman*: Jeff Haden, "How to Use the Franklin
Effect to Repair and Build Stronger Bonds," Inc.com, June 8, 2020,
https://www.inc.com/jeff-haden/how-to-use-franklin-effect-to-repair
-build-stronger-bonds.html.

p. 71   *even when people know perfectly well*: Piercarlo Valdesolo, "Flattery
Will Get You Far," *Scientific American*, January 12, 2010, https://www
.scientificamerican.com/article/flattery-will-get-you-far.

p. 73   *Their feet are another clue*: Joe Navarro, "The Feet and Legs — A
Nonverbal Primer," Joe Navarro Body Language, March 22, 2019, https://
www.jnforensics.com/post/the-feet-and-legs-a-nonverbal-primer.

p. 74   *they instructed some commuters*: Nicholas Epley and Juliana Schroeder,
"Mistakenly Seeking Solitude," *Journal of Experimental Psychology:
General 143, no. 5 (July 2014)*, https://www.researchgate.net/publication
/263899201_Mistakenly_Seeking_Solitude.

Chapter 7: Dealing with Toxic People

p. 81   *"Narcissists are running the world"*: All Judith Orloff quotes in this
chapter are from an interview for Minda Zetlin, "5 Toughest Personalities at Work — and How to Manage Them," Inc.com, May 5, 2014,
https://www.inc.com/minda-zetlin/how-to-lead-the-5-toughest
-employees.html.

p. 82   *participants were paired up in two-person teams*: Carl Vogel, "A Field
Guide to Narcissism," *Psychology Today*, January 1, 2006, https://www
.psychologytoday.com/us/articles/200601/field-guide-narcissism.

p. 82   *"Studies have shown narcissists are willing to sacrifice"*: Vogel, "A Field
Guide to Narcissism."

p. 82   *It's management orthodoxy*: Roddy Millar, "Here's Why Being Likable
May Make You a Less Effective Leader," *Fast Company*, January 12,

2020, https://www.fastcompany.com/90450649/heres-why-being
-likable-may-not-make-you-a-more-effective-leader.

p. 89   *Sherman has identified some habits*: Jeremy E. Sherman, "10 Typical
Habits of the Most Toxic People," *Psychology Today*, April 21, 2019,
https://www.psychologytoday.com/us/blog/ambigamy/201904/10
-typical-habits-the-most-toxic-people.

Chapter 8: How to Thrive (or at Least Survive) in an Unequal World

p. 94   *"My name is Dorothy"*: "Tootsie — My Name Is Dorothy," clip from the
film *Tootsie*, directed by Sidney Pollack (1982), https://www.youtube
.com/watch?v=Ch57pIuYhbM.

p. 94   *an interview Dustin Hoffman gave*: American Film Institute interview,
"Dustin Hoffman on TOOTSIE and His Character Dorothy Michaels,"
2012, https://www.youtube.com/watch?v=xPAat-T1uhE.

p. 95   *Michelle and Barack Obama's twin memoirs*: Barack Obama, *A
Promised Land* (New York: Crown, 2020), chap. 10; Michelle Obama,
Becoming (New York: Crown, 2018), chap. 21.

p. 96   *Studies show that unpaid labor*: Gus Wezerek and Kristen R. Ghodsee,
"Women's Unpaid Labor Is Worth $10,900,000,000,000," *New York
Times*, March 5, 2020, https://www.nytimes.com/interactive/2020
/03/04/opinion/women-unpaid-labor.html.

p. 96   *"This means, on average, women do seven years more"*: Melinda Gates,
The Moment of Lift: How Empowering Women Changes the World (New
York: Flatiron Books, 2019), 118.

p. 96   *the disproportionate burden on women*: Eleni X. Karageorge, "COVID-
19 Recession Is Tougher on Women," US Bureau of Labor Statistics,
Monthly Labor Review, September 2020, https://www.bls.gov/opub
/mlr/2020/beyond-bls/covid-19-recession-is-tougher-on-women.htm.

p. 96   *the number of jobs lost by women*: Claire Ewing-Nelson, "All of the
Jobs Lost in December Were Women's Jobs," National Women's Law
Center, Fact Sheet, January 2021, nwlc.org/wp-content/uploads/2021
/01/December-Jobs-Day.pdf.

p. 97   *women earned just over 77 cents*: "The Wage Gap Over Time: In Real
Dollars, Women See a Continuing Gap," National Committee on Pay
Equity, 2020 Fact Sheet, https://www.pay-equity.org/info-time.html.

p. 97   *for Black women, that number is a depressing 63 cents*: Sharon Epperson,
"Black Women Make Nearly $1 Million Less Than White Men during
Their Careers," CNBC.com, August 3, 2021, https://www.cnbc.com
/2021/08/03/black-women-make-1-million-less-than-white-men-during
-their-careers.html.

p. 97   *"I'm simply stating that the distribution of preferences and abilities"*: Kara Swisher, "Google Has Hired a Diversity VP — Just as It Struggles with a Sexist Memo from an Employee," Vox, August 5, 2017, https://www .vox.com/2017/8/5/16102476/google-diversity-vp-employee-memo [includes full text of James Damore memo].

p. 98   *women weren't being welcomed into high-tech jobs*: Alison T. Wynn and Shelley J. Correll, "Puncturing the Pipeline: Do Technology Companies Alienate Women in Recruiting Sessions?" *Social Studies of Science* 48, no. 1 (February 9, 2018), https://journals.sagepub.com/doi /pdf/10.1177/0306312718756766.

p. 98   *There's emotional labor*: Gemma Hartley, "Women Aren't Nags — We're Just Fed Up," *Harper's Bazaar*, September 27, 2017, https://www .harpersbazaar.com/culture/features/a12063822/emotional-labor -gender-equality/.

p. 98   *There's the pink tax*: Amy Fontinelle, "Pink Tax," Investopedia, May 27, 2021, https://www.investopedia.com/pink-tax-5095458.

p. 98   *women are more likely than men to be seriously injured*: Keith Barry, "The Crash Test Bias: How Male-Focused Testing Puts Female Drivers at Risk," *Consumer Reports*, October 2019, https://www.consumer reports.org/car-safety/crash-test-bias-how-male-focused-testing-puts -female-drivers-at-risk.

p. 99   *the distinction between line areas and staff areas*: "Staff versus Line Function," Community Colleges of Spokane, MMGT 231 lecture, Summer 2013, https://ccs.instructure.com/courses/833187/pages/lecture -1-dot-2-staff-vs-line-functions.

p. 101 *women ask for raises just as often as men*: Benjamin Artz, Amanda Goodall, and Andrew J. Oswald, "Research: Women Ask for Raises as Often as Men, but Are Less Likely to Get Them," *Harvard Business Review*, June 25, 2018, https://hbr.org/2018/06/research-women-ask -for-raises-as-often-as-men-but-are-less-likely-to-get-them.

p. 101 *when women ask for more money*: Tara Siegel Bernard, "Moving Past Gender Barriers to Negotiate a Raise," *New York Times*, March 24, 2014, https://www.nytimes.com/2014/03/25/your-money/moving -past-gender-barriers-to-negotiate-a-raise.html.

p. 101 *women only apply for a job*: Tara Sophia Mohr, "Why Women Don't Apply for Jobs Unless They're 100% Qualified," *Harvard Business Review*, August 25, 2014, https://hbr.org/2014/08/why-women-dont -apply-for-jobs-unless-theyre-100-qualified.

p. 101 *"If you decided not to apply for a job"*: Mohr, "Why Women Don't Apply for Jobs."

p. 102 *women applied to 20 percent fewer jobs*: Deanne Tockey and Maria

Ignatova, *Gender Insights Report: How Women Find Jobs Differently*, LinkedIn Talent Solutions, https://business.linkedin.com/content/dam/me/business/en-us/talent-solutions-lodestone/body/pdf/Gender-Insights-Report.pdf.

p. 103   *"job hunt like a man"*: Jody Allard, "I Job Hunted Like a Man. Here's What Happened," The Lily, May 2, 2018, https://www.thelily.com/i-job-hunted-like-a-man-heres-what-happened.

p. 105   *"I was always told that I'd have to work twice as hard"*: All Jessica Eggert quotes in this chapter are from an interview for Minda Zetlin, "Parental Leave Is Great, but Returning to Work Still Sucks: Here's How Employers Can Make It Better," GeekWire, November 27, 2019, https://www.geekwire.com/2019/parental-leave-great-returning-work-still-sucks-heres-employers-can-make-better.

p. 106   *VC investments that went to women-led start-ups*: Kate Clark, "US VC Investment in Female Founders Hits All-Time High," TechCrunch, December 9, 2019, https://techcrunch.com/2019/12/09/us-vc-investment-in-female-founders-hits-all-time-high.

p. 106   *thanks to the pandemic and the resulting economic crisis*: Gené Teare, "Global VC Funding to Female Founders Dropped Dramatically This Year," Crunchbase, December 21, 2020, https://news.crunchbase.com/news/global-vc-funding-to-female-founders.

p. 106   *Black female founders*: Emma Hinchliffe, "The Number of Black Female Founders Who Have Raised More Than $1 Million Has Nearly Tripled Since 2018," *Fortune*, December 2, 2020, https://fortune.com/2020/12/02/black-women-female-founders-venture-capital-funding-vc-2020-project-diane.

p. 107   *"I can be tricked by anyone who looks like Mark Zuckerberg"*: Nathaniel Rich, "Silicon Valley's Start-Up Machine," *New York Times*, May 2, 2013, https://www.nytimes.com/2013/05/05/magazine/y-combinator-silicon-valleys-start-up-machine.html.

p. 107   *investors who backed start-ups led by women*: Katie Abouzahr et al., "Why Women-Owned Startups Are a Better Bet," Boston Consulting Group, June 6, 2018, https://www.bcg.com/publications/2018/why-women-owned-startups-are-better-bet.

p. 108   *a highly unpleasant incident at a cocktail party*: Maya Guzdar, "What Happened the Day After I Was Sexually Harassed at the Pentagon," *New York Times*, September 5, 2021, https://www.nytimes.com/2021/09/05/opinion/culture/sexually-harassed-pentagon.html.

p. 109   *Women working in the Obama White House*: Juliet Eilperin, "White House Women Want to Be in the Room Where It Happens," *Washington Post*, September 13, 2016, https://www.washingtonpost.com

/news/powerpost/wp/2016/09/13/white-house-women-are-now-in
-the-room-where-it-happens.

p. 109   *a lengthy account of being sexually harassed on the job*: Susan Fowler,
"Reflecting on One Very, Very Strange Year at Uber," *Susan Fowler*
(blog), February 19, 2017, https://www.susanjfowler.com/blog/2017/2
/19/reflecting-on-one-very-strange-year-at-uber.

p. 109   *sexual harassment in Silicon Valley*: Aimee Lucido, "Reflecting on
Susan Fowler's Reflections," *Aimee Lucido* (blog), February 20, 2017,
https://medium.com/@hadrad1000/reflecting-on-susan-fowlers
-reflections-e2dccb374b47.

Chapter 9: How to Get Mentored — and Sponsored (Which Is Just as Important)

p. 112   *97 percent of people with a mentor*: "Facts and Statistics," National
Mentoring Day, nationalmentoringday.org/facts-and-statistics.

p. 112   *Sun Microsystems decided to measure the effects of mentoring*: "Workplace Loyalties Change, but the Value of Mentoring Doesn't," Knowl-
edge@Wharton, May 16, 2007, https://knowledge.wharton.upenn.edu
/article/workplace-loyalties-change-but-the-value-of-mentoring-doesnt.

p. 112   *70 percent of new companies that had mentors*: "The UPS Store Makes
'Mentoring Month' Matter for Small Business Owners," The UPS Store,
January 9, 2014, https://www.theupsstore.com/about/pressroom/small
-business-mentoring-month-2014.

p. 112   *Lyle Stevens*: All Lyle Stevens quotes in this chapter are from an interview for Minda Zetlin, "Why the Smartest Entrepreneurs Have Multiple
Mentors," Inc.com, March 2, 2015, https://www.inc.com/minda-zetlin/
why-the-smartest-entrepreneurs-have-multiple-mentors.html.

p. 113   *"I was trying to figure out"*: All Paola Doebel quotes in this chapter are
from an interview, March 11, 2021.

p. 119   *you also need sponsors*: Interview with Daina Middleton for Minda
Zetlin, "1 Important Career Lesson You Can Learn from the Movie
'Hidden Figures,'" Inc.com, March 27, 2017, https://www.inc.com
/minda-zetlin/what-you-can-learn-about-sponsors-vs-mentors-from
-the-movie-hidden-figures.html.

Chapter 10: Why You Should Make Sure to Do What You Love

p. 129   *His own father "could have been a great comedian"*: "Jim Carrey at MIU:
Commencement Address at the 2014 Graduation," May 30, 2014,
https://www.youtube.com/watch?v=V80-gPkpH6M.

p. 129   *"If my career in show business hadn't panned out"*: Jim Holt, "It's All in the Numbers: Jim Carrey Could Be at Dofasco If Hollywood Hadn't Worked Out," *Hamilton Spectator*, February 26, 2007, 14.

p. 131 *The problem with "find your passion" is two-fold*: Olga Khazan, "'Find Your Passion' Is Awful Advice," *Atlantic*, July 12, 2018, https://www.theatlantic.com/science/archive/2018/07/find-your-passion-is-terrible-advice/564932.

p. 136 *the single most common reason people quit a full-time job*: Why They "Quit You" — Top Reasons an Employee Leaves, PayScale white paper, n.d., https://www.payscale.com/content/ebook/why-people-quit-their-jobs.pdf.

p. 137 *the 3.6 percent unemployment rate in 2019*: Kimberly Amadeo, "Unemployment Rate by Year Since 1929 Compared to Inflation and GDP," The Balance, November 10, 2021, https://www.thebalance.com/unemployment-rate-by-year-3305506.

p. 137 *unemployment hit a staggering 14.7 percent*: "Unemployment Rate Rises to Record High 14.7 Percent in April 2020," Bureau of Labor Statistics, TED: The Economics Daily, May 13, 2020, https://www.bls.gov/opub/ted/2020/unemployment-rate-rises-to-record-high-14-point-7-percent-in-april-2020.htm.

p. 137 *By November 2021, unemployment was down*: "The Employment Situation — November 2021," Bureau of Labor Statistics, news release, December 3, 2021, https://www.bls.gov/news.release/pdf/empsit.pdf.

Chapter 11: How to Reach Your Biggest Goals

p. 143 *"He was shaped by it and devoted to it"*: Brian Hiatt, "Jimmy Fallon's Big Adventure," *Rolling Stone,* January 20, 2011, https://www.rollingstone.com/music/music-news/jimmy-fallons-big-adventure-182204.

p. 144 *"Looking back on those years"*: James Clear, "Introduction: How I Learned about Habits," in *Atomic Habits: An Easy and Proven Way to Build Good Habits and Break Bad Ones* (New York: Avery, 2018), Kobo edition.

p. 147 *taking small steps is the best way*: BJ Fogg, introduction to *Tiny Habits: The Small Changes That Change Everything* (Boston: Houghton Mifflin Harcourt, 2020).

p. 156 *"The team started calling me 'Dr. Yes'"*: All Richard Branson quotes in this chapter are from an email interview, April 22, 2021.

p. 159 *"Years ago, I found myself declaring"*: All Wendy Capland quotes in this chapter are from an interview for Minda Zetlin, "One Simple Secret That Will Help You Reach Your Biggest Goals," Inc.com, January 14, 2016, https://www.inc.com/minda-zetlin/one-simple-secret-that-will-help-you-reach-your-biggest-goals.html.

p. 167 *"Even if I have no idea where I'm going"*: Quoted in Minda Zetlin, "Richard Branson Says This 1 Word Will Give You an Extraordinary Life," Inc.com, December 19, 2017, https://www.inc.com/minda-zetlin /richard-branson-says-this-1-word-will-give-you-an-extraordinary -life.html.

p. 172 *"conceptualized as an approach-avoidance conflict"*: Svenja Koletzko, Marcel Herrmann, and Veronika Brandstätter, "Unconflicted Goal Striving: Goal Ambivalence as a Mediator between Goal Self-Concordance and Well-Being," *Personality and Social Psychology Bulletin* 41, no. 1 (November 2014), https://www.researchgate.net/publication/268874843 _Unconflicted_Goal_Striving_Goal_Ambivalence_as_a_Mediator _Between_Goal_Self-Concordance_and_Well-Being.

p. 172 *people with goal ambivalence*: Svenja Koletzko, *Goal Ambivalence: Implications for Self-Regulation, Health, and Well-Being*, University of Zurich, 2015.

p. 175 *we spend, on average, thirteen years and two months*: Leigh Campbell, "We've Broken Down Your Entire Life into Years Spent Doing Tasks," HuffPost, October 18, 2017, https://www.huffpost.com/entry/weve -broken-down-your-entire-life-into-years-spent-doing-tasks_n_6108 7617e4b0999d2084fec5.

p. 178 *"Managing costs and maintaining things"*: From an interview with Patrick Meehan for Minda Zetlin, "Is IT Having an Identity Crisis?" Computerworld, May 2, 2017, https://www.computerworld.com /article/3191986/is-it-having-an-identity-crisis.html.

Chapter 14: The Dirty Little Secret about Success

p. 182 *what had really been going on at the company*: Spencer Soper, Matt Day, and Henry Goldman, "Behind Amazon's HQ2 Fiasco: Jeff Bezos Was Jealous of Elon Musk," Bloomberg, February 3, 2020, https://www .bloomberg.com/news/articles/2020-02-03/amazon-s-hq2-fiasco-was -driven-by-bezos-envy-of-elon-musk.

p. 188 *"Money is only a part"*: "Money Only Buys Happiness for a Certain Amount," Purdue University, news release, February 13, 2018, https://www.purdue.edu/newsroom/releases/2018/Q1/money-only -buys-happiness-for-a-certain-amount.html.

Chapter 15: How to Build Your Own Confidence

p. 195 *"It's not really about asking for the raise"*: Monica Nickelsburg, "Satya Nadella's 'Karma' Gaffe Was 'One of the Best Things That Ever Happened for Microsoft,' Says Former Board Member Who Was on Stage

with Him," GeekWire, June 16, 2019, https://www.geekwire.com/2019
/maria-klawe-satya-nadellas-gaffe-about-raises-for-women-was-one
-of-the-best-things-that-ever-happened-for-microsoft.

p. 199   *take a small step outside your comfort zone*: From an interview with
Becky Blalock for Minda Zetlin, "13 Ways to Teach Yourself to Be
More Confident," Inc.com, April 24, 2014, https://www.inc.com/minda
-zetlin/13-easy-ways-to-boost-your-confidence.html.

Chapter 16: Why You Have to Stop Working So Hard

p. 205   *"30 hours of work"*: Neetzan Zimmerman, "Copywriter Tweets about
Working 30 Hours Straight, Dies the Next Day," Gawker, December 17,
2013, https://www.gawker.com/copywriter-tweets-about-working-30
-hours-straight-dies-1485064911.

p. 206   *The resulting Inc.com column*: Minda Zetlin, "10 Reasons to Stop Working So Hard," Inc.com, January 29, 2014, https://www.inc.com/minda
-zetlin/10-reasons-you-have-to-stop-working-so-hard.html.

p. 206   *"So it's 2AM, Friday night"*: Mita Diran (@mitdoq), Twitter, October 25,
2013, https://twitter.com/mitdoq/status/393815102379417600.

p. 208   *eight hours of sleep isn't even enough*: Georgia Frances King, "Why
Eight Hours a Night Isn't Enough, according to a Leading Sleep Scientist," Quartz, June 18, 2018, https://qz.com/1301123/why-eight-hours
-a-night-isnt-enough-according-to-a-leading-sleep-scientist.

p. 208   *being awake for twenty-four hours*: "Get Sleep: What's in It for You?
Judgment and Safety," Harvard Medical School, December 16, 2008,
healthysleep.med.harvard.edu/need-sleep/whats-in-it-for-you
/judgment-safety.

p. 209   *cerebrospinal fluid washes through our brains*: Minda Zetlin, "Here's
How Sleep Removes Poisons from Your Brain, Protecting You from
Alzheimer's as Nothing Else Can," Inc.com, November 22, 2019,
https://www.inc.com/minda-zetlin/sleep-alzheimers-beta-amy-
loids-benefits-of-deep-sleep-boston-university-research.html.

p. 211   *"Regrets of the Dying"*: Bronnie Ware, "Regrets of the Dying," *Inspiration and Chai* (blog), web.archive.org/web/20100310205804/http://
www.inspirationandchai.com/Regrets-of-the-Dying.html.

Chapter 17: Why Your Relationships outside Work
Can Make Your Career

p. 217   *having a supportive spouse might affect your career*: Patrick Monahan,
"Supportive Relationships Linked to Willingness to Pursue Opportunities,"

Carnegie Mellon University, Dietrich College of Humanities and Social Sciences, news story, August 11, 2017, https://www.cmu.edu/dietrich /news/news-stories/2017/august/supportive-spouses-brooke-feeny.html.

p. 218   *"The thriving perspective posits that people must fully embrace life"*: Brooke C. Feeney et al., "Predicting the Pursuit and Support of Challenging Life Opportunities," *Personality and Social Psychology Bulletin* 43, no. 8 (June 2017), https://www.researchgate.net/profile/Brooke-Feeney /publication/317422706_Predicting_the_Pursuit_and_Support_of _Challenging_Life_Opportunities/links/59f37803aca272607e2 9133a/Predicting-the-Pursuit-and-Support-of-Challenging-Life -Opportunities.pdf.

Chapter 18: Making Work Work for Parents

p. 226   *a Harvard Business Review piece by Stanford professor Nicholas Bloom*: Nicholas Bloom, "Don't Let Employees Pick Their WFH Days," *Harvard Business Review*, May 25, 2021, https://hbr.org/2021/05/dont -let-employees-pick-their-wfh-days.

p. 227   *"Single young men could all choose"*: Bloom, "Don't Let Employees Pick Their WFH Days."

p. 228   *on the phone with Bloom*: Interview with Nicholas Bloom, June 23, 2021.

p. 231   *"People tell you all the time that those years are short"*: Interview with April Crichlow, June 30, 2021.

p. 233   *"Is there a solution or a magic wand?"*: Interview with Angela Ficken, June 22, 2021.

p. 235   *choose what you will fail at*: Interview with Oliver Burkeman, August 27, 2021.

Chapter 19: You Have a Brain — Here's How to Make the Most of It

p. 239   *"As the more junior person, I had to change my presentation"*: Interview with Josh Davis by Hitendra Wadhwa, "Josh Davis on Managing Your Time during a Global Pandemic," *Intersections*, episode 12, July 16, 2020, https://www.youtube.com/watch?v=W8cLyoYvoac.

p. 243   *here's what we do know*: Josh Davis, *Two Awesome Hours: Science-Based Strategies to Harness Your Best Time and Get Your Most Important Work Done* (San Francisco: HarperOne, 2015), Strategy 4: Leverage Your Mind-Body Connection.

p. 245   *people who spent an hour more a day moving*: "More Evidence That Exercise Can Boost Mood," Harvard Health Publishing, May 1, 2019,

https://www.health.harvard.edu/mind-and-mood/more-evidence-that
-exercise-can-boost-mood.

p. 246 *do some vigorous exercise*: Interview with Jenny Evans for Minda
Zetlin, "2 Easy Changes That Will Stress-Proof Your Brain," Inc.com,
November 14, 2014, https://www.inc.com/minda-zetlin/two-easy
-changes-that-will-stress-proof-your-brain.html.

p. 247 *"Now that I know this, I build it into my preparations"*: Interview with
Josh Davis for Minda Zetlin, "7 Simple Tweaks That Make Your Brain
Work Remarkably Well," Inc.com, July 28, 2015, https://www.inc.com
/minda-zetlin/7-simple-tweaks-that-make-your-brain-work-remarkably
-well.html.

p. 249 *"Detecting approaching people, animals, flying objects"*: Davis, *Two
Awesome Hours*, Strategy 3: Stop Fighting Distractions.

Chapter 20: How Mindfulness Can Help You in Work and Life

p. 254 *"Mindfulness is about the training of attention"*: Interview with Chade-
Meng Tan for Minda Zetlin, "How to Be Happier at Work: 3 Tips," Inc.
com, May 22, 2012, https://www.inc.com/minda-zetlin/how-to-be
-happier-more-calm-googles-happiness-guru.html.

p. 255 *"the main component of the parasympathetic nervous system"*: Sigrid
Breit et al., "Vagus Nerve as Modulator of the Brain–Gut Axis in Psy-
chiatric and Inflammatory Disorders," *Frontiers in Psychiatry* 9 (March
13, 2018), https://www.ncbi.nlm.nih.gov/pmc/articles/PMC5859128.

p. 255 *"In one regard we are very much like computers"*: Josh Davis, *Two Awe-
some Hours: Science-Based Strategies to Harness Your Best Time and Get
Your Most Important Work Done* (San Francisco: HarperOne, 2015),
Strategy 1: Recognize Your Decision Points.

p. 257 *it takes the average worker twenty-three minutes*: Kermit Pattison,
"Worker, Interrupted: The Cost of Task Switching," Fast Company, July
28, 2008, https://www.fastcompany.com/944128/worker-interrupted
-cost-task-switching.

p. 257 *"a gift has just occurred"*: Interview with Josh Davis by Hitendra
Wadhwa, "Josh Davis on Managing Your Time during a Global Pandemic," *Intersections*, episode 12, July 16, 2020, https://www.youtube
.com/watch?v=W8cLyoYvoac.

p. 259 *a Tibetan monk named Matthieu Ricard*: Alyson Shontell, "A 69-
Year-Old Monk Who Scientists Call the 'World's Happiest Man' Says
the Secret to Being Happy Takes Just 15 Minutes a Day," Insider, January 27, 2016, https://www.businessinsider.com/how-to-be-happier
-according-to-matthieu-ricard-the-worlds-happiest-man-2016-1.

p. 261 *"a positive emotion elicited when in the presence of vast things"*: Minda Zetlin, "Doing This for 15 Minutes a Week Will Make You Happier, New Study Shows," Inc.com, October 10, 2020, https://www.inc.com /minda-zetlin/awe-walks-happiness-gratitude-nature-well-being-brain -function.html.

Chapter 21: What Do You Really Want?

p. 265 *"I just want you to understand"*: Minda Zetlin, "What One Entrepreneur Learned from Working for Steve Jobs," Inc.com, November 11, 2014, https://www.inc.com/minda-zetlin/what-one-eager-entrepreneur -learned-from-working-for-steve-jobs.html.

p. 265 *"driven by demons"*: Walter Isaacson, *Steve Jobs* (New York: Simon & Schuster, 2011), xxi.

p. 265 *"When you grow up, you tend to get told"*: Silicon Valley Historical Association interview, "Steve Jobs [*sic*] Secrets of Life," 1994, https://www .youtube.com/watch?v=kYfNvmFoBqw.

p. 266 *"no longer meet my duties and expectations"*: "Letter from Steve Jobs," August 24, 2011, Apple.com, Newsroom, https://www.apple.com /newsroom/2011/08/24Letter-from-Steve-Jobs.

p. 266 *On the last full day of his life*: "Confirmed: Steve Jobs Worked on Apple Until His Last Day," *PC*, October 19, 2011, https://www.pcmag.com /archive/confirmed-steve-jobs-worked-on-apple-until-his-last-day-28 9344.

p. 266 *"At Facebook, we offer four months of maternity and paternity leave"*: Catherine Clifford, "Billionaire Facebook Founder Mark Zuckerberg Has Signed Off for the Month of December — to Go on Paternity Leave," CNBC.com, December 4, 2017, https://www.cnbc.com/2017/1 2/04/facebook-ceo-mark-zuckerberg-is-taking-off-december-as -paternity-leave.html.

p. 267 *Four Thousand Weeks*: Oliver Burkeman, *Four Thousand Weeks: Time Management for Mortals* (New York: Farrar, Straus and Giroux, 2021); interview with Oliver Burkeman, August 27, 2021.

p. 268 *"I wish I hadn't worked so hard"*: Bronnie Ware, "Regrets of the Dying," *Inspiration and Chai* (blog), web.archive.org/web/20100310205804 /http://www.inspirationandchai.com/Regrets-of-the-Dying.html.

p. 270 *"I wish I'd had the courage"*: Ware, "Regrets of the Dying."

p. 271 *"At 30 I was out"*: "'You've Got to Find What You Love,' Jobs Says," Stanford University, News, June 14, 2005, https://news.stanford. edu/2005/06/14/jobs-061505/ [text of Jobs's commencement address].

Chapter 22: It's Your Job to Make Yourself Happy

p. 274   *"Every time you use it"*: Interview with Daylle Deanna Schwartz for Minda Zetlin, "11 Simple Ways to Make Yourself Happy Every Day," Inc.com, June 10, 2014, https://www.inc.com/minda-zetlin/11-simple -ways-to-make-yourself-happy-every-day.html.

p. 274   *"Robert Louis Stevenson wrote, 'There is no duty'"*: All Gretchen Rubin quotes in this chapter are from an interview, August 20, 2021.

p. 275   *"You do have a responsibility, but it's to meaning"*: Interview with Oliver Burkeman, August 27, 2021.

p. 275   *it truly is better to give than to receive*: Colleen Walsh, "Money Spent on Others Can Buy Happiness," *Harvard Gazette*, April 17, 2008, https://news.harvard.edu/gazette/story/2008/04/money-spent-on -others-can-buy-happiness.

p. 279   *Chade-Meng Tan recommends for everyone*: Interview with Chade-Meng Tan for Minda Zetlin, "How to Be Happier at Work: 3 Tips," Inc.com, May 22, 2012, https://www.inc.com/minda-zetlin/how-to-be -happier-more-calm-googles-happiness-guru.html.

Index

and, 93–95, 104–5; calling out, 107–10; exercises, 109–10; language of, 94; ubiquity of, 98–99; unpaid labor and, 95–96, 108; wage gap and, 32–33, 96–97, 99–101, 159, 195; at workplace, 97–98, 99–100, 104–9, 159
gender wage gap, 32–33, 96–97, 99–101, 159, 195
generosity, 90, 275–76, 279
gig economy, 22, 23
Gilmore Girls, The (TV series), 229
Glaring Omissions (writing group), 59
glycemic index, 243
goals, 172–73. *See also* career goals; life goals
Go Find Out (exercise), 139–40
Good Wife, The (TV series), 229
Google, 39, 97, 109, 254, 274
Grace and Frankie (TV series), 41
Graceland (album; Simon), 194
Grammy Awards, 235
gratitude, 253
Great Resignation, 137
Groundlings (comedy troupe), 143
Grow a Support System from Scratch (exercise), 225
growth theory, 132
grumpiness, 212, 244
guided meditation, 260
guilt, 231–33, 234, 235
Guzdar, Maya, 108

Haden, Jeff, 70
Hagen, Jean, 196
Haitian proverbs, 183–84
Hamilton Spectator, 129–30
Happier at Home (Rubin), 274
happiness: career decisions and, 131; career goals and, 146, 147–48; conditionality and, 277; exercises, 272, 279–80; factors contributing to, 275–78; fear of, 277–78; meaning as key to, 275; money and, 187–88; search for, 264,

273–75; self-care and, 11, 274; small moments of, 148; social benefits of, 274–75; studies of, 274; success and, 177, 188, 264–67, 278; thriving perspective and, 218. *See also* career goals; life goals; success
Happiness Project, The (Rubin), 50–51, 274
Harvard Business Review, 226–27
Harvard Medical School, 208
Harvey Mudd College, 195
Hastings, Reed, 163–64
Have a Conversation with Your Older Self (exercise), 215–16
Have a Conversation with Your Younger Self (exercise), 189
Have an Anti-stress Tool Kit (exercise), 39–40
Hawking, Stephen, 131
Headspace Guide to Meditation (Netflix series), 260
health, 269
heart, following one's, 267–68
heartbreak, 31
heart failure, 205, 206–7
heart rate, 255
help, asking for, 59–60, 69–70, 200
Hewlett, Bill, 267
Hewlett Packard Enterprise (HP), 101–3, 113, 159
Hispanic women, 97, 106
Hit Refresh (Nadella), 195
Hoffman, Dustin, 93–95
home, working from, 25
"Homeless" (song; Simon and Shabalala), 194
homeschooling, 96
homophobia, 93, 110
honesty, 90
Hong Kong (China), 71
housecleaning, 95
How Do I Love Me? (ebook; Schwartz), 273
HQ2, Amazon, 181–82
Huffington, Arianna, 207

Human Resources departments,
99–100
hydration, 244–45

IBM, 10, 64
identity-based organizations, 114
ignorance, and the power of "yes,"
159–60
Ignore All These Instructions (exercise), 51
Imagine Your Best Possible Future
(exercise), 152–53
Imagine Your Last Job (exercise),
140–41
immune response, 255
Improv (Los Angeles, CA), 143
Inc.com: author's colleagues at, 70,
143; author's column at, 7, 9,
157, 183, 197, 199, 206, 209, 241;
author's writing career at, xi, 4,
219–20; Jobs and, 264
Inc. magazine: author's writing career
at, xi–xii, 174, 175, 219; solopreneur community at, 104, 152;
website of, xi, 220 (*see also* Inc.
com)
Index, the (journaling approach),
42–44
individuality, 56
inequality, 93. *See also* gender bias
infinite inputs, 268
Insider, 174
insomnia, 111, 259. *See also* sleep;
sleep deprivation
Instagram, 12
integration, 26–27
intention, 253
interruptions, 90, 257–59
Intersections (podcast), 239
Iowa City (IA), 185
Isaacson, Walter, 265
isolation, 56

Jenkins, Florence Foster, 192
job dissatisfaction, 135–38. *See also*
career satisfaction

job hunting, 149
Jobs, Steve, 10, 38, 264–66, 267,
270–71
jogging, 246–47
JOMO (joy of missing out), 22
journaling: author's experience, 21–
22, 41–42; for baby-step method,
149, 151–52; bullet journal,
42–43, 45; disconnection and,
21–22; effectiveness of, for career
advancement, 41; exercises,
50–51; exercises using, 15–16, 63;
one-sentence, 50–51; power journal, 43–50, 149, 200–201; reasons
for, 41–42; for success, 189
J-35 (orca), 35–36

karma and confidence, 194–95
Keep a One-Sentence Journal (exer-
cise), 50–51
"Killing Me Softly" (Becker et al.), 20
kindness, random acts of (exercise),
279
Kipling, Rudyard, 139
Klawe, Maria, 195
Klingman, Thaddeus, 130

labor: emotional, 98; unpaid, 95–96,
108
Ladysmith Black Mambazo, 193–94
language, 94
Late Night (TV show), 142
Latinas, 106
learning mind, 122
Learn to Be a Better Support System
Yourself (exercise), 224
leisure time, 13, 210–11, 241
Lennon, John, 167
Levey, Joel, 253, 261
Levey, Michelle, 253, 261
life goals: exercises, 272; following
one's heart for, 267–68; happiness
vs. success, 264–67; human life
expectancy and, 267–68, 271–72;
meaning and, 268–72. *See also*
career goals; happiness; success

About the Author

Minda Zetlin's articles, books, and workshops offer research-backed advice to help people get the most out of their careers and their lives. She writes the highly popular Laid-Back Leader column at Inc.com and is a regular contributor to Insider and CNBC.com. She is the author or coauthor of several books, including *The Geek Gap*, written with her husband Bill Pfleging, and is a former president of the American Society of Journalists and Authors (ASJA). She and Bill live in Snohomish, Washington.